All In One
Paris Guide
&
French
Phrasebook

Above: *lanterns against the façade of Notre-Dame*

AA Publishing

Above: a French breakfast

All In One guide first published 2003
Paris Guide written by Elisabeth Morris.
© Automobile Association Developments Limited 2003
Maps © Automobile Association Developments Limited
2002

Automobile Association Developments Limited retains the
copyright in the orginal edition © 1998 and in all
subsequent editions, reprints and amendments.

French Phrasebook: English edition prepared by
First Edition Translations Ltd, Great Britain
Designed and produced by AA Publishing

First published in 1992 as Wat & Hoe Frans,
© Uitgeverij Kosmos bv - Utrecht/Antwerpen
Van Dale Lexicografie bv - Utrecht/Antwerpen

Published by AA Publishing, a trading name of Automobile
Association Developments Limited whose registered
office is Millstream, Maidenhead Road, Windsor, Berkshire
SL4 5GD. Registered number 1878835.

A CIP catalogue record for this book is available from the
British Library.

ISBN 0 7495 3849 X

The contents of this publication are believed correct at
the time of printing. Nevertheless, AA Publishing accepts
no responsibility for any errors, omissions or changes in
the details given, nor for the consequences of readers'
reliance on this information. This does not affect your
statutory rights. Assessments of the attractions and hotels
and restaurants are based upon the author's own
experience and contain subjective opinions that may not
reflect the publisher's opinion or a reader's experience.

We have tried to ensure accuracy, but things do
change, so please let us know if you have any comments
or corrections.

A01882

Colour separation: BTB Digital Imaging Ltd,
Whitchurch, Hampshire

Printed and bound in Italy by Printer Trento S.r.l.

Find out more about
AA Publishing and the
wide range of services
the AA provides by
visiting our website at
www.theAA.com

Contents

Paris Guide 4–126

About the Paris Guide 4

Viewing Paris 5–14

Top Ten 15–26
Centre Georges Pompidou	16
Les Champs-Elysées	17
La Grande Arche de la Défense	18
Les Invalides	19
Le Louvre	20–21
Notre-Dame	22
Orsay, Musée d'	23
Les Quais	24
La Tour Eiffel	25
La Villette	26

What To See 27–90

Where To... 91–116

Practical Matters 117–124

Index & Acknowledgements 125–126

French Phrasebook 1–156

Pronunciation table 6

Useful lists 7–16

Phrases by category 17–113

Word list 114–153

Basic Grammar 154–156

About the Guide

The **Paris Guide** is divided into five sections to cover the most important aspects of your visit to Paris.

Viewing Paris pages 5–14
An introduction to Paris by the author
  Paris's Features
  Essence of Paris
  The Shaping of Paris
  Peace and Quiet
  Paris's Famous

Top Ten pages 15–26
The author's choice of the Top Ten places to see in Paris, each with practical information.

What to See pages 27–90
Two sections: Paris and Ile de France, each with its own brief introduction and an alphabetical listing of the main attractions
  Practical information
  Snippets of 'Did You Know...' information
  4 suggested walks
  3 suggested tours
  2 features

Where To... pages 91–116
Detailed listings of the best places to eat, stay, shop, take the children and be entertained.

Practical Matters pages 117–24
A highly visual section containing essential travel information.

Maps
All map references are to the individual maps found in the What to See section of this guide.
For example, Notre-Dame has the reference ✚ 29E2 – indicating the page on which the map is located and the grid square in which the cathedral is to be found. A list of the maps that have been used in this travel guide can be found in the index.

Prices
Where appropriate, an indication of the cost of an establishment is given by £ signs:
£££ denotes higher prices, ££ denotes average prices, while £ denotes lower charges.

Star Ratings
Most of the places described in this book have been given a separate rating:
✪✪✪   Do not miss
✪✪   Highly recommended
✪   Worth seeing

Viewing
Paris

Elisabeth Morris's Paris   6
Paris's Features   7
Essence of Paris   8–9
The Shaping of Paris   10–11
Peace and Quiet   12–13
Paris's Famous   14

Above: a café in the Saint-Germain district

Elisabeth Morris's Paris

'Villages' such as Saint-Germain-des-Prés (above) and the conviviality of café life (below) are just part of Paris's charm

Paris never leaves me indifferent. It has the power to rouse strong feelings in me, whatever mood I am in: admiration, exhilaration, irritation and even frustration, but above all fascination as time and again I am bewitched by its charm and diversity.

Paris may seem straightforward and orderly to the first-time visitor as it unfolds its wealth of stately monuments, but it is in fact a complex city and its beauty has many facets; besides the vast open vistas there are picturesque villages like Saint-Germain-des-Prés, Le Marais or Montmartre where you may suddenly come across a tiny square steeped in a romantic old-world atmosphere or be confronted with a bold modern sculpture defiantly competing with a medieval master-piece. What never ceases to amaze me, however, is the overall sense of harmony that pervades these contrasting features and confers on the city a unique homogeneity.

Paris is a melting-pot of new, daring, even outrageous ideas in the fields of art, fashion, architecture, cuisine, lifestyle, politics and sociology. Living in the midst of this continuous creative outburst is tremendously stimulating, but I also enjoy standing back and relaxing at lunchtime in the peaceful Jardins du Palais-Royal, at the heart of the city, or taking a stroll along the river at sunset when Parisians set aside their hurried daily pursuit of an elusive happiness and unashamedly give in to their inclination for enjoyment. Paris then seems more alive and exciting than ever.

Bistros and Cafés
You may think that *bistro* is just another name for *café* but there is a subtle difference. Cafés were traditionally the haunt of fashionable society and artists. Bistros are cafés of modest appearance where locals meet regularly for a drink, a game of dice and sometimes a snack. The number of cafés and bistros has decreased considerably in recent years.

6

Paris's Features

Geography
• Situated at the heart of northern France, some 250km from the sea, Paris lies on the banks of the meandering River Seine.

The City
• The city is small and compact, entirely surrounded by the boulevard périphérique, a congested 35km-long dual carriageway. Green spaces cover an area of 366ha excluding the Bois de Boulogne and Bois de Vincennes and there is one tree for every four Parisians.

Greater Paris
• The surrounding area, known as the *banlieue*, includes densely populated suburbs, dormitory towns and traditional villages scattered through the green belt, as well as several new towns. The whole region enjoys a reasonably dry climate, fairly cold in winter, hot and sunny in summer.

An unmistakeable skyline – the Tour Eiffel beyond the pont Neuf

Administration
• Paris is a municipality administered by a council and a mayor like any other town in France, but it is also a *département* (county) headed by a *préfet*.
• Paris is divided into 20 *arrondissements* numbered from 1 to 20 starting from the Louvre in the historic centre.

Population
• The city has just over 2 million inhabitants but more than 10 million people, almost one-fifth of the French population, live in Greater Paris.

The Oldest...
• The oldest bridge is the pont Neuf (New Bridge!) dating from 1578.
• The oldest church is Saint-Germain-des-Prés, built in the 11th century.
• The oldest houses date from the 15th century; the Musée de Cluny is one of them (➤ 62).
• The oldest tree, planted in 1601, stands in the square Viviani, on the Left Bank opposite Notre-Dame.

Paris's Highest Monuments
Tour Eiffel: 317m
Tour Montparnasse: 209m
Grande Arche de la Défense: 110m
Dôme des Invalides: 105m
Panthéon: 83m
Sacré-Coeur: 80m`
Notre-Dame: 69m
Arc de Triomphe: 50m

Paris to...by Road
Amsterdam: 504km
Berlin: 1,069km
Brussels: 308km
Geneva: 538km
London: 343km
Luxembourg: 376km
Madrid: 1,310km
Rome: 1,417km

Essence of Paris

Paris is order, harmony, beauty and elegance...the result of bold town planning that was particularly successful in marrying tradition and innovation, sometimes with stunning effects, as in the case of the stark glass pyramid erected in front of the Louvre.

Paris is also passion, youthful energy and a stimulating cultural life.

But Paris is above all the capital of good living: the best of French cuisine, an enticing choice of gastronomic specialities from various countries, the glamorous world of *haute couture* and eccentric fashion, and a sparkling nightlife.

La Grande Arche dominates Le Parvis

THE 10 ESSENTIALS

If you have only a short time to visit Paris and would like to take home unforgettable memories, here are the essentials:

• **Take a boat trip along the Seine** from the pont de l'Alma and admire the stately monuments (➤ 22, 24, 41 and 43) whose splendour is dramatically enhanced at night by powerful spotlights.

• **Climb to the top of the Tour Eiffel** for an aerial view of Paris (➤ 25); guaranteed thrill from the panoramic lift.

• **Take a morning walk through the Jardin du Luxembourg** and stand beside the romantic Fontaine de Médicis (➤ 12).

• **Sit outside Les Deux Magots Café** in boulevard Saint-Germain, on the Left Bank, and watch the world go by. Street bustle peaks around lunchtime and from 6PM (➤ 71).

• **Stand on the pont de la Tournelle** near Notre Dame: look downriver for panoramic views of 'old Paris' (Ile de la Cité and beyond) and upriver for contrasting views of 'new Paris' (Bercy and Institut du Monde Arabe, ➤ 38 and 54).

• **Stroll along the quais** and browse through the *bouquinistes'* stock of old prints and books (➤ 24).

• **Take the funicular to Sacré Coeur** at the top of Montmartre for stunning views of the city (➤ 70).

• **Go to the colourful Moulin-Rouge** show and discover the glamour of traditional Parisian entertainment (➤ 58).

• **Stand on the place de la Concorde** at night and look up the Champs-Elysées. The illuminated avenue, gently rising towards the Arc de Triomphe, offers one of the most perfect urban vistas in the world (➤ 17).

• **Mingle with Parisians** doing their daily shopping in street markets along the rue Mouffetard (Quartier Latin) or the rue de Buci (Saint-Germain-des-Prés).

A trip along the Seine is an ideal way to see many of the city's sights

Place de la Concorde, the great square at one end of the Champs-Elysées

The Shaping of Paris

c250 BC
A Celtic tribe, called the Parisii, settles on the Ile de la Cité.

52 BC
The Parisii are defeated by the Romans.

2nd century AD
Building of the Gallo-Roman city of Lutetia.

c300
Lutetia is renamed Paris.

508
Clovis, king of the Franks, chooses Paris as his capital.

845
First Viking raid on Paris.

c1100
Abélard teaches in Paris and meets Héloïse. The Quartier Latin spreads to the left bank.

1163–1245
Building of Notre-Dame Cathedral.

1215
Foundation of the Paris University.

c1220
The Royal Palace of Le Louvre is completed.

1358
The merchants of Paris, headed by Etienne Marcel, rebel against royal authority and call for tax reforms.

1408
During the Hundred Years' War, Paris is occupied by the English.

1431
King Henry VI of England is crowned king of France in Notre-Dame.

1437
Charles VII liberates Paris.

c1470
The first printing-press is set up in the Sorbonne.

1559
Foundation of the French Reformed Church.

1594
King Henri IV enters Paris, cheered by the population, and thus puts an end to the Wars of Religion.

1570–1610
The Louvre is extended.

1605
The building of the place Royale (place des Vosges), Paris's oldest square, leads to the development of the Marais district.

1660–70
The Louvre is extended once more.

c1670
The first cafés become popular.

1680
Foundation of the Comédie-Française, France's most prestigious theatre. Louis XIV leaves Paris for Versailles.

1755–75
Building of the place Louis XV (place de la Concorde).

1783
First-ever balloon flight by Pilâtre de Rozier.

1789
The fall of the Bastille marks the beginning of the French Revolution.

1804
Napoleon is crowned emperor in Notre-Dame Cathedral.

1816
Gas lighting is installed in the city. The first steamships sail along the Seine.

Napoleon I dressed in his coronation robes

General Eisenhower in liberated Paris, 1944

1852–70
Baron Haussmann reshapes Paris.

1870
Paris is besieged by the Prussians and is forced to capitulate. During the civil unrest that follows, the Hôtel de Ville is burnt down and is rebuilt in less than 10 years.

1889
The Tour Eiffel is the main attraction at the World Fair.

1900
The first métro line is inaugurated.

1914
Paris is saved from German occupation by the Battle of the Marne.

1919
Inauguration of the world's first commercial airline between Paris and London.

1940
Paris is occupied by German troops.

1944
Paris is liberated.

1947
First-ever fashion parade, organised by Christian Dior.

1968
Series of student demonstrations followed by a general strike.

1973
The boulevard périphérique is completed.

1977
The office of mayor of Paris is reinstated after more than 100 years; Jacques Chirac is elected. The Centre Georges Pompidou is inaugurated.

1986
Inauguration of the Musée d'Orsay.

1989
The Grand Louvre, the Opéra-Bastille and the Grande Arche de la Défense are inaugurated for the bicentenary of the Revolution.

1996
Opening of the new Bibliothèque Nationale.

1998
The football World Cup final takes place in the newly built Stade de France in St-Denis – and is won by France.

2000
The Eiffel Tower is revamped with glittering halogen lighting.

Peace & Quiet

Paris is a compact, densely populated city and the pace of life is notoriously hectic. Fortunately, the city has its quiet spots, full of charm and mystery, ideal for relaxing after a head-spinning shopping spree in boulevard Haussmann or a marathon visit to the Louvre.

Paris's green spaces cover an area of about 2,000ha. They come in all shapes and sizes, from the tiny square du Vert Galant on the Ile de la Cité to the imposing Bois de Boulogne on the outskirts of town. Names vary according to size: *squares* are small gardens, often occupying the centre of a square such as the square Louis XIII in the place des Vosges; *jardins* are larger and usually formal in design, such as the Jardin des Tuileries; *parcs* are freer in style: they can be romantic like the parc Monceau or futuristic like the parc André Citroën. Whether you wish to take a brief pause or are longing for a day away from it all, you should find what you are looking for in the selection below.

Jardin du Luxembourg, popular with students as a retreat from the nearby Sorbonne

In the City Centre

Square du Vert Galant – this triangular green patch, situated at the western end of the Ile de la Cité, offers a splendid view of the Louvre.

Arènes de Lutèce – surrounded by greenery, the ruins of the city's Gallo-Roman amphitheatre form a picturesque setting at the heart of the busy Quartier Latin.

Square Viviani – adjacent to the small medieval church of St-Julien-le-Pauvre, on the Left Bank, it shelters Paris's oldest tree. Admire the delightful view of Notre-Dame.

Jardin du Luxembourg – situated a stone's throw from the Sorbonne, this attractive French-style garden is traditionally the favourite haunt of students and lovers, who particularly favour the area surrounding the Fontaine de Médicis, named after Marie de Médicis, who commissioned the Palais du Luxembourg (now the Senate) and the gardens.

Jardin du Palais-Royal – walking under the arches into the garden is like taking a journey back in time: the noise of traffic fades away and the visual impression is one of 18th-century elegance and harmony.

Parc Monceau – this English-style park is scattered with 18th-century follies. Combine a quiet stroll here with a visit to the nearby Musée Nissim de Camondo (➤ 63) and Musée Cernuschi (➤ 39).

Further Out

Parc des Buttes-Chaumont – complete with lake, rocky island, bridges and waterfall, this was the first park to be laid out in the city's northern districts.

Parc André-Citroën – this ultra-modern park in the 15th *arrondissement* combines architecture with nature and experiments with colours, metals and water to create different impressions and striking contrasts.

Bois de Boulogne and Bois de Vincennes – landscaped in the English style at the end of the 19th century with artificial lakes, lawns, woodland areas, footpaths and tracks for horse-riding and bicycling, these offer an ideal one-day break from city life. The Bois de Boulogne boasts two racecourses as well as cafés and restaurants while the Bois de Vincennes has a racecourse, a zoo and a working farm open to the public.

Top: *Bois de Vincennes, an extensive area of parkland on the edge of the city*
Above: *floating wooden boats in the Jardin des Tuileries.a popular pastime with Parisian children*

13

Paris's Famous

Molière

The son of an upholsterer established near Les Halles, Molière turned down a promising career in law to become an actor. His first attempts at directing his own company ended in disaster and…prison! However he persevered and success finally came in 1659 with *Les Précieuses ridicules*, the first of many incisive comedies in which he satirised human nature in general and French society in particular. He worked and lived near the Palais-Royal, where the Comédie-Française is now established; inside is the armchair in which Molière was playing the rôle of the *Malade imaginaire* when he collapsed and died in 1673.

André Le Nôtre

André Le Nôtre was Louis XIV's (the Sun King) famous landscape gardener. He conceived his gardens along archi-tectural lines and showed an extraordinary flair for harmonious proportions. He not only designed the magnif-icent parks of Vaux-le-Vicomte and Versailles, but also left his mark on Paris by redesigning the Jardin des Tuileries and creating the vast vista leading up to the Arc de Triomphe, later to become the Champs-Elysées.

Baron Haussmann

During the second half of the 19th century, Baron Haussmann's brilliant town planning transformed Paris from a squalid medieval town into a spacious, modern city. The Ile de la Cité underwent major surgery, to an extent which seems excessive today, and several wide arteries were opened up along the left and right banks; the place de l'Etoile and its 12 radiating avenues were created, and green spaces were provided all over the town centre.

Geneviève and Attila
Born just outside Paris around AD 420, Geneviève was a devout Christian. In 451, as the Huns were appoaching Paris, panic spread among the people who prepared to leave the city. But Geneviève galvanised them into organising the town's defences, and Attila and his army were forced back. Geneviève later became the patron saint of Paris.

Jacques Chirac

Jacques Chirac was mayor of Paris from 1977 to 1995. During that time, he continued the work of his famous predecessors, including the systematic cleaning of the town's monuments, created yet more green spaces and partly restored the avenue des Champs-Elysées to its former splendour. He resigned as mayor when he was elected president in 1995.

14

Top Ten

Centre Georges Pompidou	16
Les Champs-Elysées	17
Le Grande Arche de la Défense	18
Les Invalides	19
Le Louvre	20–1
Notre-Dame	22
Orsay, Musée d'	23
Les Quais	24
La Tour Eiffel	25
La Villette	26

Above and right: *a fountain and pipes at Centre Georges Pompidou*

1
Centre Georges Pompidou

Not to everyone's taste, but undeniably eye-catching

This controversial modern art centre, which recently celebrated its 20th birthday, houses under one roof all forms of contemporary art.

 29E3

✉ Place Georges-Pompidou, 75004 Paris; www.centrepompidou.fr

☎ 01 44 78 12 33

🕐 Modern art museum and exhibitions: 11–9; closed Tue. Library: weekdays 12–10; weekends 11–10. Brancusi workshop 1–7

🍴 Cafeteria (£) with good view on 5th floor

🚇 Rambuteau, Hôtel de Ville

🚌 29 38 47 58

♿ Good

✋ Free access; museum: moderate. Ticket gives access to the Brancusi workshop, the children's workshop and level 6 (panoramic view)

❓ Audio guides, cash dispenser, shops

With 25,000 visitors a day, the Centre Georges Pompidou is now one of Paris's top sights. Yet at the time it was built, close to the historic Marais which is famous for its elegant architecture, the 'refinery', as Rogers' and Piano's post-modern building was nicknamed, deeply shocked French people. In fact, the revolutionary concept of this open-plan 'house of culture for all' ensured its success and brought life back to the district. The centre has had its first major face-lift and been completely refurbished inside; its main asset, the Musée National d'Art Moderne, reached by the external escalator, gained extra exhibition space in the process. The museum is dedicated to the main trends of 20th-century art from 1905 to the present day. Modern art is displayed on level 5. Particularly well represented are Fauvism (Dufy, Derain, Matisse), Cubism (Braque, Picasso, Léger), Dadaism, Surrealism (Dali, Miró), Expressionism (Soutine, Kirchner, Modigliani and to a lesser extent Chagall), various forms of abstract art (Kandinsky, Klee, but also Poliakoff, Dubuffet and the Cobra movement), and pre-1960 American painting. The collections of contemporary art (level 4) include exponents of the new realism (Arman, César), of Pop Art (Warhol), of Minimalist art (Sol Lewitt, Buren) and of monochromes (Manzoni, Klein).

The centre also houses a library, the Institute for Acoustic and Musical Research, the Centre for Industrial Creation, a large exhibition hall, a children's workshop and a reconstruction of Brancusi's workshop.

2
Les Champs-Elysées

For most visitors this prestigious avenue epitomises French elegance, but it is also a dazzling place of entertainment and a luxury shopping mall.

In the late 17th century, Le Nôtre designed a gently rising alleyway as an extension of the Jardin des Tuileries. This later lost its rustic appearance and became a fashionable avenue lined with elegant restaurants and cafés. Nowadays it is the traditional venue for a variety of events such as the Paris Marathon, the arrival of the Tour de France and the march past on 14 July, which celebrates France's national day. But 'les Champs' (the fields) is also a place where people of all ages just relax and feel alive.

The lower section, stretching from the place de la Concorde (with breathtaking views along the whole length of the avenue) to the Rond-Point des Champs-Elysées, is laid out as an English-style park shaded by imposing chestnut trees. On the left are the Grand and Petit Palais, two temples of the arts, while on the right is a monument to the French Resistance hero, Jean Moulin, who was reburied in the Panthéon on 19 December 1964.

The upper section stretches from the Rond-Point, designed by Le Nôtre, to the Arc de Triomphe. This is the 'modern' part of the avenue, recently revamped, with its pavements now restored to their former comfortable width. Banks, cinemas, airline offices, car showrooms, and large cafés spread out on the pavements, lining the way to the place de l'Etoile. Fashion boutiques cluster along the arcades running between the Champs-Elysées and the parallel rue de Ponthieu. Some shops remain open well into the night and the bustle only quietens down in the early hours of the morning.

28B4

Avenue des Champs-Elysées, 75008 Paris

Choice of restaurants (£–£££)

Concorde, Champs-Elysées-Clemenceau, Franklin-D Roosevelt, George V, Charles-de-Gaulle-Etoile

73, Balabus (in summer)

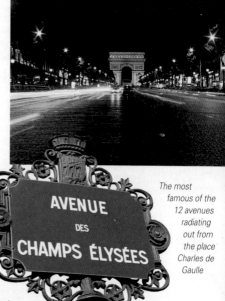

The most famous of the 12 avenues radiating out from the place Charles de Gaulle

AVENUE DES CHAMPS ÉLYSÉES

17

3
La Grande Arche de la Défense

✚ Off map 28A5

✉ 1 parvis de la Défense, 92044 Paris-La Défense

☎ 01 49 07 27 57 (Grande Arche)

🕐 Grande Arche: daily 10–7

🍴 Rooftop restuarant, snackbars and cafés in Les Quatre Temps shopping centre (£) and in the CNIT (£ and ££)

Ⓜ Grande Arche de la Défense

🚌 73, Balabus in summer

♿ Good

✋ Lift Grande Arche: moderate

❓ Video presentation, guided tours, shops

A striking modern symbol

Symbolically guarding the western approach to the city, the Grande Arche is both a recognition of tradition and a bold step towards the future.

From the arch's roof top (110m above ground), accessible by the exterior lift, a marvellous view unfolds in a straight line along an axis to the Arc de Triomphe and, beyond, to the Obelisk at La Concorde and to the Louvre, extending the magnificent vista opened up by Le Nôtre. The arch was inaugurated in 1989 for the bicentenary celebrations of the French Revolution and is now a major tourist attraction. The stark simplicity of its architectural outline and the materials used are definitely contemporary, while its sheer size is a marvel of modern technology. The Danish architect, Otto von Spreckelsen, built a perfect hollow concrete cube covered over with glass and white Carrara marble. Steps lead up to the central platform, where the lifts are to be found.

The arch dominates a vast square, known as Le Parvis, decorated with colourful sculptures, including a red 'stabile' by Calde, and flanked by another remarkable building: the CNIT (Centre of New Industries and Technology), shaped like an upside-down-shell, which serves mainly as a conference centre but is also a pleasant meeting place for business people. There are several cafés and a branch of the FNAC, the French equivalent of Virgin stores, stocking a large selection of CDs covering a wide spectrum of musical tastes.

Opposite, there is a huge shopping centre known as Les Quatre Temps, which has some of the best shopping bargains in Paris. Its focal point is the vast hyper-market Auchan.

4
Les Invalides

This is one of Paris's most imposing architectural ensembles, built around two churches and housing several museums.

The Hôtel National des Invalides was commissioned by Louis XIV as a home for wounded soldiers. It is a splendid example of 17th-century architecture, the classical austerity of its 200m-long façade being offset by the baroque features of the Eglise du Dôme, with its gilt dome glittering above the slate roofs of the stone buildings. The huge esplanade filling the gap between the river and the monumental entrance enhances the majesty of the building.

The museums are accessible from the arcaded main courtyard. The Musée de l'Armée is one of the richest museums of its kind in the worldr. It contains weapons from all over the world, armour and uniforms, mementoes of famous generals, paintings, documents and models. An interesting permanent exhibition devoted to General de Gaulle and the Second World War opened in June 2000.

The Musée des Plans-Reliefs is a fascinating collection of models of fortified French towns, originally started at Louis XIV's request.

On the far side of the courtyard is the entrance to St-Louis-des-Invalides, the soldiers' church, which contains a colourful collection of flags brought back from various campaigns; the organ here dates from the 17th century.

The magnificent Eglise du Dôme, built by Jules Hardouin-Mansart, is a striking contrast: an elegant façade with two tiers of Doric and Corinthian columns and an imposing gilt dome surmounted by a slender lantern. The splendid interior decoration is enhanced by the marble floor. The open circular crypt houses Napoleon's red porphyry tomb.

Eglise du Dôme across the Cour d'Honneur

✚	28B3
✉	Esplanade des Invalides, 75007 Paris
☎	01 44 42 37 72
🕐	10–5 (6 in summer). Closed 1 Jan, 1 May, 1 Nov, 25 Dec
🍴	Restaurant (£)
Ⓜ	Invalides, Latour Maubourg
🚌	82, 92 ♿ Good
✋	Moderate
❓	Audio-visual shows, guided tours, shops

5
Le Louvre

✝ 28C3

✉ Musée du Louvre, 75058 Paris Cedex 01. Main entrance via the pyramid

☎ Recorded information: 01 40 20 51 51; reception desk: 01 40 20 53 17; visitors with disabilities: 0140 20 59 90

🕐 Wed–Mon 9–6, late night Mon (Richelieu wing) and Wed (whole museum) 9:45; closed Tue and some bank hols

This former royal palace, which celebrated its bicentenary in 1993, is today one of the largest museums in the world.

The Palace

Excavations carried out in 1977 under the Cour Carrée, the courtyard surrounded by the oldest part of the palace, led to the discovery of the original castle built around 1200 by King Philippe-Auguste, which remained a fortress until it was razed to the ground to make way for a Renaissance palace. The tour of the foundations of this medieval Louvre, including the base of the keep, the moat and the outer wall, starts from the main entrance hall under the glass pyramid.

The first palace, built by Pierre Lescot in the style of the Italian Renaissance, was enlarged round the Cour Carrée and along the Seine during the following 200 years.

It is said that Molière performed in front of the court in the splendid Salle des Cariatides where Greek and Roman antiquities are now displayed. Louis XIV enclosed the Cour Carrée with the stately colonnade that faces the Church of St-Germain-l'Auxerrois. Soon afterwards, however, the king left for Versailles and the palace was neglected by the royal family and the court.

Building was resumed by Napoleon, who built part of the north wing and erected the exquisite Arc de Triomphe du Carrousel. During the second half of the 19th century, Napoleon III completed the Louvre along its rue de Rivoli side.

Just one of the 30,000-odd works on show

The Museum

The museum was founded in 1793 to house the royal art collections, which were subsequently enriched to the point that a large part of its vast stock could not be displayed. This prompted President Mitterrand to launch a complete renovation of the buildings and to extend the museum over the whole of the Louvre; the project became known as the 'Grand Louvre'. A huge entrance hall was created under a stunning glass pyramid, designed by Ieoh Ming Peï placed in the centre of the Cour Napoleon. This gives access to three main areas

known as Sully, Denon and Richelieu.

The collections are divided into seven departments:

• Egyptian Antiquities include a pink granite *Sphinx from Tanis*, a huge *head of Amenophis IV-Akhenaten* and the famous *Seated Scribe*.

• The most remarkable exhibits in the Oriental Antiquities Department must be the *Assyrian winged bulls*.

• The department of Greek, Etruscan and Roman Antiquities contains numerous masterpieces: do not miss the *Vénus de Milo*, the *Winged Victory* and the Graeco-Roman sculpture in the Salle des Cariatides.

• The painting collections comprise a fine selection from the Italian school (works by Giotto, Fra Angelico, Leonardo da Vinci, Veronese, Titian and Raphael), from the French school (Poussin, Watteau, Georges de la Tour), from the Dutch school (Rembrandt, Rubens and Vermeer) and works by Spanish masters (Murillo, Goya and El Greco).

• French sculpture is particularly well represented and includes fine works by Jean Goujon, Houdon and Pradier.

• *Objets d'art* are now displayed to full advantage in the Richelieu wing; among them are beautiful tapestries and historic items such as Charlemagne's sword.

• The last department is that of Graphic Art, housing drawings, prints and watercolours.

In addition, there is a display of art collections from Africa, Asia, Oceania and the Americas.

The Carrousel du Louvre is a luxury underground shopping precinct with a lovely inverted pyramid in its centre.

Two wildly disparate styles of architecture symbolise the museum's progression into the 20th century

Palais-Royal/Musée du Louvre

21, 27. 39, 48, 68, 69, 72, 76, 95

Several restaurants (£ and ££) and cafés below the pyramid and in the Carrousel du Louvre

Excellent

Moderate until 3pm, reduced fee after 3 and Sun, free on 1st Sun of the month. To avoid queuing, buy your ticket in advance; www.louvre.fr

Guided tours, lectures, concerts, film shows, shops. Information: 01 40 20 52 09

21

6
Notre-Dame

✚ 29E2

✉ Place du Parvis de Notre-Dame, 75004 Paris

☎ 01 42 34 56 10

This masterpiece of Gothic architecture is one of Paris's most famous landmarks and one of France's most visited religious monuments.

In 1163, the Bishop of Paris, Maurice de Sully, launched the building of the cathedral, which took nearly 200 years

to complete. One of the architects involved was Pierre de Montreuil, who also built the nearby Sainte-Chapelle (► 73). Later alterations deprived the church of its rood screen and of some of its original stained glass; its statues were mutilated during the Revolution because the Commune thought they were likenesses of the kings of France; the cathedral also lost all its original bells, except the 'gros bourdon', known as Emmanuel, which is traditionally heard on occasions of national importance. Restoration work was carried out in the 19th century by the famous architect Viollet-le-Duc and the area round the cathedral was cleared.

From across the vast square in front of the cathedral you can admire the harmonious proportions and almost perfect symmetry of the façade. The richly decorated portals are surmounted by statues of the kings of Judaea restored by Viollet-le-Duc. Above the central rose window, a colonnade links the elegant twin towers; there is a splendid view from the south tower, if you can face up to the 387-step climb.

The nave is 130m long, 48m wide and 35m high; the side chapels are richly decorated with paintings, sculptures and funeral monuments. Note the beautiful rose window at each end of the transept. The former vestry, on the right of the chancel, houses the Cathedral Treasure, which includes a piece of the Holy Cross.

🕐 Cathedral: daily 8–6:45, Sat, Sun 8–7:45; closed some religious feast days. Treasure: 9:30–11:30 and 1–5:30; closed Sun and religious feast days. Towers: 10–5:30 (9–9 in summer)

🍴 Left Bank (£–££)

Ⓜ Cité, St Michel

🚌 21, 24, 27, 38, 47, 85, 96

♿ Good

🎟 Cathedral: free; treasure: inexpensive; towers: moderate

A classic view of Notre-Dame Cathedral, from pont de l'Archevêché

7

Orsay, Musée d'

Once a mainline railway station, the Musée d'Orsay has been successfully converted into one of Paris's three major art museums.

Built in 1900, the Gare d'Orsay was narrowly saved from demolition by a daring plan to turn it into a museum dedicated to all forms of art from 1848 to 1914, and intended as the chronological link between the Louvre and the Musée National d'Art Moderne. The Musée d'Orsay was inaugurated by President Mitterrand in 1986.

The main hall, with the station clock, was retained to create a sense of unity between painting, sculpture, architecture, design, photography and the cinema. The collections are spread over three levels:

• The Lower Level deals with the years from 1848 to 1880; small flights of steps lead off the central alleyway to various exhibition areas where major sculptures are displayed, including a group of graceful figures by Carpeaux entitled *La Danse*. On either side is a comprehensive collection of paintings of the same period – works by Ingres, Delacroix, Corot, Courbet and the Realists, as well as the beginning of Impressionism with early works by Monet, Manet, Pissarro etc.

• On the Upper Level is the prestigious Impressionist and post-Impressionist collection, undoubtedly the main attraction of the museum: masterpieces by Manet (*Olympia*), Degas (*Blue Dancers*), Sisley (*Snow in Louveciennes*), Renoir (*Bathers*), Monet (*The Houses of Parliament, Rouen Cathedral*), Cézanne (*The Card Players*), Van Gogh (*The Church at Auvers-sur-Oise*), Gauguin and the school of Pont-Aven, Matisse, Toulouse-Lautrec and many others.

• The Middle Level is dedicated to the period from 1870 to 1914 and includes important works by Rodin (*Balzac*), paintings by the Nabis school, as well as a comprehensive section on art nouveau (Lalique, Gallé, Guimard, Mackintosh and Wright).

The iron and glass former railway hall

28C3

62 rue de Liue (entrance quai Anatole-France), 75007 Paris

01 40 49 48 14; recorded information: 01 45 49 11 11

Tue–Sat 10–6, Sun 9–6; late night: Thu 9:45 (opens 9AM in summer). Closed Mon, 1 Jan, 1 May, 25 Dec

Restaurant (Middle Level) (£) and pleasant café (Upper Level) (£)

Solférino

24, 63, 68, 69, 73, 83, 84, 94

Very good

Moderate

Guided tours, shops, concerts, film shows

8
Les Quais

✛ 28C3

✉ Quai du Louvre, quai de la Mégisserie (75001), quai de Gesvres, quai de l'Hôtel de Ville, quai des Célestins (75004), quai de la Tournelle, quai de Montebello, quai St-Michel (75005), quai des Grands Augustins, quai de Conti, quai Malaquais (75006), quai Voltaire, quai Anatole-France (75007)

🍴 Restaurants and cafés along the way, particularly near place du Châtelet and place de l'Hôtel de Ville on the Right Bank, and around place St-Michel on the Left Bank (£–£££)

🚇 Pont-Neuf, Châtelet, Hôtel de Ville, Pont-Marie, St-Michel, Solférino

🚌 24 follows the Left Bank

❓ Boat trips along the Seine from pont de l'Alma right round the islands

Street artists at work add to the timeless appeal of a stroll alongside the river

Walk along the banks of the Seine between the pont de la Concorde and the pont de Sully for some of Paris's finest views.

In 1992, the river banks from the pont d'Iéna, where the Tour Eiffel stands, to the pont de Sully, at the tip of the Ile Saint-Louis, were added to Unesco's list of World Heritage sites. Here the townscape has an indefinable charm inspired by the harmonious blend of colours: the pale greys and blues of the water and the sky, the soft green of the trees lining the embankment and the mellow stone colour of the historic buildings. Parisians have been strolling along the embankments for centuries, window-shopping, browsing through the *bouquinistes'* stalls or simply watching the activity on both sides of the river.

The Right Bank
Start from the pont du Carrousel and walk up-river past the imposing façade of the Louvre. From the pont Neuf, enjoy a fine view of the Conciergerie on the Ile de la Cité, or admire the birds and exotic fish on the quai de la Mégisserie. Continue past the Hôtel de Ville towards the lovely pont Marie leading to the peaceful Ile Saint-Louis. Cross over to the Left Bank.

The Left Bank
The familiar green boxes of the *bouquinistes* are here as well! Admire the stunning views of Notre-Dame and its magnificent flying buttresses. The quai Saint-Michel is a favourite haunt of students looking for second-hand books. Further on, stand on the pont des Arts for a romantic view of the historic heart of Paris before walking past the stately façade of the Musée d'Orsay towards the pont de la Concorde.

9
La Tour Eiffel

Paris's most famous landmark has been towering above the city for more than a hundred years, yet its universal appeal remains constant.

The Tour Eiffel was built by the engineer Gustave Eiffel as a temporary attraction for the 1889 World Exhibition. At the time, its 300-m height made it the tallest building in the world and an unprecedented technological achievement. It met with instant success, was celebrated by poets and artists, and its spindly silhouette was soon famous all over the world. In spite of this, it was nearly pulled down when the concession expired in 1909 but was saved because of its invaluable radio aerial, joined in 1957 by television aerials. It was later raised by another 20m to accommodate a meteorological station.

The iron frame weighs 7,000 tonnes, yet the pressure it exerts on the ground is only 4kg per square cm; 40 tonnes of paint are used to repaint it every seven years. To celebrate its one hundredth birthday, it was renovated and halogen lighting was installed making it even more spectacular at night than before.

There are three levels, all accessible by lift, or by stairs – first and second floors only. Information about the tower is available on the first floor (57m above ground); there are also a restaurant, a gift shop and a post office, where letters are post-marked 'Paris Tour Eiffel'.

The second floor (115m above ground) offers a fine panoramic view of Paris, several boutiques and a gastronomic restaurant appropriately named 'Jules Verne'.

For a unique aerial view of the capital go up to the third floor (276m above ground). There is also a reconstruction of Gustave Eiffel's study and a diorama retracing the history of the building.

There is a good view of the tower (with the statue of General Foch in the foreground) across the Seine from the place du Trocadéro

28A3

Champ de Mars, 75007 Paris

01 44 11 23 23

Sep–mid-Jun: 9:30AM–11PM; mid-Jun–Aug: 9AM–midnight

Restaurants (£–£££)

Bir-Hakeim

42, 69, 72, 82, 87

Good

Lift: 1st floor inexpensive, 2nd floor moderate and 3rd floor expensive

10
La Villette

Off map 29F5

Cité des Sciences et de l'Industrie, parc de la Villette, 30 avenue Corentin Cariou, 75019 Paris; Cité de la Musique, 221 avenue Jean Jaurès, 75019 Paris

Cité des Sciences: 01 40 05 80 00; Cité de la Musique: information bookings 01 44 84 44 84

Cité des Sciences: Tue–Sat 10–6, Sun 10–7; closed 1 May, 25 Dec. Cité de la Musique: Tue–Thu 12–6, Fri–Sat 12–7:30, Sun 10–6

Restaurants near by (£–££)

Cité des Sciences: Porte de la Villette; Cité de la Musique: Porte de Pantin

Cité des Sciences: 75, 139, 150, 152, PC; Cité de la Musique: 75, 151, PC

Cité des Sciences: very good; Cité de la Musique, museum: excellent

Cité des Sciences: expensive; Cité de la Musique: free, museum: moderate

Cité des Sciences: temporary exhibitions, lectures, shops; Cité de la Musique: themed tours, workshops, musical tours

La Géode, a huge hemispherical cinema

The Cité des Sciences et de l'Industrie and the Cité de la Musique revitalised the outer district of La Villette, turning it into a new cultural centre.

Situated just inside the boulevard périphérique, between the Porte de la Villette and the Porte de Pantin, the 30-ha parc de la Villette was laid out on the site of Paris's former abattoirs. This ultra-modern park includes two vast cultural complexes, one devoted to science and the other to music, themed gardens scattered with red metal follies and various children's activity areas. A long covered walk joins the main buildings.

Cité des Sciences et de l'Industrie
The abattoirs' former auction hall was transformed into a vast scientific complex surrounded by water in which the public is both spectator and actor. 'Explora' is a permanent exhibition centred on the earth and the universe, life, languages and communication, the use of natural resources and technological and industrial developments. The Cité des Enfants is a fascinating interactive world for children aged 3 to 12. There are also a planetarium, an aquarium, a 3-D cinema, a multimedia library, a research centre, a submarine, a simulation booth (Cinaxe), in which spectators are able to live through the action of a film, and La Géode, a huge sphere equipped with a hemispherical screen that shows films on scientific subjects.

Cité de la Musique
The focal point of the Cité de la Musique is the vast square in front of the Grande Halle where concerts and exhibitions are held. On the left of the square is the new music and dance conservatory while the triangular building on the right houses concerts halls and a museum (see Musée de la Musique ► 63).

What To See

Paris	30–77
Food and Drink	36–7
In the Know	50–1
Ile de France	78–90

Above: *Institut de France
clock detail*

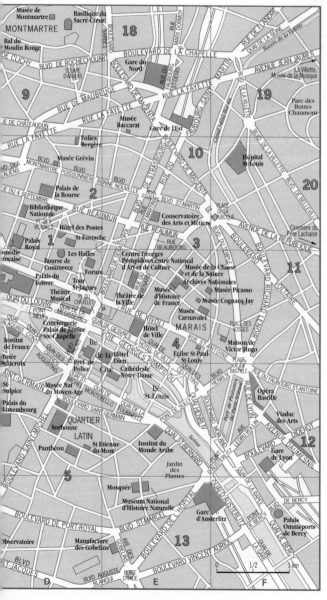

Musée de Montmartre
Basilique du Sacré-Cœur
MONTMARTRE
18
Bal du Moulin Rouge
DE CLICHY
BLVD DE ROCHECHOUART
BOULEVARD DE LA CHAPELLE
QUAI DE LA SEINE
Bassin de la Villette
SQUARE D'ANVERS
Gare du Nord
AVENUE JEAN JAURÈS
La Villette, Musée de la Musique
9
RUE DE MAUBEUGE
RUE DE MAGENTA
RUE LA FAYETTE
RUE DU FAUBOURG ST-DENIS
FAUBOURG SAINT-MARTIN
19
Parc des Buttes Chaumont
IE DE CHATEAUDUN
RUE LA FAYETTE
Musée Baccarat
Gare de l'Est
BLVD DE LA VILLETTE
20
Folies Bergère
Hôpital St-Louis
Cimetière du Père Lachaise
Musée Grévin
BLVD MONTMARTRE
BLVD POISSONNIÈRE
BLVD BONNE NOUVELLE
BLVD DE STRASBOURG
BOULEVARD DE MAGENTA
10
BOULEVARD DE BELLEVILLE
IE DU 4 SEPTEMBRE
Palais de la Bourse
2
RUE RÉAUMUR
BLVD ST-DENIS BLVD ST-MARTIN
PLACE DE LA RÉPUBLIQUE
AVENUE DE LA RÉPUBLIQUE
Bibliothèque Nationale
PLACE DES VICTOIRES
Hôtel des Postes
Conservatoire des Arts et Métiers
RUE RÉAUMUR
Palais Royal
1
St-Eustache
RUE BEAUBOURG
3
médie çaise
Bourse de Commerce
Les Halles
Centre Georges Pompidou Centre National d'Art et de Culture
Musée de la Chasse et de la Nature
BOULEVARD RICHARD LENOIR
11
Forum
Palais du Louvre
Tour St-Jacques
Archives Nationales
Musée Picasso
BOULEVARD VOLTAIRE
Théâtre Musical
PL. DU CHÂTELET
Théâtre de la Ville
Musée d'Histoire de France
Musée Cognacq-Jay
QUAI DU LOUVRE
QUAI DE LA MÉGISSERIE
RUE DE RIVOLI
Musée Carnavalet
PONT NEUF
QUAI
QUAI DE GESVRES
Hôtel de Ville
MARAIS
PLACE DES VOSGES
ALAQUAIS
QUAI DES GRANDS AUGUSTINS
Conciergerie Palais de Justice Ste-Chapelle
Île de la Cité
QUAI DE L'HÔTEL DE VILLE
RUE ST-ANTOINE
Maison de Victor Hugo
RUE DU FAUBOURG ST-ANTOINE
Institut de France
Préf. de Police
Hôtel Dieu
Église St-Paul St-Louis
4
PLACE DE LA BASTILLE
lusée lacroix
Cathédrale Notre-Dame
BLVD HENRI IV
Opéra Bastille
AINT-GERMAIN
Musée Nat du Moyen-Âge
QUAI DE MONTEBELLO
Île St-Louis
BLVD MORLAND
Viaduc des Arts
St Sulpice
BOULEVARD SAINT-GERMAIN
QUAI DE LA TOURNELLE
Institut du Monde Arabe
QUAI ST-BERNARD
AVE. DAUMESNIL
DIDEROT
12
Palais du Luxembourg
QUARTIER LATIN
Gare de Lyon
Sorbonne
St Étienne du-Mont
Jardin des Plantes
Seine
Panthéon
5
Mosquée
Museum National d'Histoire Naturelle
Gare d'Austerlitz
PONT DE BERCY
Palais Omnisports de Bercy
Observatoire
BOULEVARD DE PORT-ROYAL
Manufacture des Gobelins
BLVD ST-MARCEL
QUAI D'AUSTERLITZ
DE BERCY
BLVD ST-JACQUES
AVE. DES GOBELINS
13
BOULEVARD VINCENT AURIOL
QUAI DE BERCY
BLVD AUGUSTE BLANQUI
PLACE D'ITALIE

0   1/2   1 Km

Paris

The city of Paris has always played its role of capital of France to the full. It is the place where the French nation's future is decided, where revolutions began in the past and where major political, economic and social changes are traditionally launched. This is as true today as it ever was, in spite of many attempts at decentralisation.

Parisian life reflects the city's leading role in many different ways: the numerous trade exhibitions and international conferences taking place every year testify to its economic and potitical dynamism and healthy competitive spirit. Paris is continually on the move in all fields of human activity: its architectural heritage is constantly expanding and it is proudly setting new trends in the arts, in gastronomy and in fashion. Paris is also a cosmopolitan metropolis where many ethnic groups find the necessary scope to express their differences.

> *'If you are lucky enough to have lived in Paris as a young man, then wherever you go for the rest of your life, it stays with you, for Paris is a movable feast.'*
>
> ERNEST HEMINGWAY
> *A Movable Feast* (1964)

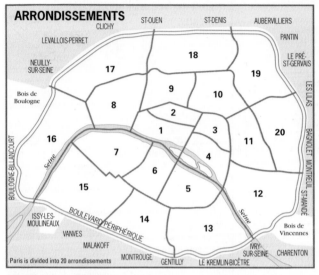

ARRONDISSEMENTS

CLICHY · ST-OUEN · ST-DENIS · AUBERVILLIERS

LEVALLOIS-PERRET · PANTIN

NEUILLY-SUR-SEINE · LE PRÉ-ST-GERVAIS

Bois de Boulogne · LES LILAS

BOULOGNE-BILLANCOURT · BAGNOLET · MONTREUIL · ST-MANDÉ

ISSY-LES-MOULINEAUX · Bois de Vincennes

VANVES · IVRY-SUR-SEINE · CHARENTON

MALAKOFF · MONTROUGE · GENTILLY · LE KREMLIN-BICÊTRE

BOULEVARD PÉRIPHÉRIQUE

17 · 18 · 19 · 8 · 9 · 10 · 2 · 1 · 3 · 11 · 20 · 16 · 7 · 4 · 6 · 5 · 12 · 15 · 14 · 13

Seine

Paris is divided into 20 arrondissements

Exploring Paris

It is tempting for visitors to allow themselves to be whisked off from one major sight to the next without ever getting the feel of the true Paris. You must wander off the beaten track to discover the city's hidden assets, which are often tucked away around unexpected corners.

La Marseillaise frieze on the Arc De Triomphe

To get the best out of Paris, you should travel by métro or bus from one main area to the next and then explore the neighbourhood on foot.

Each district has its own characteristics: Montmartre and Montparnasse are associated with artists while the Marais is inhabited by a trendy middle class; the splendid mansions of the Faubourg St-Germain have been taken over by government ministries but St-Germain-des-Prés and the Quartier Latin are still the favourite haunt of intellectuals and students. There are also several colourful ethnic areas: Chinatown in the 13th *arrondissement*, the African district north of the Gare du Nord and the Jewish quarter in the Marais.

Some areas are best avoided at night: around the Gare du Nord, Les Halles and the Grands Boulevards between République and Richelieu-Drouot.

31

What to See in Paris

PONT ALEXANDRE III ✪

This is Paris's most ornate bridge, inaugurated for the 1900 World Exhibition and named after the Tsar of Russia to celebrate the Franco-Russian alliance. Its sole arch (107m) spanning the Seine is in line with the Invalides on the Left Bank while, on the Right Bank, the avenue Winston Churchill leads straight to the Champs-Elysées, passing the Grand and Petit Palais. The bridge is decorated with exuberant allegorical sculptures surmounted by gilt horses.

ARC DE TRIOMPHE ✪✪✪

This stately monument stands in the middle of the circular place Charles de Gaulle, formerly known as the place de l'Etoile because of the 12 avenues that radiate from it. Commissioned by Napoleon, it was completed by France's last reigning monarch and finally dedicated to the memory of an unknown soldier of the Republic who died during World War I.

Looking at the harmonious proportions of its familiar silhouette and its splendid carvings you forget its megalomaniac origins. It stands in line with two other arches – the Arc de Triomphe du Carrousel near the Louvre and the Grande Arche de la Défense. At 50m high, the Arc de Triomphe is twice the height of the former and only half that of the latter.

From the top there is a 360 degree panorama, with, in the foreground, the 12 avenues reaching out like tentacles towards the city beyond.

ARMÉE, MUSÉE DE L' (➤ 19)

Sidebar (Pont Alexandre III):

➕ 28B3
✉ Cours La Reine/Quai d'Orsay
🚇 Invalides, Champs-Elysées-Clémenceau
🚌 63, 83

Sidebar (Arc de Triomphe):

➕ 28A4
✉ Place Charles de Gaulle, 75008 Paris
☎ 01 55 37 73 77
🕐 Oct–Mar: 10AM– 10:30PM; Apr–Sep: 9:30AM–11PM, closed 1 Jan, 1 May, 8 May, 14 July, 11 Nov, 25 Dec
🍴 Choice of restaurants near by (£–£££)
🚇 Charles de Gaulle-Etoile
🚌 73
♿ Very good
💷 Moderate
❓ Video, shops

A ceremony takes place at the Arc de Triomphe every Armistice Day

ART MODERNE DE LA VILLE DE PARIS, MUSÉE D' ✪✪

The Palais de Tokyo housing the modern art collections was built for the 1937 World Exhibition; significantly, one of the main exhibits is a huge work called *La Fée Electricité* , painted by Raoul Dufy for the 'Light pavilion' at the Exhibition. Most of the major artistic trends of the 20th century are represented; one room, entirely devoted to Matisse, displays two versions of his famous *La Danse*. In addition, there are interesting collections of art deco furniture, *objects d'art*, photography and textiles.

✚ 28A4
✉ 11 avenue du Président Wilson, 75116 Paris
☎ 01 53 67 40 00
🕐 Tue–Fri 10–5:30, Sat and Sun 10–7; closed Mon and bank hols
🍴 Cafe (£)
Ⓜ Iéna, Alma-Marceau
🚌 32, 42, 63, 72, 80, 92
♿ Very good
✋ Moderate
❓ Guided tours (reservations necessary)

Exciting exhibits at the Musée d'Art Moderne

ARTS ASIATIQUES-GUIMET, MUSÉE NATIONAL DES/PANTHÉON BOUDDHIQUE ✪✪

The renovated and extended Musée Guimet is now one of the most outstanding museums of Asian art in the world. Its collections, spanning 5,000 years, illustrate all the major civilisations of the Asian continent., with special emphasis on calligraphy, painting, gold plate and textiles. In addition, carefully restored monumental works from Cambodia and Afghanistan are on display for the first time.

✚ 28A4
✉ Museum: 6 place d'Iéna; Panthéon Bouddhique: 19 avenue d'Iéna, 75116 Paris
☎ 01 45 05 00 98
Ⓜ Boissière, Iéna
🚌 22, 30, 32, 63, 82
♿ Excellent ✋ Moderate, inexpensive on Sun

ARTS DÉCORATIFS, MUSÉE DES ✪✪

Founded in the 19th century in order to display 'Beauty in function', the Museum of decorative arts, housed in the Marsan wing of the Louvre, is gradually reopening its departments after undergoing major restructuring. The Medieval and Renaissance collections include remarkable altarpieces, religious paintings, 16th-century stained glass and objects of daily life. In addition, special exhibitions are organised regularly pending the reopening of the remaining 17th, 18th, 19th and 20th-century collections.

✚ 28C3
✉ 107 rue de Rivoli; 75001
☎ 01 44 55 57 50
🕐 Tue–Fri 11–6 (Wed 9), Sat–Sun 10–6; temporary exhibitions Tue–Sun 12–6
🍴 The main Louvre near by
♿ Good Ⓜ Palais-Royal
🚌 21, 27, 39, 48, 67, 69, 72, 81
✋ Moderate

ARTS ET MÉTIERS-TECHNIQUES, MUSÉE DES NATIONAL ✪✪

Reopened in 2000, this museum is devoted to the artistic aspect of scientific and technical achievements.

✚ 29E4 ✋ Moderate
✉ 60 rue Réaumur, 75003 Paris
☎ 01 53 01 82 00

33

...ne historical
...es decorating the
...alais-Bourbon, seat of
the Assemblée Nationale

ASSEMBLÉE NATIONALE PALAIS-BOURBON ✪

The façade of this neo-classical building, housing the lower house of the French parliament, echoes that of the Madeleine across the place de la Concorde. Completed by Louis XV's famous architect Gabriel, the Palais-Bourbon still bears the name of the French royal family to whom it once belonged. Guided tours (identity document required) include the chamber, where members of parliament sit on benches arranged in semicircular tiers, several reception rooms and the library, richly decorated by Delacroix.

➕ 28C3
✉ 33 quai d'Orsay, 75007
☎ 01 40 63 60 00
🕐 Guided tours only Sat 10AM, 2PM, 3PM; closed bank hols and when Parliament is sitting
Ⓜ Assemblée Nationale
🚌 63, 83, 84, 94
♿ Very good **🎫** Free
❓ Shops

BACCARAT, MUSÉE ✪

The prestigious collections of Baccarat crystal are housed in one of the last 19th-century post-houses in Paris. There are over a thousand pieces, illustrating the evolution of styles and manufacturing techniques since 1764: vases, chandeliers, perfume bottles and various other objects including candelabra ordered by Tsar Nicholas II of Russia. The most fascinating exhibits are probably the unique pieces specially created by Baccarat for various World Exhibitions since 1855.

➕ 29E5
✉ 30 bis rue de Paradis, 75010 Paris
☎ 01 47 70 64 30
🕐 10–6; closed Sun
Ⓜ Château d'eau
🚌 32, 48, 49
♿ None **🎫** Inexpensive
❓ Guided tours, shops

BALZAC, MAISON DE ✪

This is the house in which Honoré de Balzac lived from 1840 to 1847, while he was writing the series of novels *La Comédie Humaine*. The house contains numerous mementoes of his life and work, such as manuscripts, letters, original drawings and prints and a plaster cast that Rodin used as a study for the monumental statue now standing in Montparnasse. Balzac used the backdoor in the picturesque rue Berton when he needed to avoid the bailiffs!

➕ Off map 28A3
✉ 47 rue Raynouard, 75016 Paris
☎ 01 55 74 41 80
🕐 Tue–Sun 10–5:40; closed bank hols
Ⓜ Passy, La Muette
🚌 32 **♿** None
🎫 Inexpensive
❓ Guided tours, bookshop

BASTILLE ⭐⭐

The place de la Bastille is forever associated with the French Revolution, since it was here that it all began. The dreaded fortress was stormed by the people of Paris on 14 July 1789 and later razed to the ground; its outline can be seen on the paving stones covering the entire square. In the centre stands a 50m-high column erected in memory of the victims of the 1830 and 1848 Revolutions, who were buried beneath the base and whose names are carved on the shaft. The column is surmounted by the gilt winged figure of the *Spirit of Liberty* by Dumont.

The new Paris opera house, one of President Mitterrand's 'Grands projets', was inaugurated for the bicentenary of the 1789 Revolution. It was the subject of bitter controversy from the start as running costs proved too high for an establishment intended as a popular opera house. Designed by the Canadian architect Carlos Ott, the **Opéra National de Paris-Bastille** is a harmonious building with a curved façade in several shades of grey that glitters in the sun and gently glows at night. The acoustics of the main auditorium, which can accommodate 2,700 spectators, are superb and the stage is one of the most sophisticated in the world.

Just south of the opera house, a disused railway viaduct has been converted into a series of workshops and showrooms illustrating a number of traditional crafts known as the **Viaduc des Arts**; the Ateliers du Cuivre et de l'Argent (copper and silver workshops) are particularly interesting and there is a small museum.

Sidebar

✚ 29F2

Opéra National de Paris-Bastille
✉ Place de la Bastille, 75012 Paris
☎ Recorded information: 01 40 01 19 70
🕐 Listen to the recorded information; closed Sun
🍴 Bar
Ⓜ Bastille
🚌 20, 29, 65, 69, 76, 86, 87, 91
♿ Good 👤 Moderate
❓ Guided tours, shops

Viaduc des Arts
✉ 9–129 avenue Daumesnil, 75012 Paris
☎ General information: 01 44 75 80 66
🕐 Variable; most workshops open Sun
🍴 Near by (£)
Ⓜ Bastille, Ledru-Rollin, Reuilly-Diderot

Above: *the Bastille monument*

Left: *the Governor of the Bastille being led to the town hall by the revolutionaries*

Food & Drink

In France, eating is an art that reaches its highest expression in Paris, for here the diversity and know-how of traditional regional cuisine are combined with a creative spirit stimulated by a strong cosmopolitan influence. In recent years, a growing awareness of the need for healthier living has prompted the invention of *nouvelle cuisine* and contributed to change the Parisians' eating habits.

Musée du Vin
- ✉ 5 square Charles Dickens, 75016 Paris
- ☎ 01 45 25 63 26
- 🕐 Tue–Sun 10–6
- 🍴 Nice bistro (£)
- 🚇 Passy
- ♿ Good
- 💰 Moderate; free for visitors eating in the restaurant
- ↔ Maison de Balzac (➤ 34)
- ❓ Guided tours, bookshop, gift shop

Opposite: *watching the world go by from pavement cafés is a national pastime; traditional baguettes, bought daily;* tarte au citron, *a popular dessert; expresso coffee – small, dark and strong*

Below: *fresh fish in Le Marais*

Eating Parisian Style

The traditional French breakfast of bread, butter and jam with a large cup of *café au lait* (white coffee) has to a large extent given way to cereals and milk with black coffee, tea or chocolate. The traditional fresh croissants are often a weekend treat, when people breakfast *en famille.*

The majority of working people have lunch out. Cafés and bistros overflow onto the pavements in spring and summer and overworked waiters are continually calling out *un steak frites* (steak and chips) at the tops of their voices, as Parisians order their favourite lunchtime dish. The trendiest places to have lunch are *bars à huîtres* (oyster bars, serving a variety of seafood) and cyber cafés where you can have a snack and a drink while surfing the Internet!

Dinner at home around 8PM is the first relaxing meal of the day, enjoyed with family or friends; it starts with hors-d'oeuvre, finishes with cheese or a sweet and may include a freshly prepared dish bought from a local *traiteur* (delicatessen), accompanied by a glass of wine.

Shopping for Food

Parisians are still very fond of their local street markets where they can buy fresh vegetables and fruit as well as cheese, charcuterie, fish and meat. One traditional item which is still going strong is the *baguette*, the light and crisp bread that is better in Paris than anywhere else in France!

Eating Out

Eating out is one of the Parisians' favourite forms of entertainment as conviviality is as important as the food itself. Friday night and Saturday night are the most popular evenings, while families with children tend to go out for Sunday lunch. Parisian cuisine includes a wide choice of regional and traditional dishes, although the tendency nowadays is to lighten sauces. Typical Parisian dishes are *soupe à l'oignon gratinée* (onion soup *au gratin*) and *pieds de cochon* (grilled pig's trotters), traditionally eaten near Les Halles when this was the chief food market in Paris. Oysters and seafood in general are also very popular, judging by the numerous take-away seafood stalls outside restaurants in the city centre.

Wine is a must with any good meal, preceded by an aperitif, which may consist of port, whisky or champagne. A *digestif* (brandy, Cointreau or any other liqueur) is served with coffee at the end of the meal.

Musée du Vin

Anyone interested in wine should visit this museum, appropriately housed in the old cellars of Passy Abbey. It illustrates the history of wine in France and the main wine-producing areas, and has a collection of tools, bottles, and wax figures. An added inducement is the opportunity for some wine-tasting.

The Galerie Vivienne, a charming arcade linked to the Bibliothèque National de France

✚ 29D4
✉ Richelieu: 58 rue de Richelieu, 75002 Paris; François Mitterrand: quai François Mauriac, 75013 Paris
☎ Richelieu: 01 53 79 53 79, recorded information: 01 53 79 81 10; François Mitterand: 01 53 79 59 59
🕐 Richelieu: 10–7; closed Mon. Cabinet des Médailles: daily 1–5; Sun 12–6. François Mitterrand: visits of the building on Tue–Sat 2, Sun 3 by appointment only. Reading rooms Tue–Sat 10–8, Sun noon–7
🍴 Restaurant in Galerie Vivienne (£)
Ⓜ Richelieu: Bourse, Palais-Royal-Musée du Louvre; François Mitterrand: Quai de la Gare
🚌 Richelieu: 29, 39, 48; François Mitterrand: 62, 89
♿ Very good
💷 Richelieu: moderate; François Mitterrand: free

BIBLIOTHÈQUE NATIONALE DE FRANCE ✪

The national library is seen by the French as a symbol of their culture. Until 1996, the BN, as Parisians call it, was housed in Cardinal Mazarin's former palace situated at the back of the Palais-Royal, extended many times and now stretching from the rue de Richelieu to the rue Vivienne. However, with around 13 million books and as many prints and photographs, it had long been overcrowded. The building of a new library along the river, in the redevelopment area of Bercy, was President Mitterrand's last 'Grand Projet'. The BNF, as it is now called, occupies two sites known as 'Richelieu' and 'François Mitterrand'.

The new library houses the huge stock of printed books and documents and is intended to serve as a public library and a research centre equipped with the most modern means of data transmission. Four corner towers looking like open books surround an imposing base with a central garden where the reading rooms are situated.

The Richelieu building houses manuscripts, prints and medals and holds temporary exhibitions in the Galerie Mansart, the Galerie Mazarine (which has a magnificent painted ceiling) and the Crypte. The Cabinet des Médailles et des Antiques houses coins and medals from antiquity to the present day as well as various *objets d'art*, cameos and bronzes from the former royal collections.

Two charming arcades linked to the library, the Galerie Vivienne and the Galerie Colbert, offer an unexpected insight into Parisian social life in the 19th century.

CARNAVALET, MUSÉE ✪✪

This museum retraces the history of Paris from antiquity to the present day, and is worth visiting for the building alone: a beautiful Renaissance mansion, one of the oldest in Le Marais, remodelled in the 17th century. The Hôtel Carnavalet was the residence of Madame de Sévigné, who depicted Parisian society at the time of Louis XIV with a great deal of humour. Note the 16th-century lions guarding the entrance and Louis XIV's statue by Coysevox in the centre of the courtyard. In 1989, the museum was linked to the nearby Hôtel Le Peletier de St Fargeau, which dates from the late 17th century. The Hôtel Carnavalet deals with the period from the origins of the city to 1789, with mementoes of Madame de Sévigné and splendid Louis XV and Louis XVI furniture. The Hôtel Le Peletier de St Fargeau houses collections from 1789 to the present day. The Revolution is extensively illustrated, while the 19th and 20th centuries are represented by a number of reconstructions such as Marcel Proust's bedroom and the art nouveau reception room of the Café de Paris.

✚ 29E3
✉ 23 rue de Sévigné, 75003 Paris
☎ 01 44 59 58 58
🕐 Tue–Sun 10–5:40; closed some bank hols
🍴 Restaurants and cafés near by in rue des Francs-Bourgeois(£–£££)
Ⓜ Saint-Paul
🚌 69, 96
♿ None
🖐 Moderate
❓ Guided tours, shops

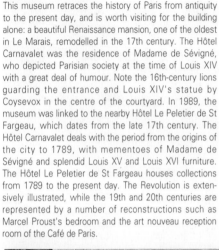

The courtyard of the Musée Carnavalet, built in 1540 although since remodelled

CENTRE GEORGES POMPIDOU (➤ 16, TOP TEN)

CERNUSCHI, MUSÉE ✪

The banker and art collector Henri Cernuschi bequeathed his elegant private mansion to the city of Paris at the end of the 19th century. Situated on the edge of the parc Monceau, the building houses Cernuschi's superb collection of ancient Chinese art on the ground floor (terracottas, bronzes, jades and ceramics) and contemporary traditional Chinese paintings on the first floor.

✚ 28B5
✉ 7 avenue Velasquez, 75008 Paris
☎ 01 45 63 50 75
🕐 Tue–Sun 10–5:40; closed bank hols
Ⓜ Villiers 🚌 30, 94
♿ Good 🖐 Inexpensive

Magnificent bronzes, pools and fountains front the Palais de Chaillot

✚ 28A3

✉ Place du Trocadéro, 75116 Paris

☎ Musée de l'Homme: 01 44 05 72 72; Musée de la Marine: 01 53 65 69 69

🕐 Musée de l'Homme: Wed–Mon 9:45–5:15; closed bank hols. Musée de la Marine: Wed–Mon 10–5:45; closed 1 May

Ⓜ Trocadéro

🚌 22, 30, 32, 63, 72, 82

♿ Musée de l'Homme: none; Musée de la Marine: good

🍴 Both museums: moderate

❓ Both museums have a bookshop; guided tours in Musée de la Marine

CHAILLOT, PALAIS DE ✪✪

This imposing architectural complex on top of a hill overlooking the river and facing the Tour Eiffel across the pont d'Iéna offers magnificent views and houses two interesting museums.

Designed for the 1937 World Exhibition, the building consists of two separate pavilions with curved wings, on either side of a vast terrace decorated with monumental statues. Just below, the tiered Jardins du Trocadéro extend to the edge of the river. The ornamental fountain is particularly impressive at night when the powerful spray of water shines under the spotlights.

The Musée de l'Homme is devoted to anthropology and ethnography, dealing with Man and his development in various geographical contexts. It illustrates the arts and cultures of different civilisations from Africa, the Near East, the Arctic, Asia, Oceania and America by means of tools, weapons, jewellery, frescoes, sculptures, ceramics, handicrafts and musical instruments.

The Musée de la Marine is devoted to French maritime history from the 18th century onwards. The extensive collections show the development of navigational skills and include beautiful models of 18th-century sailing ships; they also provide an insight into the modern navy and retrace the history of maritime transport and great expeditions across the world.

The east wing was seriously damaged by fire in 1997 and the two museums it contained are now closed. The Musée des Monuments Français is scheduled to reopen in 2003 whereas the Musée du Cinéma Henri Langlois will probably move to new premises in the former American Center in Bercy.

CHAMPS-ELYSÉES, LES (➤ 17, TOP TEN)

CINÉMA, MUSÉE DU (SEE ABOVE)

CITÉ, ILE DE LA ⭐⭐⭐

The Ile de la Cité is not only the historic centre of Paris, it is also a place of exceptional natural beauty and an architectural gem.

The Celtic tribe the Parisii settled on the largest island in an area known as Lutetia, which under the Romans expanded onto the Left Bank of the Seine. Nevertheless, the island (the Cité), which the king of the Franks chose as his capital in 508, remained for 1,000 years the seat of royal, judicial and religious power. During the Middle Ages, the Ile de la Cité was an important intellectual centre as its cathedral schools attracted students from all over Europe. Even after the kings of France left the royal palace for larger premises on the right bank, the Cité lost none of its symbolic importance and remains to this day the 'guardian' of 2,000 years of history.

The appearance of the Cité has, of course, changed considerably over the years; in the 19th century, the centre of the island was cleared and the vast square in front of Notre-Dame Cathedral created. At the other end of the island, the Conciergerie (► 44) and Sainte-Chapelle (► 73) are the only remaining parts of the medieval royal palace, now incorporated in the huge Palais de Justice.

✝ 29E2

✉ Ile de la Cité, 75001 and 75004 Paris

🍴 Restaurants and cafés (£–££) on the island and on the Right and Left banks

Ⓜ Cité, pont Neuf, St-Michel, Châtelet, Hôtel de Ville

🚌 21, 38, 96

A view of Ile de la Cité and pont Neuf

41

A Walk Along the Sein
& On the Islands

This relatively compact area offers stately historic buildings, breathtaking views, provincial charm and the liveliness of a great city.

Start from the place du Châtelet on the Right Bank.

The monumental fountain was commissioned by Napoleon on his return from Egypt.

Walk along the quai de Gesvres, then across the pont Notre-Dame.

The flower market on the place Louis Lépine is a refreshing sight. On Sunday, flowers are replaced by birds.

Walk east along the embankment, turn right into rue des Ursins then left and left again.

The narrow streets of the medieval cathedral precinct have retained a few old houses. At the tip of the island is an underground memorial to the victims of Nazi concentration camps.

Cross over to the Ile Saint-Louis and turn left, following the quai de Bourbon.

Enjoy the peaceful atmosphere of this sought-after residential area (➤ 72).

Turn right into rue des Deux Ponts and cross over to the Left Bank. Walk to the square Viviani then cross rue St-Jacques into rue St-Séverin.

This is one of the oldest parts of the Quartier Latin. The Gothic Church of St-Séverin has a magnificent interior.

From the place St-Michel, cross back on to the Ile de la Cité.

Sainte-Chapelle (➤ 73) is very close. The place Dauphine at the western end of the island is another haven of peace. Admire the view from the pont Neuf, Paris's oldest bridge.

Cross over to the Right Bank and the pont Neuf métro station.

Distance
4km

Time
2–4 hours depending on church visits

Start point
Place du châtelet
✚ 29D3
Ⓜ Châtelet or 🚌 21, 38, 85, 96

End point
Pont Neuf
✚ 29D3
Ⓜ Pont Neuf or 🚌 21, 58, 67, 70

Lunch
Le Vieux Bistrot
✉ 14 rue du Cloître-Notre-Dame, 75004 Paris
☎ 01 43 54 18 95

Left: *Pont Neuf*
Below: *Place du Châtelet salutes Napoleon's Egyptian campaign*

Macabre associations always attract crowds, and La Conciergerie, Paris's oldest prison, is no exception

COGNACQ-JAY, MUSÉE ✪✪

The collections of 18th-century European art bequeathed to the city of Paris by Ernest Cognacq and his wife Louise Jay, founders of the Samaritaine department stores, are displayed in one of the beautiful mansions of Le Marais. The refinement of the Enlightenment period is illustrated by the works of French artists Watteau, Chardin, Fragonard and La Tour, and also by Tiepolo, Guardi and Reynolds. The Rembrandt adds a welcome contrasting note. Various *objets d'art*, including Saxe and Sèvres porcelain, are exhibited in glass cabinets.

29E3
Hôtel Donon, 8 rue Elzévir, 75003 Paris
01 40 27 07 21
10–5:40; closed Mon and bank hols
Near by (£–££)
Saint-Paul 29
None Inexpensive
Guided tours, bookshop

LA CONCIERGERIE ✪✪

For most people, the name 'Conciergerie' suggests crowds of innocent prisoners waiting to be taken to the guillotine. Nowadays, its familiar round towers covered with conical slate roofs and the square clock tower, which housed the first public clock in Paris, are one of the most picturesque sights of the Île de la Cité. The Conciergerie is the last remaining authentic part of a 14th-century royal complex, administered by a 'concierge' or governor. The twin towers marked the main entrance to the palace. In the late 14th century, the Conciergerie was turned into a prison but it only acquired a sinister connotation during the Revolution, when it held a number of famous prisoners, including Queen Marie-Antoinette, Madame du Barry and the poet André Chénier, as well as Danton and Robespierre.

The visit includes the original guards' room, a magnificent great hall with Gothic vaulting and kitchens with monumental fireplaces. There is also a reconstruction of Marie-Antoinette's cell.

28D3
1 quai de l'Horloge, 75001 Paris
01 53 73 78 50
Apr–Sep 9:30–6:30, Oct–Mar 10–5; closed 1 Jan, 1 May, 1 Nov, 11 Nov, 25 Dec
Cité, Châtelet
96
None
Moderate
Guided tours, bookshop

CONCORDE, PLACE DE LA ✪✪✪

This is undoubtedly the most impressive square in Paris: its stately elegance, its size and its magnificent views are simply breathtaking. Built in the mid-18th century to celebrate Louis XV 'the beloved', it was designed by Gabriel who erected two classical pavilions on either side of the rue Royale; its octagonal shape is emphasised by eight allegorical statues representing major French cities.

The pink granite obelisk from Luxor, offered to the French nation by the viceroy of Egypt in 1836, is at the centre of the square, flanked by two graceful fountains. Two magnificent vistas open up: one towards the Champs-Elysées and Le Louvre beyond the beautiful gates of the Jardin des Tuileries, the other towards the Madeleine at the end of the rue Royale and the Assemblée Nationale across the pont de la Concorde.

✠ 28C4
✉ 75008 Paris
🚇 Concorde
🚌 42, 73, 84, 94

Decorative architecture and statuary (left and above) grace place de la Concorde

EUGÈNE DELACROIX, MUSÉE NATIONAL ✪

The old-world charm of the tiny rue de Furstenberg, hidden behind the Church of St-Germain-des-Prés, is the perfect setting for a museum devoted to one of the major French Romantic painters. Delacroix lived and worked here until the end of his life and, besides a few paintings, the place is full of mementoes of the artist, letters, sketches...and his palette. It is well worth taking time to explore the picturesque neighbourhood and the open market in rue de Buci.

✠ 29D3
✉ 6 rue de Furstenberg, 75006 Paris
☎ 01 44 41 86 50
🕐 9:30–5; closed Tue, 1 Jan, 1 May, 14 Jul, 15 Aug, 25 Dec
🚇 St-Germain-des-Prés
🚌 39, 48, 63, 95
♿ None Inexpensive

28C3

75007 Paris

For the museums' opening times, see the relevant entries

Cafés and restaurants near by in boulevard St-Germain (£–££)

Varenne, Rue du Bac

69, 83, 84, 94

FAUBOURG SAINT-GERMAIN ✪✪

This 'suburb' is today one of the most elegant districts of central Paris.

Its name came from the nearby Abbaye de St-Germain-des-Prés to which it belonged in medieval times. University students loved to stroll through fields and meadows stretching down to the river west of the abbey and the area remained in its natural state until the 18th century, when it became fashionable for the aristocracy and the wealthy middle class to have mansions built there by the famous architects of the time. Today, a few streets have retained some of their past elegance even though most of the mansions have now been taken over by ministries and foreign embassies.

The rue de Varenne (a distortion of *garenne*, the French word for warren, which confirms the area's rural origins!), is lined with the famous Hôtel Matignon, built in 1721 and now the Prime Minister's residence, and the Hôtel Biron, better known as the Musée Rodin (➤ 70). The parallel rue de Grenelle is equally interesting for its wealth of authentic architecture, including the Hôtel de Villars, which is now the town hall of the 7th *arrondissement*. Further along the street, on the opposite side, there is an interesting museum (No 59) devoted to the sculptor Maillol (➤ 55) and, next to it, the beautiful Fontaine des Quatre Saisons (Fountain of the Four Seasons).

Typical Parisian apartments, four to six storeys high, in Faubourg-Saint-Germain. Uniformly painted in shades of white and grey, the mansions date from the 17th and 18th centuries

Faubourg St-Honoré is not for those on a budget

FAUBOURG ST-HONORÉ ✪✪

This other 'suburb', this time on the Right Bank, is centred on the very long street of the same name, running parallel to the Champs-Elysées and famous for its *haute couture* establishments and luxury boutiques as well as for the Palais de l'Elysée, the official residence of the French president.

Leading fashion houses have been established in the area for over a hundred years: Louis Féraud, Christian Lacroix and Lanvin are still in the rue du Faubourg St-Honoré, but the majority are now in the avenue Montaigne across the Champs-Elysées. Opposite the British Embassy, No 54 opens into a couple of courtyards surrounded by boutiques selling beautiful furniture, *objets d'art*, paintings etc. Many modern art galleries line the perpendicular avenue Matignon, while the avenue Gabriel, which runs along the Champs-Elysées gardens past the American Embassy, makes a peaceful stroll through this select area.

➕ 28B4
✉ 75008 Paris
🚇 St-Philippe-du-Roule, Madeleine
🚌 52
❓ A stamp market takes place near the Rond-Point des Champs-Elysées on Thu, Sat and Sun 9–7

FRAGONARD, MUSÉE ✪

The history of perfume from the time of the ancient Egyptians to the present is the fascinating subject of this museum, housed within the premises of the Fragonard perfumery, in two different places, both near the opera house. The way in which plant and animal substances are used to create an infinite variety of essences and the delicate process of perfume-making are explained in a historical context, amidst collections of bottles, test tubes, labels, paintings etc.

➕ 28C4
✉ 9 rue Scribe, 75009 Paris; 39 boulevard des Capucines, 75002 Paris
☎ 01 47 42 04 56
🕐 9–5:30; closed Sun from Oct–Mar and 25 Dec
🚇 Opéra None
💷 Free
❓ Guided tours, shop

47

+ 29E1
✉ 42 avenue des Gobelins, 75013 Paris
☎ 01 44 08 52 00
⏰ Tue, Wed, Thu guided tours only at 2 and 2:45; closed bank hols
Ⓜ Les Gobelins
🚌 27, 47, 83, 91
♿ None
🎟 Moderate

GOBELINS, MANUFACTURE NATIONALE DES ✪

The former royal tapestry factory, founded by Colbert in 1664 to make beautiful tapestries for the royal household, is still going strong. Priceless works of art, based on paintings by artists such as Le Brun and Boucher and, more recently, Lurçat and Picasso, have been produced in the workshops over the last three centuries. Techniques have hardly changed since the 17th century and looms are either upright (*haute lice* method) or horizontal (*basse lice* method). The 17th-century buildings also house the Savonnerie carpet factory, founded in 1604, and the Beauvais tapestry factory, founded at the same time as the Gobelins.

LA GRANDE ARCHE DE LA DÉFENSE (➤ 18, TOP TEN)

+ 28B4
✉ Galeries Nationales: avenue du Général Eisenhower, 75008 Paris; Palais de la Découverte, avenue Franklin-Roosevelt, 75008 Paris
☎ Galeries Nationales: 01 44 13 17 17; Palais Découverte: 01 56 43 20 21
⏰ Galeries Nationales: variable; Palais Découverte: 9:30–6, Sun 10–7; closed Mon
🍴 Café-bar (£)
Ⓜ Champs-Elysées-Clemenceau
🚌 28, 42, 49, 72, 73, 80, 83
♿ Galeries Nationales: excellent; Palais: none
🎟 Galeries Nationales: variable; Palais Découverte: moderate

GRAND PALAIS ✪✪

Built at the same time as the Pont Alexandre III for the 1900 World Exhibition, this enormous steel and glass structure, concealed behind stone walls, is typical of the *belle époque* style: Ionic columns line the imposing façade and colossal bronze statues decorate the four corners.

Major international art exhibitions – Tutankhamun, Renoir, Gauguin and Picasso, to name but a few – are traditionally held in the Galeries Nationales, on the Champs-Elysées side of the building.

The west part of the Grand Palais houses the Palais de la Découverte, inaugurated in 1937 to bring science within the grasp of the general public and keep them informed of the latest scientific developments. There are interactive experiments, documentary films and a planetarium. Recent additions are the Electrostatic exhibition and the Sun room.

Elaborate statues adorn the Grand Palais

The Passage des Panoramas shopping arcade in boulevard Montmartre

GRANDS BOULEVARDS ⭐

These busy arteries, stretching from the place de la République to the Madeleine and lined with cinemas, theatres, cafés and shops, have today fallen victim to their long tradition of popular entertainment, choked by traffic jams and disfigured by aggressive neon signs, cheap snack bars and general neglect.

The 'boulevards' were laid out as a tree-lined promenade in the 17th century, when some of the city's medieval fortifications were demolished; two ceremonial arches, the Porte St-Martin and the Porte St-Denis, replaced the town gates.

The popularity of the boulevards peaked during the 19th century, with popular attractions in the east (theatre, dancing, circus and busking) and a more refined choice of entertainment in the west, especially after the building of the opera house. Several shopping arcades were also opened, including the Passage des Panoramas in boulevard Montmartre, opposite **Musée Grévin**, the famous waxworks museum, and at the end of the century, one of the first cinemas was inaugurated in boulevard St-Denis by the Lumière brothers.

Today, the boulevards still attract crowds of cinema- and theatre-goers but their general shabby appearance also encourages a rowdy element, particularly between the Porte St-Martin and the rue de Richelieu. Fortunately, complete renovation is underway.

Grands Boulevards
➕ 28C4
✉ From east to west: boulevards St-Martin, St-Denis, de Bonne Nouvelle, Poissonnière, Montmartre, des Italiens, des Capucines and de la Madeleine
🚇 République, Strasbourg-St-Denis, Bonne Nouvelle, Rue Montmartre, Richelieu-Drouot, Opéra, Madeleine

Musée Grévin
➕ 29D4
✉ 10 boulevard Montmartre, 75009 Paris
☎ 01 47 70 85 05
🕐 10–7
🍴 Near by along the boulevards (£–££)
🚇 Rue Montmartre
🚌 20, 48, 74, 85
♿ None
💰 Expensive
❓ Shop

In the Know

If you only have a short time to visit Paris, or would like to get a real flavour of the city, here are some ideas:

10
Ways To Be A Local

Stand on the place Charles-de-Gaulle during the rush hour to get the feel of the Parisian pace of life.

Go into a crowded café at lunchtime and rub shoulders with hard-working Parisians.

Go to 'Les Champs' (Champs-Elysées) on Saturday night and meet Parisians enjoying themselves.

Soak in the atmosphere of old Paris along the canal St-Martin.

Buy a baguette and some cheese in the rue Mouffetard for an outdoor lunch in the nearby square des Arènes de Lutèce.

Sample the village atmosphere in Le Marais on Sunday afternoon, together with thousands of Parisians.

Talk to the *bouquinistes* along the Seine, usually only too willing to comment on local news and people.

Mingle with Parisian youth along boulevard St-Germain.

Learn how to bargain at the Marché aux Puces, Porte de Clignancourt.

Don't talk to a Parisian about local driving.

10
Good Places To Have Lunch

Le Caveau du Palais (££) ✉ 19 place Dauphine, 1st, ☎ 01 43 26 04 28; view of the lovely place Dauphine.

Brasserie de l'Île Saint-Louis (£) ✉ 55 quai de Bourbon, 4th, ☎ 01 43 54 02 59; *choucroute garnie.*

Le Polidor (£) ✉ 41 rue Monsieur-le-Prince, 6th, ☎ 01 43 26 95 34; French cuisine in the heart of the Latin Quarter.

La Victoire suprême du coeur (££) ✉ 41 rue des Bourdonnais, 1st, ☎ 01 40 41 93 95; international vegetarian cuisine.

Georges (££–£££) ✉ Centre Pompidou (6th floor), 4th, ☎ 01 44 78 47 99; fabulous views of Paris.

Le Toupary (££) ✉ Samaritaine, 5th floor, 2 quai du Louvre, 1st,

☎ 01 40 41 29 29; panoramic view.

Bofinger (££) ✉ 5 rue de la Bastille, 4th, ☎ 01 42 72 87 82; *belle époque* setting.

Restaurant du Palais-Royal (££) ✉ 43 rue de Valois, 1st, ☎ 01 40 20 00 27; overlooking the Jardin du Palais-Royal.

A Priori Thé (£) ✉ 35–7 Galerie Vivienne, 2nd, ☎ 01 42 97 48 75; old-world surroundings.

Châlet des Iles (££) ✉ Bois de Boulogne, Lac Inférieur, 16th, ☎ 01 42 88 04 69; for a refreshing lunch after an invigorating row on the lake!

Famous and Picturesque Cafés

• Café de la Paix, 12 boulevard des Capucines,  Opéra
• Fouquet's, 99 Champs-Elysées, George V
• Café Marly, Le Louvre, Palais-Royal
• Café de Flore, 172 boulevard St-Germain, St-Germain-des-Prés
• Les Deux Magots, 6 place St-Germain-des-Prés, St-Germain-des-Prés
• Le Procope, 13 rue de l'Ancienne-Comédie, Odéon
• Café de la Mairie, 8 place St-Sulpice, St-Sulpice
• Café Martini, 11 rue du Pas de la Mule, Chemin-Vert
• La Closerie des Lilas, 171 boulevard du Montparnasse, Vavin
• Le Sancerre, 35 rue des Abbesses, Abbesses

Top Activities

Walking (pedestrian areas): footpath along the river; quartier Montorgueil north of Les Halles.
Cycle tours: Paris à Vélo, c'est Sympa! 37 bd Bourdon, 4th, 01 48 87 60 01.
Rowing on the lake in Bois de Boulogne.
Horse riding: Société d'Equitation de Paris, 01 45 01 20 06.
Theme parks: Disneyland Paris (➤ 81), Parc Astérix (➤ 85).
Parc Floral de Paris Bois de Vincennes, 12th; flowers, medicinal plants etc.
Aquaboulevard 4–6 rue Louis-Armand, 15th, 01 40 60 10 00; fun with water.
Hot-air ballooning: France Montgolfières, 01 47 00 66 44.
Helicopter rides: Paris Hélicoptère, 01 48 35 90 44.
Leisure park: Base de Plein Air, St-Quentin-en-Yvelines, 01 30 62 20 12, RER C.

Bird's-Eye Views

• Tour Eiffel (➤ 25)
• Sacré-Coeur (➤ 70)
• Tour Montparnasse (➤ 62)
• Grande Arche de la Défense (➤ 18)
• Towers of Notre-Dame (➤ 22)
• Arc de Triomphe (➤ 32)
• Dôme of Les Invalides (➤ 19)
• Centre Georges Pompidou (6th floor, ➤ 16)
• Palais de Chaillot (➤ 40)
• Institut du Monde Arabe (➤ 54)

Forum des Halles

➕ 29D3

✉ Rue Pierre Lescot, rue Rambuteau, rue Berger, 75001 Paris

🍴 In the complex (£)

🚇 Les Halles

🚌 29, 38, 47

♿ Lifts to all levels

LES HALLES ✪

Paris's legendary food market has long gone from the centre of the capital, but the name is here to stay, tinged for many Parisians with a certain nostalgia, for when the 19th-century steel and glass 'pavillons de Baltard' were removed in 1969 and the noisy activity of the market suddenly stopped, the character of this popular district changed beyond recognition. A vast gaping hole was left between one of the most beautiful churches in Paris and a lovely Renaissance fountain. A commercial and cultural complex was built underground with a central patio surrounded by glass-roofed galleries that barely reach ground level. Above ground, a garden was laid over the remaining space, with a children's area and shaded walks and yet more graceful steel and glass structures.

The underground complex, spread over several levels, comprises shops, including a group of fifty young fashion designers (Poste Berger, level –1), restaurants, an auditorium, a gymnasium and a swimming pool, as well as a tropical greenhouse.

A huge stone head leaning against a hand decorates the semicircular paved area in front of the Eglise St-Eustache. The latter was built over a period of a hundred years, in a blend of late Gothic, Renaissance and neo-classical styles. From the church, a path leads across the gardens to the square des Innocents and the beautiful Renaissance fountain, built and carved in the mid-16th century by Pierre Lescot and Jean Goujon, who also worked on the Louvre.

HISTOIRE NATURELLE, MUSÉE NATIONAL D' (➤ 68)

HOMME, MUSÉE DE L' (➤ 40)

Eglise St-Eustache, with the incongruous giant head and hand sculpture

Place de l'Hôtel de Ville, formerly called place de Grève (grève is French for shore)

Above: *the town hall clock*

HÔTEL DE VILLE ✪

The town hall of the city of Paris has been standing on this site since the 14th century. Destroyed by fire during the Paris Commune in 1871, it was rebuilt almost straight away in neo-Renaissance style. On the exterior are 136 statues representing famous historic figures.

Near by stands the 52m-high Tour St-Jacques, the only remaining part of a demolished church. In 1648, Pascal used the tower to verify his experiments on the weight of air. Later, a meteorological station was set up at the top and the tower became the property of the city of Paris.

On the east side of the town hall, the Eglise St-Gervais-St-Protais is a splendid example of a successful blend of Flamboyant Gothic and classical styles.

 29E3
✉ Place de l'Hôtel de Ville, 75004 Paris
☎ 01 42 76 40 40
🕐 Guided tour by appointment only
🚇 Hôtel de Ville
🚌 47, 67, 70, 72, 74, 96,
♿ Good
🎟 Free

INSTITUT DE FRANCE ✪

The imposing classical building facing the Louvre across the river was commissioned by Cardinal Mazarin, as a school for provincial children, and designed by Le Vau; it is surmounted by a magnificent dome and houses the Institut de France, an institution created in 1795 to unite under one roof five prestigious academies, including the famous (and oldest) Académie Française founded in 1635 by Richelieu. It also houses the Bibliothèque Mazarine, Mazarin's own collection of rare editions.

 29D3
✉ 23 quai de Conti, 75006 Paris
☎ 01 44 41 44 41
🕐 Sat, Sun guided tours at 3PM
🚇 Pont Neuf, Louvre, Odéon
🚌 24, 27, 39, 48, 58, 70, 95
♿ None 🎟 Inexpensive

53

+ 29E2

⊠ 1 rue des Fossés St-
Bernard, 75005 Paris

☎ 01 40 51 38 38

⊙ 10–6; closed Mon, 1 May

🍴 Café on 9th floor (£–££)

Ⓜ Jussieu

🚌 24, 63, 67, 86, 87, 89

♿ Good 👆 Inexpensive

❓ Guided tours, shops

+ 28B5

⊠ 158 boulevard
Haussmann, 75008 Paris

☎ 01 42 89 04 91

⊙ 10–6

🍴 Tea-room (£)

Ⓜ Miromesnil, St-Philippe-
du-Roule

🚌 22, 28, 43, 52, 54, 80, 83,
84, 93

♿ None 👆 Moderate

+ 28C4

⊠ 1 place de la Concorde,
75001 Paris

☎ 01 47 03 12 50

⊙ Wed–Fri 12–7, Sat–Sun
10–7, Tue 12–9:30

🍴 Café (£) Ⓜ Concorde

🚌 24, 42, 52, 72, 73, 84, 94

♿ Very good 👆 Moderate

❓ Shop

Opposite page: *Eglise de
la Madeleine, not
instantly recognisable as
a church*

Right: *home of André-
Jacquemart's European
art collection; the former
owners' private
apartments are also
on show*

INSTITUT DU MONDE ARABE ✪

The Institute of Arab and Islamic Civilisation is a remarkable
piece of modern architecture designed by the French
architect Jean Nouvel. Its glass and aluminium façade,
reminiscent of a *musharabia* (carved wooden screen),
discretely refers to Arab tradition. The seventh floor houses
a museum of Islamic art and civilisation from the 8th
century to the present day. The ninth floor offers a
panoramic view of the Ile de la Cité and Ile St-Louis near by.

LES INVALIDES (➤ 19, TOP TEN)

JACQUEMART-ANDRÉ, MUSÉE ✪✪

This elegant 19th-century mansion, recently refurbished,
houses the remarkable collections of European art
bequeathed by the wealthy widow of a banker to the
Institut de France. French 18th-century art includes
paintings by Boucher, Chardin, Greuze and Watteau, as well
as sculptures by Houdon and Pigalle, furniture, Beauvais
tapestries and *objets d'art*. There are also 17th-century
Dutch and Flemish masterpieces and an exceptionally fine
collection of Italian Renaissance art including works by
Mantegna, Donatello, Botticelli and Uccello.

JEU DE PAUME, GALERIE NATIONALE DU ✪

One of two pavilions built in the late 19th century at the
entrance of the Jardin des Tuileries, the Jeu de Paume, on
the rue de Rivoli side, was intended for the practice of a
game similar to tennis. From the early 20th century, both
pavilions were used for art exhibitions and the Jeu de
Paume later housed the national collection of Impressionist
paintings until it was transferred to the new Musée
d'Orsay. Entirely refurbished in 1991, the Jeu de Paume
now holds temporary exhibitions of contemporary art.

MUSÉE

LE LOUVRE (► 20–1, TOP TEN)

MADELEINE, EGLISE DE LA ✪✪

Work started on this imposing neo-classical building in 1764, shortly after the completion of the place de la Concorde, but troubled times lay ahead and the partly constructed building was abandoned until 1806, when Napoleon decided to erect a temple to the glory of his 'Great Army'. He ran out of time to complete his ambitious project. It was then decided that the edifice would be a church after all and it was consecrated in 1845. The result is an impressive Graeco-Roman temple completely surrounded by tall Corinthian columns. Steps lead up to the entrance, which is surmounted by a monumental pediment. The interior is decorated with sculptures by Rude and Pradier; the magnificent organ was made by Cavaillé-Coll in 1846 and several well-known composers, including Camille Saint-Saëns, held the post of organist.

✚ 28C4
✉ Place de la Madeleine, 75008 Paris
☎ 01 44 51 69 00
🕐 7:30–7, Sun 7:30–1:30 and 3:30–7; bank hols variable
Ⓜ Madeleine
🚌 24, 42, 52, 84, 94
♿ None
💷 Free
❓ Shops

MAILLOL, MUSÉE ✪✪

This atttractive museum, situated in the rue de Grenelle next to a beautiful 18th-century fountain, is interesting on two accounts: it displays a great many works by the French painter and sculptor Aristide Maillol (1861–1944) as well as a private collection of works by Ingres, Cézanne, Dufy, Matisse, Bonnard, Degas, Picasso, Gauguin, Rodin, Kandinsky, Poliakoff etc.

Maillol's obsessive theme was the nude, upon which he conferred an allegorical meaning; he produced smooth rounded figures, some of which can be seen in the Jardin des Tuileries.

✚ 28C3
✉ 59–61 rue de Grenelle, 75007 Paris
☎ 01 42 22 59 58
🕐 11–6; closed Tue and bank hols
🍴 Cafeteria (£)
Ⓜ Rue du Bac
🚌 63, 68, 83, 84
♿ Good
💷 Moderate
❓ Shop

LE MARAIS ✪✪✪

The sedate old-world atmosphere of this historic enclave at the heart of the city, its architectural beauty and cultural diversity are unique.

As its name suggests, Le Marais was once an area of marshland on the Right Bank of the Seine. In the 13th century, the area was drained and cultivated by monks and Knights Templar. However, it was the construction of the place des Vosges at the beginning of the 17th century and the subsequent rapid urbanisation of the district that produced a wealth of beautiful domestic architecture and gave Le Marais its unique character. When fashions changed in the late 18th century, the district gradually became derelict and had to wait until the 1970s to be rediscovered and renovated.

Today Le Marais, which extends from the Hôtel de Ville to the place de la Bastille, offers visitors narrow picturesque streets, cafés and bistros, elegant mansions, tiny boutiques and a lively population that includes an important Jewish community. It is also one of the favourite haunts of the gay community.

Around every corner is another delightful mansion. These houses are no longer privately owned: some have been turned into museums, sometimes with striking results (Musée Picasso, ➤ 67). One of the most imposing, the Hôtel de Soubise, houses the **Musée de l'Histoire de France**, where historic documents are displayed amidst a profusion of Louis XV decoration. An unusual museum dedicated to hunting and nature (**Musée de la Chasse et de la Nature**) is housed in the Hôtel de Guénégaud des Brosses, built by François Mansart. Here hunting arms dating from prehistory until the 19th century are on display, plus paintings and decorative arts on the subject of hunting.

MARINE, MUSÉE DE LA (➤ 40)

Capturing the mansions, fountains and plane trees of the place des Vosges

Musée de l'Histoire de France

🕀 29E3
✉ Hôtel de Soubise, 60 rue des Francs-Bourgeois, 75003 Paris
☎ 01 40 27 60 96
🕐 Mon–Fri 10–5:45, Sat–Sun 1:45–5:45; closed Tue and bank hols
Ⓜ Hôtel de Ville
🚌 29, 75, 96
♿ None
💶 Inexpensive
❓ Shop

Musée de la Chasse et de la Nature

🕀 29E3
✉ Hôtel de Guénégaud des Brosses, 60 rue des Archives, 75003 Paris
☎ 01 42 72 86 43
🕐 11–6; closed Mon and bank hols
Ⓜ Hôtel de Ville
🚌 29, 75
♿ None   💶 Moderate
❓ Bookshop

A Walk Through Le Marais

Picturesque streets and carefully restored architectural gems make this an enjoyable walk.

Walk north from place de l'Hôtel de Ville along rue des Archives.

The Eglise des Billettes, on your right, has the last remaining medieval cloister in Paris.

Turn right into rue Ste-Croix de la Bretonnerie, then third left and first right.

Rue des Rosiers, at the heart of the Jewish quarter, is lined with a colourful array of traditional shops and restaurants.

Turn left into rue Pavée then left again.

Rue des Francs-Bourgeois is the liveliest street in the Marais, with unusual boutiques selling clothes, antiques and trinkets.

Turn right into rue des Archives, then first right and continue to the tiny place de Thorigny.

The Musée Picasso (► 67) is on the left; on the right stands the Musée de la Serrure housing a remarkable collection of keys, locks and door knockers (🕐 10–12 and 2–5; closed Mon morning, Sat, Sun).

Walk down rue Elzévir on the right, past the Musée Cognacq-Jay (► 44) then left up the rue Payenne and right down rue Sévigné.

This whole area is delightfully peaceful, with gardens surrounded by railings. Have a look inside the courtyard of the Hôtel Carnavalet (► 39).

Walk east to the end of rue des Francs-Bourgeois.

Soak in the unique atmosphere of the place des Vosges (► 75). Come out from the southern end.

Turn right in the rue St-Antoine. The walk ends in front of Eglise St-Paul-St-Louis.

Distance
3.5km

Time
2–4 hours depending on museum visits

Start point
Place de l'Hôtel de Ville
✚ 29E3
🚇 Hôtel de Ville

End point
Eglise St-Paul-St-Louis
✚ 29E3
🚇 St Paul

Lunch
Café Martini
✉ 11 rue du Pas-de-la-Mule, 4th
☎ 01 42 77 05 04

Fashionable though the area may be, long-established shops and businesses still survive in Le Marais

Off map 28A4
2 rue Louis Boilly, 75016 Paris
01 42 24 07 02
10–5:30; closed Mon, 1 May, 25 Dec
Cafés and restaurants (£–££) in nearby Place de la Muette
La Muette
32, 63, PC
Good
Moderate
Shops

MARMOTTAN-MONET, MUSÉE ✪✪

Although situated off the beaten track, this gallery is a must for anyone interested in the Impressionist movement and in Monet in particular.

The museum was named after Paul Marmottan, who bequeathed his house and his private collections of Renaissance and 18th- and 19th-century art to the Institut de France. These were later enriched by several bequests, including 100 paintings by Monet donated by his son: detailed studies of Monet's garden in Giverny, particularly a group of *nymphéas* (water lilies) paintings, provide insights into the artist's approach (see also Musée de l'Orangerie, ► 64) and there are paintings of Rouen Cathedral (done in different light conditions according to the time of day) and of the River Thames in London. Most important of all, perhaps, is a relatively early work, called *Impression, Soleil levant* (1872), which created a sensation at the time and gave its name to the Impressionist movement.

There are also interesting works by Monet's contemporaries, Renoir, Pissarro, Sisley, Morisot and Gauguin.

Off map 28A4
Palais Galliéra, 10 avenue Pierre Ier de Serbie, 75016 Paris
01 56 52 86 00
10–6; closed Mon
Iéna 32, 63, 72, 92
None Moderate
Children's workshops

MODE ET DU COSTUME, MUSÉE DE LA ✪

This museum of fashion is appropriately housed in a neo-Renaissance mansion dating from the late 19th century, the Palais Galliéra. Its rich collections of urban fashion, are shown in temporary exhibitions from the 18th century to the present and are continually being extended with donations from prestigious fashion houses (Dior, Yves St-Laurent, etc) and well-known personalities. In addition to the costumes (several thousands in all), there are etchings and photographs connected with fashion.

29D5
75018 Paris
Several (£–£££)
Abbesses, Lamarck-Caulaincourt
Montmartrobus

Musée de Montmartre
12 rue Cortot, 75018 Paris
01 46 06 61 11
11–6; closed Mon, 1 Jan, 1 May, 25 Dec
None Inexpensive
Temporary exhibitions, bookshop

MONTMARTRE ✪✪✪

This unassuming village overlooking Paris became a myth during the 19th century, when it was taken over by artists and writers attracted by its picturesque surroundings and Bohemian way of life. La 'Butte' (the mound) managed to retain its village atmosphere and now that the area has become a major tourist attraction, an undefinable nostalgia lingers on, perpetuating Montmartre's magic appeal.

In its heyday, the district was the favourite haunt and home of many famous artists. They met in cafés and in cabarets such as the Moulin-Rouge (1889), whose singers and dancers acquired world-wide fame through Toulouse-Lautrec's paintings and posters. Halfway up the hill, a wooden construction (13 place Emile-Goudeau) known as the Bateau-Lavoir, where, amongst others, Picasso,

Braque and Juan Gris had their studios, was the modest birthplace of Cubism; destroyed by fire in 1970, it has since been rebuilt. At the top of the hill stands the village square, place du Tertre, close to the Sacré-Coeur basilica (► 70). The **Musée de Montmartre** has works and memorabilia by the artists who lived here, and the narrow cobbled streets of the 'Butte' still have some amazing sights to offer, including a vineyard in the picturesque rue des Saules and two windmills in the twisting rue Lepic.

Today's artists follow in the footsteps of the famous 19th- and early 20th-century painters who made Montmartre their home

59

A Walk Through Montmartre

A walk through Montmartre is more like a pilgrimage. Allow 3 hours and time for the unexpected such as having your portrait done in place du Tertre!

Start from the square d'Anvers and walk north along rue de Stienkerque.

Facing you are the impressive steps leading to the Sacré-Coeur basilica. On the left, a funicular makes the climb easier.

Walk west along rue Tardieu to place des Abbesses.

This is the focal point of social life in Montmartre. Le Sancerre near by (if you can get in), is the most popular bar in the area. The métro entrance is in typical art nouveau style.

Continue northwest and turn right into rue Ravignan leading to place Emile–Goudeau.

The tiny square is one of the most authentic spots in Montmartre. The wooden Bateau-Lavoir, immortalised by Picasso, Braque and Gris, stood at No 13.

Continue up the winding street to rue Lepic then turn right towards the intersection of rue des Saules and rue St–Rustique.

The Auberge de la Bonne Franquette was the favourite haunt of the Impressionists, of Toulouse-Lautrec and Utrillo.

Rue Poulbot on the right leads to place du Calvaire (view), right round to place du Tertre.

The whole square is congested with easels and would-be artists. Go round the right side of the 12th-century Eglise St-Pierre to the Sacré-Coeur basilica (➤ 70).

Walk back to rue des Saules and follow it down to the other side of the hill.

At the corner of rue St-Vincent, watch out for the Montmartre vineyard and the Au Lapin Agile nightclub, the rendezvous of young artists and writers in the early 1900s.

Rue St–Vincent on the left leads to rue Caulaincourt where the walk ends.

Distance
2.2km

Time
3–4 hours

Start point
Square d'Anvers
✚ 29D5
🚇 Anvers

End point
Rue Caulaincourt
✚ Off map 29D5
🚇 Lamarck-Caulaincourt

Lunch
Au Clair de la Lune
✉ 9 rue Poulbot
☎ 01 42 58 97 03

Opposite page:
Montmartre by night

Left: *rue de la Gaîté, Montparnasse*
Right: *the Musée de la Musique*

MONTPARNASSE   😊😊

Fashions change quickly in artistic circles and, soon after the turn of the century, young artists and writers left Montmartre to settle on the Left Bank, in an area which had been known as Montparnasse since medieval times. Modigliani, Chagall, Léger and many others found a home and a studio in La Ruche, the counterpart of the Bateau-Lavoir in Montmartre (► 59). They were later joined by Russian political refugees, musicians and, between the wars, American writers of the 'lost generation', among them Hemingway. They met in cafés along the boulevard Montparnasse, which have since become household names: La Closerie des Lilas, La Rotonde, Le Select, La Coupole and Le Dôme.

Since the 1960s the district has been systematically modernised and a new business complex built south of the boulevard. The 200m-high **Tour Montparnasse** stands in front of one of the busiest stations in Paris. The tower's 56th and 59th floors are open to the public and offer a restaurant and panoramic views. To the south-west, the circular place de Catalogne, surrounded by rows of glass columns, was designed by Ricardo Bofill.

➕ 28C1
✉ 75014 Paris
🚇 Montparnasse-Bienvenüe, Vavin

Tour Montparnasse
✉ rue de l'Arrivée, 75015 Paris
☎ 01 45 38 52 56
🕐 9:30AM–10:30PM (11:30PM in summer)
🍴 Le Ciel de Paris (££)
♿ Good 💷 Moderate

MOYEN-AGE, MUSÉE NATIONAL DU   😊😊

This splendid museum of medieval art, also known as the Musée de Cluny, is housed in a 15th-century Gothic mansion – one of the last remaining examples of medieval domestic architecture in Paris.

The building stands at the heart of the Quartier Latin, on the site of Gallo-Roman baths dating from the 3rd century AD. The ruins are surrounded by a public garden. Inside the main courtyard, the elegant stair tower and corner turrets are particularly noteworthy.

The museum illustrates all the arts and crafts of the medieval period, the most famous exhibit being a set of tapestries known as 'La Dame à la Licorne', made in a Brussels workshop at the end of the 15th century. There is also an exceptionally fine collection of sculptures, including the heads of the kings of Judaea which decorated the façade of Notre-Dame Cathedral and were knocked down during the Revolution.

➕ 29D2
✉ 6 place Paul Painlevé, 75005 Paris
☎ 01 53 73 78 00
🕐 9:15–5:45; closed Tue and bank hols
🍴 In boulevard St Michel near by (£–££)
🚇 Cluny-La Sorbonne
🚌 21, 27, 38, 63, 85, 86, 87
♿ None
💷 Moderate
❓ Guided tours, shops, concerts

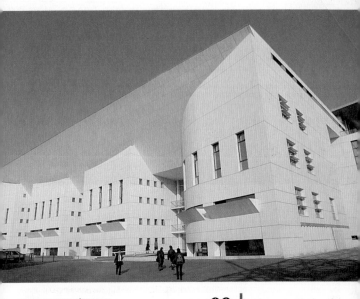

MUSIQUE, MUSÉE DE LA ✪✪

Recently reopened within the Cité de la Musique (➤ 26), the museum is now able to present a permanent exhibition consisting of some 900 musical instruments (out of a stock of around 4,500) dating from the Renaissance to the present day as well as a whole range of works of art and *objets d'art* inspired in some way by music. In order to highlight the museum's collections, regular concerts and lectures and various cultural events take place in the 230-seat auditorium.

➕ Off map 29F5
✉ 221 avenue Jean-Jaurès, 75019 Paris
☎ 01 44 84 44 84
🕐 Tue, Wed, Thu 12–6, Fri and Sat 12–9:30, Sun 10–6; closed Mon
Ⓜ Porte de Pantin
🚌 75, 151, PC
♿ Very good ✋ Moderate
❓ Guided tours, shops

NISSIM DE CAMONDO, MUSÉE ✪✪

This museum offers a delightful journey back into the 18th century.

In 1935, Count Moïse de Camondo bequeathed his private residence on the edge of the parc Monceau to the French nation in memory of his son Nissim, killed in action in 1917. The interior is arranged as an authentic 18th-century private home, including wall panelling, Aubusson and Savonnerie tapestries, paintings by Vigée-Lebrun and Hubert Robert, sculptures by Houdon and Sèvres and Chantilly porcelain.

➕ 28B5
✉ 63 rue de Monceau, 75008 Paris
☎ 01 53 89 06 40
🕐 10–5; closed Mon, Tue, 1 Jan, 14 Jul, 25 Dec
Ⓜ Villiers
🚌 84, 94
♿ None
✋ Moderate
❓ Guided tours

NOTRE-DAME (➤ 22, TOP TEN)

🔀 28C4

✉ place de l'Opéra, 75009 Paris

☎ 01 40 01 22 63

🕐 10–4:30; closed 1 Jan, 1 May and matinee performances

🚇 Opéra

🚌 20, 21, 22, 27, 29, 42, 52, 53, 56, 68, 81, 95

♿ None

💷 Moderate

❓ Guided tours at noon, shops

Above: the Opéra Garnier, epitome of late 19th-century ostentation

🔀 28C3

✉ place de la Concorde, Jardin des Tuileries, 75001 Paris

☎ 01 42 61 30 82 (fax)

🕐 Closed for restructuring

🚇 Concorde

🚌 24, 42, 52, 72, 73, 84, 94

♿ Very good

💷 Moderate

❓ Guided tours, shops

OPÉRA GARNIER

A night at the opera to see *Giselle* or *Sleeping Beauty* is one of the great moments of a visit to Paris, not only for the quality of the productions but also for the sheer splendour of what is still referred to as *the* opera, in spite of the fact that there are now two opera houses in Paris!

The Palais Garnier (named after its architect) was built in 1875 in neo-classical style, but the decoration is unmistakably late 19th century and includes a group of statues called *La Danse* by Carpeaux, a copy of the original now held in the Musée d'Orsay. Inside, the grand staircase and the foyer are magnificent. The main hall has recently been refurbished so that the ceiling decorated by Chagall can now be fully appreciated.

The museum contains paintings, watercolours and pastels illustrating the history of opera and ballet from the 18th century to the present day, mainly through portraits of famous singers, dancers and composers. Temporary exhibitions are also regularly organised.

ORANGERIE, MUSÉE NATIONAL DE L' 😀😀

The Orangerie, originally the greenhouse for the Tuileries Palace, now houses a private art collection bequeathed to the State by the widow of an art dealer. The collection consists mainly of Impressionist and 20th-century paintings – and a set of monumental paintings offered by Monet to his country, representing the famous nymphéas (water lilies, see also Musée Marmottan ➤ 58) in the artist's garden at Giverny. Unfortunately the Orangerie is to remain closed for refurbishing until December 2002.

ORSAY, MUSÉE D' (➤ 23, TOP TEN)

PALAIS-ROYAL ✪✪

This is more than just another historic building, it is a pleasant, relatively peaceful area with the Jardin du Palais-Royal in its centre. Here, cultural institutions occupy a prominent place, next to charming arcades and picturesque old streets. The palace built by Richelieu and bequeathed to the king on the cardinal's death now houses the ministry of culture and two important constitutional bodies, but the gardens are accessible through archways situated all round. Enclosed by arcading on three sides and an elegant double colonnade along the fourth, they are a haven of peace, where Parisians working in the area love to window-shop during their lunch hour along the row of quaint little boutiques hidden under the arcades.

An 18th-century addition to the original building houses the Comédie-Française, France's National Theatre, where all the classics are performed. From the place André Malraux in front, the Opéra Garnier can be seen at the top of the avenue de l'Opéra.

To the east of the Palais-Royal, off the rue Croix des Petits Champs, the Galerie Véro-Dodat is one of several elegant arcades in the area. Further up the street, the place des Victoires, designed by Mansart in the 17th century, is worth a detour for its classical architecture and for its fashion boutiques.

🚩 29D4
✉ Place du Palais-Royal, 75001 Paris
🕐 Jardin: 8AM–11PM (midnight in summer)
🍴 In the gardens (££)
Ⓜ Palais-Royal
♿ Jardin: free access

The peaceful arcades of the Palais-Royal (left) and (above) innovative sculpture in the main courtyard

29D2
Place du Panthéon, 75005 Paris
01 44 32 18 00
Apr–Sep 9:30–6:30; Oct–Mar 10–6:15; closed 1 Jan, 1 May, 25 Dec
Cardinal-Lemoine
84, 89
None
Moderate
Shops

PANTHÉON

Commissioned by Louis XV, the building was meant to replace St Genevieve's Church in the Quartier Latin; designed by Soufflot, who gave it the shape of a Greek cross surmounted by a high dome, it is now one of Paris's landmarks. Completed on the eve of the Revolution, it became a Pantheon for France's illustrious dead, among them Voltaire, Rousseau, Hugo, Zola, and more recently Jean Moulin (head of the French Resistance during World War II) and André Malraux (writer and highly successful Minister of Culture).

The domed Panthéon, imposing enough from a distance, but rather austere within

29E2
21 boulevard Morland, 75004 Paris
01 42 76 33 97
Tue–Sat 10:30–6:30, Sun 11–7; closed Mon
Sully-Morland 67, 86, 87
Good
Free

PAVILLON DE L'ARSENAL

The late 19th-century iron and glass building houses an information centre devoted to Paris's urban planning and architecture throughout its troubled history. The permanent exhibition ' Paris, la ville et ses projects' (Paris, a city in the making) shows the evolution of the cityscape by means of a large model that offers a virtual journey into old and new maps of Paris from the 18th century to today...a fascinating experience!

Off map 29F4
Boulevard de Ménilmontant, 75020 Paris
01 55 25 82 10

PÈRE-LACHAISE, CIMETIÈRE DU

Situated on the eastern edge of the city, the Cimetière du Père-Lachaise is Paris's most famous cemetery. The rising ground and abundant vegetation give the place a romantic atmosphere in spite of the great number of unsightly

funeral monuments. Many famous people are buried here, including Musset, Chopin, Molière, Oscar Wilde, Delacroix, Balzac, even the unhappy lovers Héloïse and Abélard. In the south-east corner stands the Mur des Fédérés where the last 'communards' were shot in 1871.

Mon–Fri 8–6, Sat 8:30–6, Sun 9–6 (5:30 in winter)

Père-Lachaise

Free

Guided tours (in English) Sat 3 in summer

PETIT PALAIS, MUSÉE DU ⊕

Built, like the Grand Palais facing it, for the 1900 World Exhibition, the Petit Palais houses the Fine Arts collections of the city of Paris, which mostly come from private bequests. The museum is closed until late 2003.

28B4

1 avenue Winston Churchill, 75008 Paris

PICASSO, MUSÉE ⊕⊕⊕

This is one of the most comprehensive museums devoted to the great 20th-century Spanish artist who lived and died in France. The collection was brought together after Picasso's death and consists of works donated to the State by his family in lieu of death duties, and his private collection – together totalling more than 200 paintings, sculptures, prints, drawings and ceramics.

The Hôtel Salé, situated at the heart of the historic Marais, was chosen to house this important collection. Like many other mansions in the area, it had been neglected and underwent extensive renovation to turn it into a museum. The interior decoration is very discreet, focusing attention on the beautiful stone staircase with its elegant wrought-iron banister.

Displayed in chronological order, the works illustrate the different phases of Picasso's artistic creation and the various techniques he used, from the blue period tainted with a certain pessimism (*Autoportrait bleu*), through the more optimistic pink period, to the successive Cubist periods. The tour of the museum is a fascinating journey in the company of one of the most forceful creative minds of this century. Picasso's private collection includes works by Renoir, Cézanne, Rousseau, Braque etc.

29F3

Hôtel Salé, 5 rue de Thorigny, 75003 Paris

01 42 71 25 21

Apr–Sep 9:30–6 (5:30 Oct–Mar); closed Tue, 1 Jan, 25 Dec

St-Paul, Chemin Vert

29, 69, 75, 76, 93

Very good

Moderate

Guided tours, shop

Above: *Picasso's Femmes à Leur Toilette (1938), from the museum*

67

29E2

✉ 57 rue Cuvier, 75005 Paris

☎ 01 40 79 30 00

🕐 Gardens: 7:30–sunset; closed Tue, 1 May. Museum: 10–5. Zoo: 9–5

🍴 Cafeteria (£) 🚇 Jussieu

♿ Good

🎫 Gardens: free; museum and zoo: moderate

❓ Lectures, exhibitions, workshops for children, shop

Jardin des Plantes

29D2

Sorbonne

✉ 47 rue des Ecoles and place de la Sorbonne (church), 75005 Paris

☎ 01 40 46 22 11

🕐 By appointment

🚇 Cluny-La Sorbonne

♿ None 🎫 Moderate

St-Etienne-du-Mont

✉ Place du Panthéon, 75005 Paris

🕐 9–7:30; closed Mon and all day in Jul & Aug

PLANTES, JARDIN DES ●●

The botanical gardens owe their name to the 'royal garden of medicinal plants' created in the 17th century and extended by Buffon in the 18th century. Today they form the experimental gardens of the Musée National d'Histoire Naturelle (Natural History Museum) and make an ideal spot for a leisurely stroll; children love the ménagerie (zoo). There are also hothouses, an alpine garden and several exhibition halls, the most fascinating being the Grande Galerie de l'Evolution, illustrating the evolution of life on earth and Man's influence on it. Here, the display of endangered and extinct species is particularly interesting. Also featured are the scientists closely associated with evolution and the latest discoveries in the field of genetics.

LES QUAIS (► 24, TOP TEN)

QUARTIER LATIN ●●

This lively district remains to this day the undisputed kingdom of Parisian students. Situated on the Left Bank between the Carrefour de l'Odéon and the Jardin des Plantes, it was known in medieval times as the 'Montagne Ste-Geneviève' after the patron saint of Paris, and was later given the name of 'Quartier Latin' because Latin was spoken at the university until the late 18th century.

The **Sorbonne**, the most famous French university college, was founded in 1257; the present building dates from the late 19th century when well-known artists such as Puvis de Chavannes decorated the interior. The adjacent 17th-century church is a model of Jesuit style.

The **Church of St-Etienne-du-Mont**, dating from the late 15th century, combines Gothic Flamboyant and Renaissance styles.

A Walk Through the Quartier Latin & St-Germain-des-Prés

These lively Left Bank districts are the favourite haunt of Parisian youth.

Start at the crossroads of boulevard St–Germain and boulevard St–Michel.

Soak in the Left Bank atmosphere as you walk up the 'Boul Mich', a nickname used by generations of students. The small cafés on place de la Sorbonne are packed with students.

Take the next street on the left to reach the Church of St-Etienne-du-Mont (➤ 68).

It is well worth going inside to admire the Gothic chancel, Renaissance nave and magnificent rood screen.

Behind the church, follow rue Descartes to the right.

Beyond the charming place de la Contrescarpe lies the rue Mouffetard, known as 'la Mouffe', with its untidy shops and picturesque signs.

Go through the Passage des Postes (No 104) and turn right into rue Lhomond which leads back to boulevard St-Michel.

Stroll through the Jardin du Luxembourg past the beautiful Fontaine de Médicis. Come out by the west gate.

Walk down rue Bonaparte past place St-Sulpice and its superb fountain to boulevard St-Germain.

Near by are the picturesque rue de Furstenberg, rue Cardinale, rue de l'Echaudé and rue de Buci, with its lively market.

Rue St-André-des-Arts leads to the square of the same name with its quaint Fontaine Wallace. The walk ends here.

Distance
5km

Time
3–4 hours depending on stops

Start point
Crossroads of boulevard St-Germain and boulevard St-Michel
✠ 29D2
Ⓜ Cluny-La Sorbonne

End point
Place St-André-des-Arts
✠ 29D2
Ⓜ St-Michel

Lunch
Brasserie Lipp
✉ 151 boulevard St-Germain, 6th
☎ 01 45 48 53 91

Daily exercise in place St-Sulpice

🕂 28B3
✉ 77 rue de Varenne, 75007 Paris
☎ 01 44 18 61 10
🕐 9:30–4:45 (5:45 in summer, park 6:45); closed Mon, 1 Jan, 25 Dec
🍴 Cafeteria (£)
🚇 Varenne
🚌 69, 82, 87, 92
♿ Very good
💵 Inexpensive
❓ Guided tours, shops

One of Rodin's most famous pieces, The Thinker

RODIN, MUSÉE ✪✪✪

One of the lovely mansions in the elegant Faubourg St-Germain, built by Gabriel in 1728, houses a unique collection of works by the sculptor Auguste Rodin (1840–1917). Rodin spent the last few years of his life in the Hôtel Biron as a guest of the French nation; when he died the collection of his works reverted to the State and the mansion was turned into a museum.

His forceful and highly original style brought him many disappointments and failures: his *Man with a Broken Nose* (now in the museum) was refused at the 1864 Salon and Rodin had to wait for another 15 years before his talent was fully acknowledged through his *St John the Baptist*. His major works are displayed inside the museum (*The Kiss, Man Walking*) and in the peaceful gardens (*The Thinker, The Burghers of Calais, The Gates of Hell*).

SACRÉ-COEUR, BASILIQUE DU ✪✪

The white domes and campaniles of this neo-Byzantine basilica stand out against the Parisian skyline, high above the rooftops of the capital. Its construction at the top of Montmartre was undertaken as a sign of national reconciliation and hope after the bitter defeat suffered by France in the 1870 war against Prussia. Funds were raised by public subscription and work started in 1875, but the basilica took nearly 45 years to build and was inaugurated only in 1919, at the end of another war!

🕂 29D5
✉ Place du Parvis du Sacré-Coeur, 75018 Paris
☎ 01 53 41 89 00
🕐 Basilica: 6:45AM–11PM; dome and crypt: 9–6
🚇 Anvers
🚌 30, 54, 80, 85, Montmartrobus
♿ Very good
💵 Basilica: free; dome and crypt: inexpensive
❓ Shops

Sacré-Coeur, among the city's most famous landmarks: the dome is the second highest point after La Tour Eiffel

The view over Paris from the terrace in front of the building is breathtaking; an impressive number of steps leads down to the place St-Pierre; from the dome, an even more stunning panoramic view stretches for 50km around the city. The interior of the basilica is profusely decorated with mosaics.

ST-GERMAIN-DES-PRÉS ✪✪

The oldest church in Paris stands at the heart of the lively Left-Bank district of St-Germain-des-Prés. The Benedictine Abbey of St-Germain-des-Prés, founded in the 6th century, was throughout the Middle Ages so powerful a religious and cultural centre that it became a town within the town. It was completely destroyed during the Revolution; only the church was spared. In spite of many alterations, the church is a fine example of Romanesque style: the tower dates from the 11th century as does the nave; note that the carved capitals on the pillars are copies of the originals kept in the Musée National du Moyen-Age (► 62). The chancel and ambulatory date from the 12th century.

Facing the church is the Café des Deux Magots which, like its neighbour the Café de Flore, was the favourite haunt of intellectuals, in particular Sartre and Simone de Beauvoir, immediately after World War II.

It is well worth exploring the old streets on the north and east sides of the church and strolling along boulevard St-Germain. The area between boulevard St-Germain and the river and between the rue du Bac and the rue de Seine is full of antique shops and art galleries.

✚ 28C3
✉ Place St-Germain-des-Prés, 75006 Paris
☎ 01 43 25 41 71
🕐 8–7
🍴 Cafés and restaurants near by (£–££)
Ⓜ St-Germain-des-Prés
🎫 Free

Despite unsympathetic 19th-century restoration, the interior of the Church of Saint-Germain-des-Prés has retained its Romanesque beauty

29E2

75004 Paris

In rue St-Louis-en-l'Ile
(££)

Pont Marie

67

SAINT-LOUIS, ILE

The peaceful atmosphere of this island is apparent as soon as you walk along its shaded embankment, lined with elegant private mansions which stand as silent witnesses of a bygone era. The island was formed at the beginning of the 17th century, when two small islands were united and joined to the mainland by a couple of bridges linked by the rue des Deux Ponts, which still exists; at the same time, private residences were built along the embankment and the straight narrow streets. The whole project was completed in a remarkably short time between 1627 and 1664. Since then, time seems to have stood still on the Ile Saint-Louis, which to this day retains its provincial character.

A few architectural gems can be seen along quai de Bourbon and quai d'Anjou, which offer fine views of the Right Bank. From the western tip of the island you can see Notre-Dame and the Ile de la Cité. Concerts are regularly given in the classical Church of St-Louis-en-l'Ile, richly decorated inside.

29D2

Place St-Sulpice, 75006
Paris

01 46 33 21 78

8–7

St-Sulpice

Free

ST-SULPICE, ÉGLISE

The church and square of St-Sulpice form a harmonious architectural ensemble, mostly dating from the 18th century except for part of the church and the central fountain.

The original church, founded by the Abbey of St-Germain-des-Prés, was rebuilt and extended in the 17th century but was not completed until the mid-18th century. The Italian-style façade, designed by Servandoni, is surmounted by two slightly different towers crowned by balustrades and is in marked contrast to the rest of the building. Among the wealth of interior decoration are several statues by Bouchardon and outstanding murals by Delacroix (first chapel on the right) as well as a splendid organ by Cavaillé-Coll, traditionally played by the best organists in France.

Servandoni had also submitted plans for the square in front of the church, but they were abandoned and a monumental fountain designed by Visconti was eventually placed in its centre in 1844.

In place St-Sulpice, the Fontaine des Quatre Points Cardinaux features the busts of four respected churchmen. Although their figures face the four cardinal points of the compass, none of the men ever became cardinals!

Even without the support of flying buttresses, the soaring Gothic masterpiece of Sainte-Chapelle has stood the test of time

SAINTE-CHAPELLE ✪✪✪

The full splendour of this magnificent Gothic chapel can only be appreciated from inside, as Sainte-Chapelle is unfortunately closely surrounded by the Palais de Justice buildings. Commissioned by Saint-Louis to house the Crown of Thorns and a fragment of the true Cross, it was built in less than three years by Pierre de Montreuil (who also worked on Notre-Dame) and consecrated in 1248.

The building consists of two chapels, the lower one intended as a parish church for the palace staff and the upper one reserved for the royal family. The latter is a striking example of technical prowess: walls have been replaced by 15m-high stained-glass panels linked by slender pillars which also support the vaulting. The stained-glass windows, which cover an area of more than 600sq m, are mainly original and illustrate scenes from the Old and New Testaments.

LA TOUR EIFFEL (➤ 25, TOP TEN)

 29D3

✉ 4 boulevard du Palais, 75001 Paris

☎ 01 53 73 78 50

🕐 10–5 (9:30–6:30 Apr–Sep); closed 1 Jan, 1 May, 1 Nov, 11 Nov, 25 Dec

Ⓜ Cité

🚌 96

♿ None

💰 Moderate

❓ Shop

28C3
Rue de Rivoli, 75001
Paris
Summer: 7AM–9PM;
winter: 7:30AM–7:30PM
Cafeterias (£)
Tuileries (access from rue
de Rivoli); Palais-Royal
(access from the Louvre)
Free

TUILERIES, JARDIN DES

This formal French-style garden was laid out by Le Nôtre in the 17th century, and was even then a popular public garden. The practice of hiring chairs goes back to the 18th century. The garden deteriorated over the years through extensive use and the increasing effects of pollution, but has now been entirely renovated as part of the Grand Louvre project. The stately central alleyway stretches in a straight line from the flower beds near the Arc de Triomphe du Carrousel to the place de la Concorde, where an octagonal ornamental pool is surrounded by various statues (the seasons, rivers) and flanked by terraces. On either side of the alleyway are groups of allegorical statues. There is a lovely view of the river and the gardens with the Louvre in the background from the Terrasse du Bord de l'Eau running along the riverbank.

The Tuileries, a popular place for whiling away a few hours, whether it be sailing model boats, strolling or sunbathing

28C4
75001 Paris
Opéra
72

VENDÔME, PLACE

This square illustrates Louis XIV's style at its best, classical and elegant without being too emphatic! It was designed by Jules Hardouin-Mansart at the end of the 17th century and an equestrian statue of the king was placed in its centre. However, the statue was destroyed during the Revolution and in 1810 Napoleon had a tall bronze-clad column erected in its place, somewhat spoiling the architectural harmony created by the combination of arcades, pilasters and rows of dormer windows interrupted by the occasional pediment. In 1849, Frédéric Chopin died in No 12. Today the square is the headquarters of Paris's top jewellers.

A rather comical game of musical chairs went on for over 60 years to decide who should stand at the top of the column: Napoleon dressed as Caesar was replaced by Henri IV then by a huge *fleur de lys* before Napoleon reappeared...in less pompous attire, but not for long! A copy of the original statue commissioned by Napoleon III started another round; in 1871 the Commune took it down in anger but the Third Republic had it reinstated as a demonstration of tolerance...'much ado about nothing!'

VICTOR HUGO, MAISON DE (SEE BELOW)

LA VILLETTE (➤ 26, TOP TEN)

VOSGES, PLACE DES ✪✪✪

Totally unspoilt, this is Paris's oldest square and perhaps the loveliest for its moderate size, its discreet charm, its delightful brick and stone architecture and its peaceful central garden.

We owe this brilliant piece of town planning to 'Good King Henri' (Henri IV) whose initiative launched the development of Le Marais. The square is lined with identical pavilions over continuous arcading, dormer windows breaking up the monotony of the dark slate roofs; in the centre of the south and north sides stand two higher pavilions, known respectively as the Pavillon du Roi and Pavillon de la Reine. The square changed names during the Revolution and was finally called 'place des Vosges' in 1800 in honour of the first *département* to pay its taxes!

No 6, where Victor Hugo (1805–85) lived for 16 years, is now a museum (**Maison de Victor Hugo**), containing family mementoes, furniture, portraits, drawings by the writer himself as well as recon-structions of the various homes Hugo lived in.

Flat out in the place des Vosges: too much sightseeing?

🞧 29F3
✉ 75004 Paris
🚇 St-Paul, Bastille, Chemin Vert
🚌 20, 65, 69, 76

Maison de Victor Hugo
✉ 6 place des Vosges
☎ 01 42 72 10 16
🕐 10–5:40, closed Mon
🍴 Restaurants near by
🚇 Bastille
♿ None
💵 Inexpensive
↔ Musée Carnavalet, place de la Bastille

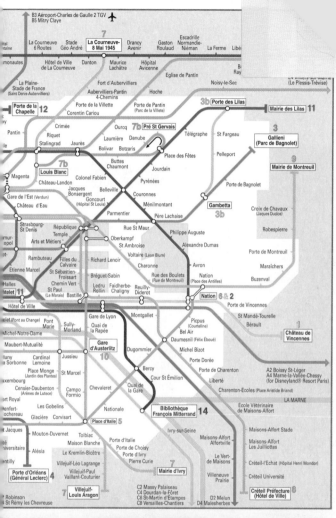

Ile de France

'Ile de France', as the Paris region is called, means the heart of France; and this is exactly what it has always been and still is, the very core of the country, a prosperous and dynamic region, inhabited by one French person in five, with Paris in its centre. Roads, motorways and international railway lines converge on this central region, which has become one of Europe's main crossroads, with two major international airports.

Besides its tremendous vitality, the Ile de France offers visitors attractive natural assets, a rich cultural heritage and a gentle way of life. The countryside is domestic rather than spectacular, graced by picturesque villages, country inns, manor houses, historic castles, abbeys, cathedrals and beautiful parks and gardens.

> *'Here is the island shaded by poplars and Rousseau's grave...the castle by the still waters of the lake and the lawn which stretches like a savannah beneath the line of shadowy hills.'*
>
> GÉRARD DE NERVAL,
> *Sylvie* (new edition 1946,
> first published 1854)

Château de Dampierre

A Drive in the Painters' Footsteps

Distance
89km

Time
8–9 hours

Start point
Porte de Clichy

End point
Porte de la Chapelle

Lunch
Maison de Van Gogh
✉ Place de la Mairie 95430 Auvers-sur-Oise
☎ 01 30 36 60 60

Musée Pissaro
✉ 17 rue du Château, 95300 Pontoise
☎ 01 30 32 06 75
🕐 Wed–Sun 2–6; closed bank hols

Maison de Van Gogh
✉ Place de la Mairie 95430 Auvers-sur-Oise
🕐 10–6; closed Mon

Château d'Auvers-sur-Oise
✉ Rue de Léry
☎ 01 34 48 48 50
🕐 Tue–Sun 10:30–4:30 (6, Apr–Oct); last admission 1½ hours before closing
❓ Audio-visual show recreating life at the time of the Impressionists

Abbaye de Royaumont
✉ 95270 Asnières-sur-Oise
☎ 01 30 35 59 00
🕐 10–6

This drive takes you along the valley of the River Oise in the footsteps of the Impressionist painters who immortalised the little town of Auvers-sur-Oise.

Start from Porte de Clichy and drive north to Cergy-Pontoise (A15) and leave at exit 9 to Pontoise.

Camille Pissarro worked in Pontoise between 1872 and 1884; housed in a large house overlooking the river, the Musée Camille Pissarro contains works by the artist and some of his contemporaries.

Continue northeast along the D4 to Auvers-sur-Oise.

Several Impressionist painters settled here in the 1870s encouraged by Doctor Gachet, himself an amateur painter: Corot, Cézanne, Renoir and above all Van Gogh, whose painting of the village church has acquired world-wide fame. He died in the local inn, known as the Auberge Ravoux, and is buried in the cemetery, next to his brother Theo.

Cross the river and drive north along the D922 to L'Isle-Adam.

From the old bridge, there are lovely views of the river and its pleasure boats; on the way out towards Beaumont, have a look at the 18th-century Chinese folly, known as the Pavillon Cassan.

Follow the D922 to Viarmes and turn left on the D909 to the Abbaye de Royaumont.

Founded by St-Louis in 1228, this is the best preserved Cistercian abbey in the Ile de France.

Turn back. The D909 joins the N1 which takes you back to Porte de la Chapelle and the boulevard périphérique.

What to See in the Ile de France

CHANTILLY, CHÂTEAU DE ✪✪

Surrounded by a lake and beautiful gardens designed by Le Nôtre, the Château de Chantilly is one of the most attractive castles in the Paris region. It houses the Musée Condé, named after one of its most distinguished owners, Le Grand Condé. The 16th-century Petit Château contains the 'Princes' apartments' and a library full of precious illuminated manuscripts including *Les Très Riches Heures du Duc de Berry*, dating from the 15th century; the Grand Château, destroyed during the Revolution and rebuilt in Renaissance style at the end of the 19th century, houses a magnificent collection of paintings by Raphaël, Clouet, Ingres, Corot, Delacroix, as well as porcelain and jewellery.

Facing the famous racecourse, the impressive 18th-century stables have been turned into a museum, the Musée Vivant du Cheval, illustrating the various crafts, jobs and sports connected with horses.

Chantilly – everything you could wish for in a château

✉ 40km north of Paris. BP 70243, 60631 Chantilly Cedex
☎ Château and Musée Conde: 03 44 62 62 62; Musée Vivant du Cheval: 03 44 57 13 13
🕐 Mar–Oct 10–6, Nov–Feb 10:30–12:45 and 2–5; closed Tue
🍴 Near the station (£)
🚉 Gare du Nord to Chantilly-Gouvieux
♿ Moderate

Did you know ?

In 1671, while Louis XIV was visiting Chantilly at the invitation of Le Grand Condé, the most famous French chef, Vatel, killed himself because the fish he had ordered for the royal meal did not arrive on time!

DISNEYLAND PARIS ✪✪

The famous theme park imported from the USA is now fully integrated into the French way of life and attracts an increasing number of families from all over Europe. It offers fantasy, humour, *joie de vivre*, excitement and the latest technological devices to ensure that your visit is a memorable one. Besides the theme park, there is a whole range of 'typically' American hotels to tempt you to stay on for a day or two. A second park is planned for 2002.

✉ 30km east of Paris. BP100 77777 Marne-la-Vallée
☎ In the UK: 0990 03 03 03; in France: 01 60 30 60 30
🕐 Varies with the season
🍴 Inside the park (£–£££)
🚉 RER A Marne-la-Vallée/Chessy
♿ Good 🖐 Moderate

ECOUEN, CHÂTEAU D' ✪✪

This elegant Renaissance castle dating from the first half of the 16th century is reminiscent of the famous castles of the Loire Valley; its painted fireplaces are especially noteworthy. It houses the Musée National de la Renaissance, whose collections of paintings, sculptures, enamels, tapestries, embroideries, ceramics, furniture, jewellery and stained glass illustrate the diversity of Renaissance art. Particularly fine is the 75m-long tapestry depicting David and Bathsheba's love story, made in a Brussels workshop at the beginning of the 16th century.

✉ 19km north of Paris. 95440 Ecouen
☎ 01 34 38 38 50
🕐 9:45–12:30 and 2–5:15; closed Tue
🍴 In the château (£)
🚉 Gare du Nord to Ecouen-Ezanville
♿ Very good
💰 Inexpensive
❓ Guided tours, shops

FONTAINEBLEAU, CHÂTEAU DE ✪✪✪

As the name suggests, a fountain or spring, now in the Jardin Anglais, is at the origin of this splendid royal residence, which started out as a hunting pavilion at the heart of a vast forest. It was François I who made Fontainebleau into the beautiful palace it is today, although it was later remodelled by successive monarchs.

The imposing horseshoe staircase decorating the main façade was the scene of Napoleon I's moving farewell to his faithful guard in 1814 (see the Musée Napoléon I). Beyond this building lies the Etang des Carpes (carp pool) with a lovely pavilion in its centre, and further on the formal French gardens redesigned by Le Nôtre. The oldest part of the palace, including the keep of the medieval castle, surrounds the Cour Ovale.

The richly decorated State Apartments contain a remarkable collection of paintings, furniture and *objets d'art*, in addition to the fine coffered ceiling of the Salle de Bal and the frescoes in the Galerie François I.

✉ 65km southeast of Paris. 77300 Fontainebleau
☎ 01 60 71 50 70
🕐 Winter: 9:30–12:30 and 2–5; summer: 9:30–5 (6 in Jul and Aug). Closed Tue, 1 Jan, 1 May
🍴 In the town nearby (£–£££)
🚉 Gare de Lyon to Fontainebleau-Avon and 🚌 A or B
♿ Very good 💰 Moderate
❓ Guided tour, shops

Fontainbleau, a favourite retreat of royalty from the 16th century

A Drive In & Around the Forêt de Fontainebleau

The forest of Fontainebleau extends over a vast area along the left bank of the Seine, to the southeast of the capital.

Start at the Porte d'Orléans and follow the A6 motorway towards Evry and Lyon. Leave at the Fontainebleau exit and continue on the N37 for 7km; turn right to Barbizon.

This village gave its name to a group of landscape painters who settled there in the mid-19th century, among them Jean-François Millet. They were joined later by some of the future Impressionists Renoir, Sisley and Monet.

The **Auberge Ganne**, which they decorated with their paintings, is now a museum.

Leave Barbizon towards Fontainebleau.

Take time to visit the castle (➤ 82), or at least the park, and to stroll around the town.

Drive southeast along the D58 for 4km bearing left at the Y-junction. Turn right onto the Route Ronde (D301).

This scenic route takes you through the forest and offers many possibilities for walking and cycling.

Turn left on the D409 to Milly-la-Forêt.

This small town nestling round an imposing covered market is a traditional centre for growing medicinal plants. The Cyclop (1km north) is a monumental modern sculpture which took 20 years to complete.

Follow the D372 for 3.5km and bear left for Courances.

The **Château de Courances** looks delightful, set like a jewel in a magnificent park designed by Le Nôtre, with pools, canals and small waterfalls.

Return to the main road and continue for 5km, then rejoin the motorway back to Paris.

Distance
143km

Time
7–9 hours depending on length of visits

Start/end point
Porte d'Orléans

Lunch
Le Caveau des Ducs
✉ 24 rue de Ferrare, 77300 Fontainebleau
☎ 01 64 22 05 05

Auberge Ganne
✉ 92 Grande Rue, 77630 Barbizon
☎ 01 60 66 22 27
🕐 Apr–Sep 10–12:30 and 2–6 (5 in winter), weekends 10–6 (5 in winter); closed Tue
♿ Moderate

Château de Courances
✉ 91240 Milly-la-Forêt
☎ 01 64 98 41 18
🕐 Apr–Oct: Sat, Sun and bank hols 2–6:30
♿ Moderate
❓ Guided tours

Barbizon's main street

✉ 25km west of Paris.
25 route du Mesnil,
78990 Elancourt
☎ 08 36 68 53 35
🕐 Apr–11 Nov 10–7; closed
on selected days
Sep–Nov
🍴 Two restaurants (£–££)
🚉 Gare Montparnasse
♿ Good
💰 Moderate
❓ Audio-visual show,
outdoor activities

✉ 14km west of Paris.
Avenue du Château,
92500 Rueil-Malmaison
☎ 01 41 29 05 55
🕐 9:30–12:30, 1:30–5:45;
weekends 10–6:30;
closed Tue, 1 Jan, 25 Dec
🚉 RER Rueil-Malmaison
♿ Good
💰 Moderate
❓ Guided tours, shop

---

*Château de Malmaison
with one of the garden
statues*

FRANCE MINIATURE ✪

This open-air museum comprises a huge three dimensional map of France on which 166 miniature historic monuments have been arranged into a harmonious whole, partly re-creating the atmosphere inherent to each place; for instance the Château de Chenonceau reflected in the calm waters of the Loire suggests the peaceful atmosphere of the Loire Valley. There are models of the Tour Eiffel, the Sacré Coeur, the solitary Mont-St-Michel, the pont du Gard and Gallo-Roman arenas, as well as many beautiful castles, all made to a scale of 1:30. Here and there, a typical French village focuses on ordinary daily life.

MALMAISON, CHÂTEAU DE ✪✪

The memory of Napoleon and his beloved Josephine lingers on around 'La Malmaison' and the nearby Château de Bois-Préau.

Josephine bought the 17th-century castle in 1799 and had the wings and the veranda added. The couple spent several happy years in Malmaison, and after their divorce Josephine continued to live in it up until her death in 1814. In the summer of 1815, Napoleon went to La Malmaison once more before sailing for St-Helena. The castle then passed through many hands before it was bought by a banker, restored and donated to the State in 1904. It contains various collections of 18th- and 19th-century paintings (David, Greuze etc), porcelain and furniture.

The Château de Bois-Préau was offered to France by a wealthy American, Edward Tuck, and now forms an annexe to the collections in La Malmaison.

PARC ASTÉRIX ⭐

This Gallic version of a made-in-USA theme park is based on the comic adventures of a friendly little Gaul named Astérix and his companions, who are determined to resist the Roman invaders. The story became famous worldwide through a series of more than 50 strip cartoons by Goscinny and Uderzo, which have since been translated into many languages.

Inside the park, visitors are invited to share Astérix's adventures as they wander through the Gauls' Village, the Roman City and Ancient Greece, travel on the impressive roller-coaster of the Great Lake and journey back and forth in time along the rue de Paris!

> ✉ 30km north of Paris. BP 8, 60128 Plailly
> ☎ 03 44 62 34 04
> 🕐 Variable
> 🍴 Several choices (£–££)
> Ⓡ RER B3 from Châtelet or Gare du Nord to Roissy-Charles-de-Gaulle 1 then 🚌 Courriers Ile-de-France every half hour
> ♿ Excellent 🅿 Moderate
> ❓ Gift shops, picnic areas, pushchair rental

SAINT-CLOUD, PARC DE ⭐

This beautiful park, situated on the outskirts of Paris, extends over a vast hilly area overlooking the Seine. The castle designed by Jules-Hardouin Mansart for 'Monsieur', Louis XIV's brother, was destroyed by fire in 1870 and razed to the ground in 1891. It had been Bonaparte's favourite official residence when he was consul of the Republic.

The park was designed by Le Nôtre, who took advantage of the steep terrain to build a magnificent 'grande cascade', in which water flows gracefully from one pool to the next over a distance of 90m. At the top the site of the former castle is now a terrace offering lovely views of the capital. Near by is the Jardin du Trocadéro, an English-style garden with an ornamental pool and an aviary. There are many shaded alleyways offering delightful walks through the 460-ha park.

> ✉ 11km west of Paris. 92210 Saint-Cloud
> ☎ 01 41 12 09 90
> 🕐 7:30AM–8:50PM (7:50PM Nov–Feb, 9:50 May–Aug). Partly closed owing to damage caused by December 1999 storms
> 🍴 Cafés (£)
> Ⓡ Pont de Saint-Cloud
> 🅾 Free

Fun for all the family at Parc Astérisk

✉ 9km north of Paris.
1 rue de la Légion
d'Honneur, 93200 Saint-
Denis

☎ 01 48 09 83 54

🕐 Winter: 10–5 (Sun 12–5);
summer: 10–7 (Sun
12–7). Closed 1 Jan, 1
May, 1 Nov, 11 Nov, 25
Dec

🚇 Saint-Denis Basilique

♿ None

💵 Moderate

❓ Guided tours

SAINT-DENIS, BASILIQUE　　●●●

So many great architects and artists have contributed to make the Basilique St-Denis what it is today that the building is in itself a museum of French architecture and sculpture of the medieval and Renaissance periods.

An abbey was built on the site where Saint-Denis died following his martyrdom in Montmartre. Designed in the early 12th century by Abbot Suger, the nave and transept of the abbey church were completed in the 13th century by none other than Pierre de Montreuil, who also worked on Notre-Dame. It was for centuries the burial place of the kings and queens of France as well as of illustrious Frenchmen such as Du Guesclin. There is a wealth of recumbent figures and funeral monuments dating from the 12th to the 16th centuries, most of them the work of great artists: Beauneveu (Charles V, 14th century), Philibert Delorme (François I, 16th century), Germain Pilon (Catherine de Médicis, 16th century), Jean Bullant and Il Primaticcio (16th century). The basilica underwent restoration by Gabriel in the 18th century and again by Viollet-le-Duc in the 19th century.

✉ 23km west of Paris.

Château de Saint-Germain-en-Laye

✉ BP 3030, 78103 Saint-
Germain-en-Laye Cedex

☎ 01 39 10 13 00

🕐 9–5:15; closed Tue, some
bank hols

🚇 RER Saint-
Germain-en-Laye

♿ Very good

💵 Moderate

❓ Guided tours,
shops

SAINT-GERMAIN-EN-LAYE　　●●

The historic city of Saint-Germain-en-Laye clusters round its royal castle, once the favourite residence of Louis XIV. François I commissioned the present Château Vieux (Old Castle) and retained Saint-Louis's chapel and the 14th-century square keep, now surmounted by a campanile. Le Nôtre later designed the gardens and the magnificent 2,400m-long Grande Terrasse. The Sun King stayed in St-Germain for many years and during that time private mansions were built around the castle for members of his court. When the court moved to Versailles in 1682, the castle was somewhat neglected but it was eventually restored by Napoléon III and turned into the Musée des Antiquités Nationales, which houses interesting archaeological collections illustrating life in France from earliest times to the Middle Ages.

The Grand Terrace of the Château de Saint-Germain-en-Laye

SCEAUX, CHÂTEAU DE ●●

Very little remains of this castle, built for Colbert: the main entrance decorated with sculptures by Coysevox, the Orangerie to the left, the old stables opposite and the Pavillon de l'Aurore tucked away on the right. But the splendid park has been preserved: it is one of the most 'romantic' ever designed by Le Nôtre, with its tall trees reflected in the secluded octagonal pool, its peaceful Grand Canal and its impressive Grandes Cascades.

The castle, rebuilt in the 19th century, houses the Musée de l'Ile de France illustrating ancient regional arts and crafts and the history of castles in the Paris Region.

✉ 10km south of Paris. Château de Sceaux, 92330 Sceaux
☎ 01 46 61 06 71
🕐 Park: daily 8–6 (winter), 7AM–8:30PM (summer). Museum: 10–5 (6 in summer); closed Tue, 1 Jan, Easter, 1 May, 1 Nov, 11 Nov, 25 Dec
🍴 Cafeteria (£)
🚇 RER B Bourg-La-Reine
♿ Good
💰 Inexpensive
❓ Guided tours

A fine Sèvres urn at the porcelain museum

SÈVRES, MUSÉE NATIONAL DE LA CÉRAMIQUE DE ●

The name of this Paris suburb was made famous by the porcelain factory transferred here in 1756 from its previous location in Vincennes. The unique 'Sèvres blue' ware, also known as 'lapis blue', became its trademark. The Musée National de la Céramique was founded at the beginning of the 19th century to house various collections of Sèvres and Saxe porcelain, Italian Renaissance ceramics, antique terracotta objects, glazed earthenware from the Far East and ceramics from elsewhere.

✉ 11km southwest of Paris. Place de la Manufacture, 92310 Sèvres
☎ 01 41 14 04 20
🕐 10–5:15; closed Tue, 1 Jan, Easter Mon, Whit Mon, 1 Nov, 25 Dec
🚇 Métro: Pont de Sèvres
♿ Good 💰 Inexpensive
❓ Guided tours

VAUX-LE-VICOMTE, CHÂTEAU DE ●●●

This architectural gem, a 'little Versailles' built before Versailles was even designed, cost its owner, Nicolas Fouquet, his freedom and eventually his life – although much appreciated by the king for his competence in financial matters, he had dared to outdo his master! Fouquet, who had excellent taste, had commissioned the best artists of his time: Le Vau for the building, Le Brun for the decoration and Le Nôtre for the gardens. Louis XIV was invited to a dazzling reception given for the inauguration of the castle in 1661. The king did not take kindly to being outshone: Fouquet was arrested and spent the rest of his life in prison, while Louis XIV commissioned the same artists to build him an even more splendid castle, Versailles.

The castle stands on a terrace overlooking magnificent gardens featuring canals, pools and fountains; walking to the end of the terrace allows an overall view of the gardens and the castle. In the stables is a museum (Musée des Equipages) devoted to horse-drawn carriages.

✉ 51km southeast of Paris. Domaine de Vaux-le-Vicomte, 77950 Maincy
☎ 01 64 14 41 90
🕐 Mid-Mar to Mid-Nov: Mon–Fri 10–1, 2–6, Sat, Sun 10–6. Candlelit visits: Mid–May to Mid–Oct Thu, Sat 8PM–midnight
🍴 Cafeteria (£)
🚇 Gare de Lyon to Melun then taxi
♿ None
💰 Expensive
❓ Shops

✉ 20km southwest of Paris. 78000 Versailles

☎ 01 30 83 78 00/01 30 83 77 77

🕐 Château: 9–5:30 (6:30 in summer); closed Mon, some bank hols. Trianons: noon–5:30 (6:30 in summer); Parc: 7–5:30 (up to 9:30pm depending on the season) ceremonies

🍴 Cafeteria (£) and restaurant (££)

🚃 Gare St-Lazare to Versailles Rive Droite

♿ Good

💰 Expensive

❓ Guided tours, shops

VERSAILLES, CHÂTEAU DE ✪✪✪

The physical expression of a king's superego, Versailles turned out to be one of the most splendid castles in the world through the genius of the artists who built and decorated it. What began as a modest hunting lodge became the seat of government and political centre of France for over a hundred years. A town grew up around the castle to accommodate the court. Several thousand men worked on the castle for 50 years, thousands of trees were transplanted, and 3,000 people could live in it.

The castle is huge (680m long) and it is impossible to see everything in the course of one visit. Aim for the first floor where the State Apartments are, including the famous Galerie des Glaces, as well as the Official Apartments and the Private Apartments of the royal couple, situated on either side of the marble courtyard. The north wing contains the two-storey Chapelle St-Louis built by Mansart and the Opéra, added later, by Gabriel.

The focal point of the park is the Bassin d'Apollon, a

Versailles: the south wing (left) and the Apollo Basin (above)

Below: *Château de Vincennes*

magnificent ornamental pool with a bronze sculpture in its centre representing Apollo's chariot coming out of the water. Two smaller castles, Le Grand Trianon and Le Petit Trianon, are also worth a visit and Le Hameau, Marie-Antoinette's retreat, offers a delightful contrast.

VINCENNES, CHÂTEAU DE ✪✪

This austere castle, situated on the eastern outskirts of Paris, was a royal residence from the Middle Ages to the mid-17th century. Inside the defensive wall, there are in fact two castles: the 50m-high keep (currently undergoing repair) built in the 14th century, which later held political prisoners, philosophers, soldiers, ministers and churchmen; and the two classical pavilions built by Le Vau for Cardinal Mazarin in 1652, Le Pavillon de la Reine, where Anne d'Autriche, mother of Louis XIV lived, and Le Pavillon du Roi, where Mazarin died in 1661. The Chapelle Royale, started by Saint-Louis and completed by François I, stands in the main courtyard.

✉ 6km east of Paris. Avenue de Paris, 94300 Vincennes

☎ 01 48 08 31 20

🕐 10–noon, 1:15–5 (6 in summer); closed 1 Jan, 1 May, 1 Nov, 11 Nov, 25 Dec

Ⓜ Métro: Porte de Vincennes

♿ None

💷 Moderate

❓ Guided tours, shops

89

A Drive Through the Vallée de Chevreuse

This drive will take you through the wooded Vallée de Chevreuse to Rambouillet, its castle and its park.

From the Porte de Saint-Cloud, follow signs for Chartres/Orléans. After 17km, leave for Saclay and take the N306 towards Chevreuse.

The little town of Chevreuse is dominated by the ruins of its medieval castle which houses the Maison du Parc Naturel Régional de la Haute Vallée de Chevreuse (Natural Regional Park Information Centre).

From Chevreuse, drive southwest on the D906 to Rambouillet.

The 14th-century fortress is now an official residence of the presidents of the Republic. In the park, criss-crossed by canals, look for the Laiterie de la Reine (Marie-Antoinette's dairy).

Drive back on the D906 for 10km and turn left on the D91 towards Dampierre.

The 16th-century stone and brick Château de Dampierre was remodelled by Jules Hardouin-Mansart for Colbert's son-in-law and still belongs to the de Luynes family.

Continue on the D91 across the River Yvette, negotiating the picturesque '17 bends' to the ruined Abbaye de Port-Royal-des-Champs (parking on left-hand side of the road).

During the 17th century, this former Cistercian abbey was at the centre of a religious battle between Jesuits and Jansenists. The Musée National des Granges de Port-Royal is in the park.

Continue along the D91 to Versailles and return to the Porte de Saint-Cloud by the Route de Paris (D10).

Above: *statue in the parkland of Château de Rambouillet*

Distance
93km

Time
7–9 hours depending on visits

Start/end point
Porte de Saint-Cloud

Lunch
Cheval Rouge
✉ 78 rue Général de Gaulle, 78120 Rambouillet
☎ 01 30 88 80 61

Maison du Parc, Chevreuse
☎ 01 30 52 09 09
🕐 Weekdays 10–12 and 2–6

Château de Rambouillet
☎ 01 34 83 00 25

Château de Dampierre
☎ 01 30 52 53 24

Musée National des Granges de Port-Royal
☎ 01 39 30 72 72

Where To...

Eat and Drink   92–9
Stay   100–3
Shop   104–9
Take the Children   110–11
Be Entertained   112–16

Above: *at the Jardin des Tuileries*

Paris

Prices

Prices for a three-course meal vary from around 11 euros to over 152 euros; the average price for each restaurant listed is shown by the pound symbol:

£ = budget (up to 23 euros)

££ = moderate (23 euros–53 euros)

£££ = expensive to luxury (over 53 euros)

Nowhere is the saying 'Variety is the spice of life' truer than in Paris, for the city with a well-deserved reputation of being the gastronomic capital of the West has such a wide choice of eating establishments that selecting one can prove a hard task, even for Parisians. In Paris, the reality behind the word 'restaurant' is particularly complex since you can eat a three-course meal for as little as 9 euros in one of the local bistros, their red and white chequer-board tablecloths having become emblems of Parisian life, or for as much as 152 euros in one of the temples of *haute cuisine*.

In between, there is an amazing array of cafés serving the inevitable *steak-frites* and *jambon-beurre* sandwiches, of *brasseries* with splendid late 19th-century settings, of chain restaurants marrying constant quality with a definite French touch, of wine bars and seafood places, of regional restaurants proudly reminding gourmets that French gastronomy is not the prerogative of Parisian chefs, and of cosmopolitan restaurants specialising in African, Lebanese or Vietnamese cuisine – to name but a few – and in Tex-Mex fare, increasingly popular with young French crowds.

Bistros are traditionally versatile and a great favourite of Parisians and visitors alike. Up to now, their ambitions had remained modest. However, in recent years, a new generation of bistros has emerged on the Paris scene: the famous chefs of several exclusive restaurants have opened up-market bistros serving *haute cuisine* in less formal surroundings and at more affordable prices. Needless to say that these new bistros are very much in fashion: such is the case of La Régalade (► 97) and l'Epi Dupin (► 96), both on the Left Bank, where young chefs Yves Camdeborde and François Pasteau regale an increasing number of enthusiastic customers.

Right Bank Restaurants

L'Alsace (££)

Alsatian specialities and seafood; terrace in summer.

✉ 39 avenue des Champs-Elysées, 75008 Paris ☎ 01 53 93 97 00 🕐 24 hours 🚇 Franklin-D Roosevelt

L'As du Fallafel (£)

Delicious Middle-Eastern food at the heart of the Jewish quarter.

✉ 34 rue des Rosiers, 75004 Paris ☎ 01 48 87 63 60 🕐 Lunch, dinner; closed Fri dinner, Sat lunch 🚇 St-Paul

Les Amognes (££)

Bistro serving imaginative cuisine; relaxed atmosphere.

✉ 243 rue du Faubourg St-Antoine, 75011 Paris ☎ 01 43 72 73 05 🕐 Lunch, dinner; closed Mon lunch, Sun and 10–31 Aug 🚇 Faidherbe Chaligy

Bar à Huîtres (£–££)

Fashionable seafood brasserie.

✉ 33 boulevard Beaumarchais, 75003 Paris ☎ 01 48 87 98 92 🕐 Lunch, dinner, open until 2AM 🚇 Bastille

Beauvilliers (£££)
Gourmet cuisine served in an elegant Napoleon III setting; terrace in summer.
✉ 52 rue Lamarck, 75018 Paris ☎ 01 42 54 54 42 🕔 Lunch, dinner; closed Mon lunch, Sun 🚇 Lamarck Caulaincourt

Bistro de Gala (££)
In the 'Grands Boulevards' area, serving traditional French cuisine.
✉ 45 rue du Faubourg Montmartre, 75009 Paris ☎ 01 40 22 90 50 🕔 Lunch, dinner; closed Sat lunch, Sun and 2 weeks in Aug 🚇 Le Peletier

Blue Elephant (££)
Thai cuisine in appropriate setting near Bastille.
✉ 43 rue de la Roquette, 75011 Paris ☎ 01 47 00 42 00 🕔 Lunch, dinner; closed Sat lunch 🚇 Voltaire

Bon (££)
Trendy new restaurant; some vegetarian dishes.
✉ 25 rue de la Pompe, 75016 Paris ☎ 01 40 72 70 00 🕔 Lunch, dinner 🚇 La Muette

Brasserie Flo (£–££)
1900-style Alsatian inn specialising in *choucroute* (sauerkraut) and seafood.
✉ 7 Cour des Petites Ecuries, 75010 Paris ☎ 01 47 70 13 59 🕔 Lunch, dinner 🚇 Château d'Eau

La Butte Chaillot (££)
Refined cuisine; striking contemporary setting.
✉ 110bis avenue Kléber, 75016 Paris ☎ 01 47 27 88 88 🕔 Lunch, dinner 🚇 Trocadéro

Cercle Ledoyen 'Rez de Chaussée (££)
More reasonably priced than the famous Ledoyen establishment upstairs.
✉ 1 avenue Dutuit, Carré des Champs-Elysées, 75008 Paris ☎ 01 53 05 10 02 🕔 Lunch, dinner; closed Sun, Christmas 🚇 Champs-Elysées Clémenceau

Chez Clément Élysées (£)
Home style cooking.
✉ 123 avenue des Champs-Élysées, 75008 Paris ☎ 01 40 73 87 00 🕔 Lunch, dinner 🚇 Charles de Gaulle-Étoile

Chez Vong (££)
Authentic Chinese cuisine from Canton.
✉ 10 rue de la Grande Truanderie, 75001 Paris ☎ 01 40 39 99 89 🕔 Lunch, dinner; closed Sun 🚇 Les Halles

Le Dôme du Marais (££)
Imaginative cuisine based on fresh seasonal produce; historic surroundings.
✉ 53 bis rue des Francs-Bourgeois, 75004 Paris ☎ 01 42 74 54 17 🕔 Lunch, dinner; closed Sun 🚇 Hôtel de Ville

Entre Ciel Terre (£)
Inventive vegetarian cuisine.
✉ 5 rue Hérold, 75001 Paris ☎ 01 45 08 49 84 🕔 Lunch, dinner; closed Sat, Sun and 20 Jul–20 Aug 🚇 Palais-Royal, Bourse

L'Etrier (£–££)
Traditional French cuisine; good value. Book a table.
✉ 154 rue Lamarck, 75018 Paris ☎ 01 42 29 14 01 🕔 Lunch, dinner; closed Mon, Sun and Aug 🚇 Guy Môquet

Grand Véfour (£££)
Haute cuisine, and 18th-century décor; beautiful view of the Jardin du Palais-Royal.

How to Get The Best Value for Money
Whenever possible, choose one of the fixed *menus* rather than à la carte. Also note that *menus* are cheaper at lunchtime and that, unless otherwise specified, service is included in the prices quoted. Wines are generally expensive but house wines are often worth trying and are more reasonably priced.

Les Halles Tradition

In the days when the Paris food market was situated where the Forum des Halles now stands, there were many restaurants in the vicinity, such as Au Pied de Cochon, which served pig's trotters and onion soup to workers kept busy throughout the night. It later became fashionable for people out on the town to end up in one of those places in the early hours of the morning.

✉ 17 rue de Beaujolais, 75001 Paris ☎ 01 42 96 56 27 🕐 Lunch, dinner; closed Sat, Sun and Aug 🚇 Palais-Royal

Les Grandes Marches (££)

Late 19th-century décor and pleasant terrace overlooking place de la Bastille for this brasserie specialising in seafood.

✉ 6 place de la Bastille, 75012 Paris ☎ 01 43 42 90 32 🕐 Lunch, dinner 🚇 Bastille

Le Jardin (£££)

Mediterranean-style haute cuisine; speciality: lobster roasted with spices.

✉ Hôtel Royal Monceau, 37 avenue Hoche, 75008 Paris ☎ 01 42 99 98 70 🕐 Lunch, dinner; closed Sat, Sun and bank hols 🚇 Charles de Gaulle-Etoile

Jipangue (££)

Excellent Japanese cuisine at reasonable prices.

✉ 96 rue La Boétie, 75008 Paris ☎ 01 45 63 77 00 🕐 Lunch, dinner; closed Sun 🚇 St-Philipe-du-Roule

Lucas Carton (£££)

Haute cuisine in an authentic late 19th-century décor by Majorelle; try the roast duck with honey and spices and the delicious saddle of lamb.

✉ 9 place de la Madeleine, 75008 Paris ☎ 01 42 65 22 90 🕐 Lunch, dinner; closed Sat lunch, Sun, Aug and Christmas 🚇 Madeleine

Nos Ancêtres les Gaulois (££)

Convivial atmosphere; menu includes as much wine as you can drink

✉ 39 rue St-Louis-en-l'Ile, 75004 Paris ☎ 01 46 33 66 07 🕐 Dinner only, lunch on Sun 🚇 Pont-Marie

Pavillon Puebla (££–£££)

In the lovely parc des Buttes Chaumont; elegant Napoleon III décor; speciality: lobster *à la catalane*.

✉ Parc des Buttes Chaumont (entrance on the corner of avenue Bolivar and rue Botzaris), 75019 Paris ☎ 01 42 08 92 62 🕐 Lunch, dinner; closed Sun, Mon 🚇 Buttes Chaumont

Piccolo Teatro (£)

Refreshing and inspired vegetarian dishes. Try the excellent soups.

✉ 6 rue des Ecouffes, 75004 Paris ☎ 01 42 72 17 79 🕐 Lunch, dinner; closed Mon, Christmas 🚇 St-Paul

Au Pied de Cochon (££)

Traditional 'Les Halles' restaurant; try the pig's trotters and onion soup.

✉ 6 rue Coquillière, 75001 Paris ☎ 01 40 13 77 00 🕐 24 hours 🚇 Châtelet Les Halles

La Poule au Pot (££)

A bistro maintaining the traditions of Les Halles.

✉ 9 rue Vauvilliers, 75001 Paris ☎ 01 42 36 32 96 🕐 Dinner; open until 6AM; closed Mon 🚇 Louvre Rivoli

Le Rouge Gorge (££)

Charming wine bar with lots of atmosphere.

✉ 8 rue St-Paul, 75004 Paris ☎ 01 48 04 75 89 🕐 Lunch, dinner; closed Sun dinner 🚇 St-Paul

Stresa (££)

Trendy Italian restaurant; booking advisable.

✉ 7 rue de Chambiges, 75008 Paris ☎ 01 47 23 51 62 🕐 Lunch, dinner; closed Sat dinner, Sun, Aug and Christmas 🚇 Alma-Marceau

The Studio (£)
Specialities from Texas in a 16th-century setting at the heart of the Marais.
✉ 41 rue du Temple, 75004 Paris ☎ 01 42 74 10 38
🕐 Lunch, dinner; closed Mon lunch 🚇 Hôtel de Ville

Terminus Nord (££)
A 1920s-style brasserie near the Gare du Nord; speciality: duck's *foie gras* with apple and raisins, bouillabaisse.
✉ 23 rue de Dunkerque, 75010 Paris ☎ 01 42 85 05 15
🕐 Lunch, dinner 🚇 Gare du Nord

Train Bleu (££)
Brasserie with late 19th-century décor illustrating the journey from Paris to the Mediterranean.
✉ Place Louis Armand, Gare de Lyon, 75012 Paris ☎ 01 43 43 09 06 🕐 Lunch, dinner 🚇 Gare de Lyon

Le Viaduc Café (££)
Trendy bistro in the new Viaduc des Arts complex of workshops near Bastille.
✉ 43 avenue Daumesnil, 75012 Paris ☎ 01 44 74 70 70
🕐 Lunch, dinner 🚇 Bastille

Le Vieux Bistrot (££)
Facing the north side of Notre-Dame; traditional French cooking includes *boeuf bourguignon* (beef stew).
✉ 14 rue du Cloître-Notre-Dame, 75004 Paris ☎ 01 43 54 18 95 🕐 Lunch, dinner 🚇 Cité

Wally le Saharien (££)
North African specialities with mountains of couscous.
✉ 36 rue Rodier, 75009 Paris ☎ 01 42 85 51 90 🕐 Lunch, dinner; closed Mon lunch and Sun 🚇 Cadet

Left Bank Restaurants

Le Bamboche (££)
Typical fish dishes from Provence.
✉ 15 rue de Babylone, 75007 Paris ☎ 01 45 49 14 40
🕐 Lunch, dinner; closed Sat lunch and Sun 🚇 Sèvres-Babylone

Bistrot Côté Mer (££)
Appropriate Breton decor for this fine fish restaurant.
✉ 16 boulevard St-Germain, 75005 Paris ☎ 01 43 54 59 10
🕐 Lunch, dinner
🚇 Maubert-Mutualité

Les Bookinistes (££)
Fashionable restaurant along the embankment; up-and-coming young chef has made *nouvelle cuisine* into an art.
✉ 53 quai des Grands-Augustins, 75006 Paris
☎ 01 43 25 45 94 🕐 Lunch, dinner; closed Sat lunch, Sun
🚇 Saint-Michel

Brasserie Saint-Benoît (£-££)
Traditional French cuisine served in rustic surroundings; small terrace
✉ 26 rue St-Benoît, 75006 Paris ☎ 01 45 48 29 66
🕐 Lunch, dinner; closed Sun lunch 🚇 St-Germain-des-Prés

Le Chat Grippé (££)
Imaginative cuisine with mouth-watering flavours.
✉ 87 rue d'Assas, 75006 Paris ☎ 01 43 54 70 00 🕐 Lunch, dinner; closed Sat, Mon lunch, Sun and Aug 🚇 Vavin

Le Ciel de Paris (££)
On the 56th floor of the Tour Montparnasse; live music from 9PM.

Fast Food and Brunch
When the first McDonald's opened in Paris, most people thought it would be a flop! Well, fast food has become part of the French way of life and now the mecca of gastronomy is about to adopt another Anglo-Saxon habit – the brunch. More and more bistros in central Paris now specialise in this 'new' kind of meal, definitely 'in'.

French and Cosmopolitan Cuisine

Most restaurants selected here serve either traditional French regional cuisine or what is loosely called *nouvelle cuisine*, as Paris's top chefs innovate in an effort to adapt to changing tastes and eating habits. There is a new emphasis on fish and seafood and it is now possible to enjoy a gastronomic meal without meat! There is also a strong tradition of world cuisine, essentially Italian, North African, Vietnamese, and Japanese.

✉ Tour Montparnasse, 33 avenue du Maine, 75015 Paris ☎ 01 40 64 77 64 🕐 Lunch, dinner 🚇 Montparnasse-Bienvenüe

D'Chez Eux (££)

Traditional bistro specialising in *cassoulet* (haricot-bean stew with Toulouse sausages).
✉ 2 avenue Lowendal, 75007 Paris ☎ 01 47 05 52 55 🕐 Lunch, dinner; closed Sun and first 3 weeks of Aug 🚇 Ecole Militaire

Chez Françoise (£)

Inn-type restaurant specialising in duck.
✉ 12 rue de la Butte aux Cailles, 75013 Paris ☎ 01 45 80 12 02 🕐 Lunch, dinner; closed Sun, Mon and Sep 🚇 Place d'Italie

Chez Toutoune (££)

Provençal cooking at good prices; convivial atmosphere.
✉ 5 rue de Pontoise, 75005 Paris ☎ 01 43 26 56 81 🕐 Lunch, dinner; closed Mon 🚇 Maubert-Mutualité

Côté Seine (£–££)

Attractively situated along the embankment between Notre-Dame and the pont Neuf. Very good value for money; booking advisable.
✉ 45 quai des Grands-Augustins, 75006 Paris ☎ 01 43 54 49 73 🕐 Dinner 🚇 Saint-Michel

La Coupole (££)

Famous brasserie from the 1920s with art-deco setting; excellent seafood. Reasonable late-night menu (after 11PM).
✉ 102 boulevard du Montparnasse, 75014 Paris ☎ 01 43 20 14 20 🕐 Lunch, dinner; open until 2AM 🚇 Vavin

La Dinée (££)

Imaginative cuisine with an emphasis on fish; young chef already hailed by gourmets.
✉ 85 rue Leblanc, 75015 Paris ☎ 01 45 54 20 49 🕐 Lunch, dinner; closed Sat, Sun and 2 weeks in Aug 🚇 Javel

Le Divellec (£££)

One of the top seafood restaurants in Paris complete with nautical décor.
✉ 107 rue de l'Université, 75007 Paris ☎ 01 45 51 91 96 🕐 Lunch, dinner; closed Sat, Sun, Christmas 🚇 Invalides

Le Dôme (££–£££)

Brasserie specialising in seafood; try the *bouillabaisse* from Provence.
✉ 108 boulevard du Montparnasse, 75014 Paris ☎ 01 43 35 34 82 🕐 Lunch, dinner 🚇 Vavin

L'Epi Dupin (£)

Sought-after, reasonably priced restaurant with regular change of menu; book well in advance. Best ingredients from Rungis market.
✉ 11 rue Dupin, 75006 Paris ☎ 01 42 22 64 56 🕐 Lunch, dinner; closed Sat, Sun, Mon lunch and 3 weeks in Aug 🚇 Sèvres-Babylone

Jacques Cagna (£££)

High-class traditional French cuisine in 17th-century residence with wood panelling and beams; Dutch paintings to match.
✉ 14 rue des Grands-Augustins, 75006 Paris ☎ 01 43 26 49 39 🕐 Lunch, dinner; closed Sat, Mon lunch, Sun, 1–21 Aug and Christmas 🚇 Saint-Michel

Lapérouse (£££)

This historic building seems to inspire the adventurous young chef!

✉ 51 quai des Grands Augustins, 75006 , Paris ☎ 01 43 26 68 04 🕐 Lunch, dinner; closed Sat lunch, Sun and Aug 🚇 Saint-Michel

Mavrommatis (£–££)

Refined traditional Greek cuisine; terrace in summer.

✉ 42 rue Daubenton, 75005 Paris ☎ 01 43 31 17 17 🕐 Lunch, dinner; closed Mon 🚇 Censier-Daubenton

Moulin à Vent (££)

Bistro insisting on traditional features such as steak, roast poultry etc.

✉ 20 rue des Fossés Saint-Bernard, 75005 Paris ☎ 01 43 54 99 37 🕐 Lunch, dinner; closed Sat lunch, Sun, Mon and Aug 🚇 Jussieu

Le Procope (£–££)

An 18th-century literary café known to Voltaire and Benjamin Franklin, now a historic monument.

✉ 13 rue de l'Ancienne Comédie, 75006 Paris ☎ 01 40 46 79 00 🕐 Lunch, dinner 🚇 Odéon

La Régalade (££)

Haute cuisine at relatively low prices in unassuming setting; book well in advance.

✉ 49 avenue Jean Moulin, 75014 Paris ☎ 01 45 45 68 58 🕐 Lunch, dinner; closed Sat lunch, Sun and Mon 🚇 Alesia

Le Reminet (£–££)

Refined bistro-style fare; terrace in summer. Extraordinarily good deserts. Friendly service.

✉ 3 rue des Grands-Degrés, 75005 Paris ☎ 01 44 07 04 24

🕐 Lunch, dinner, closed Mon, Tue, 1–21 Jan and 15–31 Aug 🚇 St-Michel

Susan's place (£)

Convivial Tex Mex restaurant also serving vegetarian dishes.

✉ 51 rue des École, 75005 Paris ☎ 01 43 54 23 22 🕐 Lunch, dinner; closed Sun lunch, Mon 🚇 Maubert-Mutualité

Le Télégraphe (££)

Close to the Musée d'Orsay, this trendy restaurant offers refined, imaginative cuisine in an art-deco setting. Pleasant garden for summer meals.

✉ 41 rue de Lille, 75007 Paris ☎ 01 42 92 03 04 🕐 Lunch, dinner, closed Sat, Sun lunch and 3 weeks in Aug 🚇 Saint-Germain-des-Prés

Thoumieux (£–££)

High-class brasserie specialising in home-made duck *cassoulet*.

✉ 79 rue Saint-Dominique, 75007 Paris ☎ 01 47 05 49 75 🕐 Lunch, dinner 🚇 Latour-Maubourg

Tour d'Argent (£££)

Haute cuisine served in exceptional surroundings with remarkable view of Notre-Dame and the river; speciality: *canard* (duck) *Tour d'Argent*.

✉ 15–17 quai de la Tournelle, 75005 Paris ☎ 01 43 54 23 31 🕐 Lunch, dinner; closed Mon 🚇 Pont-Marie

La Truffière (££)

Very refined cuisine making use of truffles, as the name suggests.

✉ 4 rue Blainville, 75005 Paris ☎ 01 46 33 29 82 🕐 Lunch, dinner; closed Mon, 1–20 Aug 🚇 Place Monge

Where to Eat

Restaurants usually serve meals from midday to 2PM and from 7.30 to 10.30PM. *Brasseries* (the word means breweries) are restaurants where one can often eat at any time of the day and which have *choucroute* on their menu, served with a glass of draught beer. Bistros are usually more modest (although some of them are very fashionable) and convivial, boasting quick friendly service.

Ile de France

Prices
The same price rating as for Paris has been applied to restaurants in nearby towns; however, you can expect to get much better value for money outside the capital; it is also important to remember that service finishes earlier in the evening than in Paris, usually around 9:30.

Chantilly
🚃 Gare du Nord to Chantilly-Gouvieux

Château de la Tour (££)
Refined cuisine and wood-panelled décor; terrace in summer.
✉ Chemin de la Chaussée, 60270 Gouvieux (1km from Chantilly) ☎ 03 44 62 38 38
🕐 Lunch, dinner

Condé Ste Libiaire (3km from Disneyland)
🚃 RER A Marne-la-Vallée/Chessy

La Vallée de la Marne (£-££)
Peaceful setting; dining-room overlooks the garden on the banks of the River Marne. Fresh local produce.
✉ 2 quai de la Marne, 77450 Condé-Ste Libiaire ☎ 01 60 04 31 01 🕐 Lunch, dinner; closed Mon dinner, Tue

Fontainebleau
🚃 Gare de Lyon to Fontainebleau-Avon then 🚌 A or B

L'Atrium (£-££)
Pizzeria in the town centre; with attractive year-round terrace dining.
✉ 20 rue France, 77300 Fontainebleau ☎ 01 64 22 18 36
🕐 Lunch, dinner

Le Beauharnais (££)
Haute cuisine in high-class restaurant well placed facing the Château.
✉ Grand Hôtel de l'Aigle Noir, 27 place Napoléon Bonaparte, 77300 Fontainebleau ☎ 01 60 74 60 00 🕐 Lunch, dinner

Le Caveau des Ducs (££)
Elegant restaurant in vaulted cellars; terrace in summer.
✉ 24 rue de Ferrare, 77300 Fontainebleau ☎ 01 64 22 05 05 🕐 Lunch, dinner

Drive In and Around the Forêt de Fontainebleau

Barbizon
L'Angélus (££)
Convivial gastronomic restaurant with a terrace in summer.
✉ 31 rue Grande, 77630 Barbizon ☎ 01 60 66 44 30
🕐 Lunch, dinner; closed Tue

Hostellerie du Bas-Préau (£££)
Haute cuisine meals served in the garden. Queen Elizabeth II and Emperor Hiro Hito have both stayed here.
✉ 22 rue Grande, 77630 Barbizon ☎ 01 60 66 40 05
🕐 Lunch, dinner

Bourron-Marlotte (9km south of Fontainebleau)
Les Prémices (££)
Within the Fontainebleau forest; dishes are served on the terrace in summer.
✉ 12 bis rue Blaise de Montesquiu. 77780 Borron-Marlotte ☎ 01 64 78 33 00
🕐 Lunch, dinner; closed Sun dinner, Mon and first two weeks in August

Rueil-Malmaison
🚃 RER Rueil-Malmaison

Le Fruit Défendu (££)
Picturesque inn along the Seine; traditional French cuisine.
✉ 80 boulevard Belle-rive, 92500 Rueil-Malmaison
☎ 01 47 49 60 60 🕐 Lunch, dinner; closed Sun dinner, Mon

Saint-Cloud

🚇 Gare Saint-Lazare to Saint-Cloud

Quai Ouest (££)

This 'Floating warehouse' serving appetising fish and poultry dishes is the place to go when the sun is out.

✉ 120 quai Marcel Dassault, 92210 Saint-Cloud ☎ 01 46 02 35 54 🕐 Lunch, dinner

Saint-Denis

🚇 Métro Saint-Denis-Basilique

Campanile Saint-Denis Basilique (£)

One of a chain of inn-style modern hotels serving reliably good cuisine.

✉ 14 rue Jean-Jaurès, 93200 Saint-Denis ☎ 01 48 20 74 31 🕐 Lunch, dinner

Saint-Germain-en-Laye

🚇 RER Saint-Germain-en-Laye

Cazaudehore-La Forestière (£££)

Sophisticated garden setting for refined summer meals; the menu even includes frogs' legs!

✉ 1 avenue du Président Kennedy, 78100 Saint-Germain-en-Laye ☎ 01 30 61 64 64 🕐 Lunch, dinner; closed Mon except hols

Ermitage des Loges (££)

Reasonably priced, cuisine with an emphasis on fish and seafood. Summer eating is in the garden

✉ 11 avenue des Loges, 78100 Saint-Germain-en-Laye ☎ 01 39 21 50 95 🕐 Lunch, dinner

Feuillantine (£)

You will find tasty cuisine at moderate prices in this elegant commuterland setting close to the impressive château.

✉ 10 rue Louviers, 78100 Saint-Germain-en-Laye ☎ 01 34 51 04 24 🕐 Lunch, dinner

10km from Vaux-Le-Vicomte

🚇 Gare de Lyon to Melun

La Mare au Diable (££)

Lovely old house with beams (see panel); terrace for summer meals.

✉ RN6, 77550 Melun-Sénart ☎ 01 64 10 20 90 🕐 Lunch, dinner; closed Sun dinner, Mon

Versailles

🚇 Gare Saint-Lazare to Versailles Rive-Droite; RER C to Versailles Rive Gauche

Le Boeuf à la Mode (£)

Old-fashioned brasserie with sunny terrace serving excellent duck and vegetable spaghettis.

✉ 4 rue au Pain, 78000 Versailles ☎ 01 39 50 31 99 🕐 Lunch, dinner

La Cuisine Bourgeoise (££)

Tasty refined cuisine served in cosy surroundings; perfect on a day out to Versailles.

✉ 10 boulevard du Roi, 78000 Versailles ☎ 01 39 53 11 38 🕐 Lunch, dinner; closed Sat lunch, Sun, Mon and 3 weeks in Aug

Le Potager du Roy (£–££)

Very good-value bistro; elegant surroundings.

1 rue du Maréchal-Joffre, 78000 Versailles ☎ 01 39 50 35 34 🕐 Lunch, dinner; closed Sun dinner and Mon

Drive through the Vallée De Chevreuse

Saint-Lambert

Les Hauts de Port Royal (££)

Beautifully restored coaching-inn; terrace overlooking the park of the Abbaye de Port-Royal; the food matches the setting.

✉ 2 rue de Vaumurier, 78470 Saint-Lambert ☎ 01 30 44 10 21 🕐 Lunch, dinner; closed Sun dinner and Mon

La Mare au Diable

Memories of George Sand linger on in this 15th-century manor house, named after one of her most famous 'rural' novels; it was here that the young romantic Aurore Dupin met her future husband and later decided on her pen-name.

Paris

Prices

Prices indicated below are per room:

£ = budget (under 90 euros)

££ = moderate (90 euros–180 euros)

£££ = expensive to luxury (over 180 euros)

Note that luxury hotels such as the Ritz or the Crillon can charge over 610 euros for a double room. Payment can be made by credit cards in most hotels except in some budget hotels.

Hôtel de l'Abbaye (£££)

A roaring log fire and a delightful inner garden ensure comfort whatever the season.

✉ 10 rue Cassette, 75006 Paris
☎ 01 45 44 38 11 🕐 All year
🚇 Saint-Sulpice

Hôtel d'Angleterre Saint-Germain-des-Prés (££–£££)

The largest rooms of this quiet luxury hotel overlook the secluded garden.

✉ 44 rue Jacob, 75006 Paris
☎ 01 42 60 34 72 🕐 All year
🚇 St-Germain-des-Prés

Hôtel Caron de Beaumarchais (££)

Recently restored 18th-century town house in the Marais; refined period decoration and air conditioning in all rooms.

✉ 12 rue Vieille-du-Temple, 75004 Paris ☎ 01 42 72 34 12
🕐 All year 🚇 Hôtel de Ville

Hôtel Esmeralda (£)

Some rooms in this old-fashioned yet cosy hotel offer delightful views of Notre-Dame. Beware no lift!

✉ 4 rue Saint-Julien-le-Pauvre, 75005 Paris ☎ 01 43 54 19 20 🕐 All year 🚇 Saint-Michel

Hôtel Franklin-Roosevelt (££)

Bright comfortable bedrooms with striking murals and functional bathrooms; warm welcome.

✉ 18 rue Clément Marot, 75008 Paris ☎ 01 53 57 49 50 🕐 All year 🚇 Franklin-D Roosevelt

Hôtel Galileo (££)

Modern refined hotel near the Champs-Elysées with air conditioning and well-appointed bedrooms, a few with verandas.

✉ 54 rue Galilée, 75008 Paris
☎ 01 47 20 66 06 🕐 All year
🚇 George V

Hôtel du Jeu de Paume (££–£££)

Exclusive hotel on the Ile Saint-Louis, housed in converted Jeu de Paume (inside tennis court), with striking galleries and mezzanines.

✉ 54 rue Saint-Louis-en-l'Ile, 75004 Paris ☎ 01 43 26 14 18
🕐 All year 🚇 Pont-Marie

Hôtel du Lys (£)

Simple hotel at the heart of the Quartier Latin; no lift but modern bathrooms, warm welcome and reasonable prices; book well in advance.

✉ 23 rue Serpente, 75006 Paris
☎ 01 43 26 97 57 🕐 All year
🚇 Saint-Michel, Odéon

Hôtel Montalembert (£££)

Luxury hotel, with discreet yet original decoration, sound-proofing and air conditioning; very expensive.

✉ 3 rue de Montalembert, 75007 Paris ☎ 01 45 49 68 68
🕐 All year 🚇 Rue du Bac

Hôtel de Nevers (£)

Simple but charming, in a former convent building; private roof terraces for top-floor rooms.

✉ 83 rue du Bac, 75007 Paris
☎ 01 45 44 61 30 🕐 All year
🚇 Rue du Bac

Hôtel du Panthéon (££)

An elegant hotel conveniently situated in the university district, with well-appointed air-conditioned bedrooms.

✉ 19 place du Panthéon, 75005

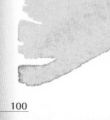

Paris 📞 01 43 54 32 95 🕒 All year 🚇 Cardinal-Lemoine

Pavillon de la Reine (£££)
In one of the historic buildings lining the place des Vosges; tradition reigns supreme throughout: oak-wood panelling, tapestries and four-poster beds.
✉ 28 place des Vosges, 75003 Paris 📞 01 40 29 19 19 🕒 All year 🚇 Saint-Paul, Bastille

Hôtel Place des Vosges (£)
Picturesque quiet hotel just off the place des Vosges.
✉ 12 rue de Birague, 75004 Paris 📞 01 42 72 60 46 🕒 All year 🚇 Saint-Paul, Bastille

Hôtel Le Régent (££)
Air conditioning and bright well-appointed bedrooms in this cleverly restored 18th-century house in Saint-Germain-des-Prés.
✉ 61 rue Dauphine, 75006 Paris 📞 01 46 34 59 80 🕒 All year 🚇 Odéon

Hôtel Relais du Louvre (££)
Warm colours, antique furniture and modern comfort, a stone's throw from the Louvre.
✉ 19 rue des Prêtres Saint-Germain-l'Auxerrois, 75001 Paris 📞 01 40 41 96 42 🕒 All year 🚇 Louvre-Rivoli

Résidence les Gobelins (£)
A haven of peace near the lively rue Mouffetard; warm welcome.
✉ 9 rue des Gobelins, 75013 Paris 📞 01 47 07 26 90 🕒 All year 🚇 Les Gobelins

Hôtel Les Rives de Notre-Dame (£££)
Elegant and comfortable, with sound-proofed bedrooms overlooking the quai Saint-Michel and the Ile de la Cité.
✉ 15 quai Saint-Michel, 75005 Paris 📞 01 43 54 81 16 🕒 All year 🚇 Saint-Michel

Hôtel Ritz Paris (£££)
Sometimes called the palace of kings and the king of palaces, the Ritz shares with the Crillon the top of the list of Paris's luxury hotels. Overlooking the place Vendôme, it boasts a beautiful swimming pool and luxury fitness centre; prices are accordingly very high.
✉ 15 place Vendôme, 75001 Paris 📞 01 43 16 30 30 🕒 All year 🚇 Opéra

Tim Hôtel Montmartre (££)
In the old part of Montmartre, halfway up the hill, with lovely views; attention to detail makes it a comfortable if simple place to stay.
✉ 11 rue Ravignan, 75018 Paris 📞 01 42 55 74 79 🕒 All year 🚇 Abbesses

Hôtel Le Tourville (££)
Refined decoration for this modern hotel in the elegant 7th *arrondissement*, close to Les Invalides; luxury at reasonable prices.
✉ 16 avenue de Tourville, 75007 Paris 📞 01 47 05 62 62 🕒 All year 🚇 Ecole Militaire

Hôtel des Trois Collèges (£)
Roof beams and dormer windows add a picturesque touch to this simple yet comfortable hotel close to the Sorbonne.
✉ 16 rue Cujas, 75005 Paris 📞 01 43 54 67 30 🕒 All year 🚇 Cluny-la-Sorbonne

Historic Hotels
The Hôtel d'Angleterre was the seat of the British Embassy in the 18th century, at the time of American Independence; more recently, it was one of the temporary homes of Ernest Hemingway. The Jeu de Paume, recently converted into a hotel, was built in the early 17th century as part of the development of the Ile Saint-Louis. It was the first one of its kind in Paris. The exclusive Hôtel Ritz has had many famous guests, including the Duke of Windsor and Ernest Hemingway.

Ile de France

Country Hotels

The hotels listed in this section have been selected as much for their picturesque, even outstanding setting and surroundings as for their high level of comfort. The price range is the same as that of Paris hotels but these country hotels offer much better value for money.

Chantilly
🚇 Gare du Nord to Chantilly-Gouvieux

Château de Montvillargenne (££)
Large mansion in vast own grounds; covered swimming pool, sauna, sports facilities.
✉ 1 avenue François Mathet, 60270 Gouvieux ☎ 03 44 62 37 37 🕐 All year

Château de la Tour (££)
Late 19th-century mansion, with swimming pool, terrace and large park.
✉ Chemin de la Chaussée, 60270 Gouvieux ☎ 03 44 62 38 38 🕐 All year

Le Relais d'Aumale (£–££)
Former hunting-lodge of the Duc d'Aumale, at the heart of the Forêt de Chantilly.
✉ 37 place des Fêtes, Montgresin 60560 Orry la Ville ☎ 03 44 54 61 31 🕐 All year

Disneyland
🚇 RER Marne-la-Vallée/Chessy

Cheyenne (£–££)
Each of the hotels has its own authentic American theme; this one is self-explanatory.
☎ 01 60 45 62 00; UK booking centre: 0990 03 03 03 🕐 All year

Disneyland Hotel (£££)
This Victorian-style hotel is the most sophisticated and expensive of the six hotels in the Disneyland complex and the closest to the theme park.
☎ 01 60 45 65 00; UK booking centre: 0990 03 03 03 🕐 All year

Esbly Marne-la-Vallée
La Pierre Tourneville (£)
Budget hotel belonging to the Hotel Akena chain, convenient for Disneyland Paris; only five minutes by car.
✉ 77450 Isles-les-Villenoy ☎ 01 60 04 42 42 🕐 All year

Fontainebleau
🚇 Gare de Lyon to Fontainebleau-Avon

Grand Hôtel de l'Aigle Noir (££)
Napoleon III-style decoration for this hotel facing the castle; fitness club, indoor swimming pool and very good restaurant.
✉ 27 place Napoléon Bonaparte, 77300 Fontainebleau ☎ 01 60 74 60 00 🕐 All year

Hôtel Le Richelieu (£)
Reasonably priced yet comfortable hotel, one of the Logis de France traditional establishments.
✉ 4 rue Richelieu, 77300 Fontainebleau ☎ 01 64 22 26 46 🕐 All year

Drive in and Around the Forêt de Fontainebleau

Barbizon
Hôtel Les Charmettes (£)
Picturesque timber-framed Logis de France hotel.
✉ 40 Grande-Rue, 77630 Barbizon ☎ 01 60 66 40 21 🕐 All year

Hostellerie de la Clé d'Or (£)
Former coaching-inn; bedrooms overlook the peaceful garden; terrace for summer meals.
✉ 73 Grande-Rue, 77630 Barbizon ☎ 01 60 66 40 96 🕐 All year

Hôtel Les Pléiades (£)

A former painter's house turned into a hotel in the 'painters' village! Splendid terrace for summer meals; refined cuisine.

✉ 21 Grande-Rue, 77630 Barbizon ☎ 01 60 66 40 25
🕐 All year

Saint-Germain-en-Laye

🚉 RER Saint-Germain-en-Laye

Hôtel Cazaudehore-La Forestière (££)

Relaxation is the keynote in this large hotel.

✉ 1 avenue du Président Kennedy, 78100 Saint-Germain-en-Laye ☎ Hotel: 01 39 10 38 38, restaurant: 01 34 51 93 80
🕐 All year

Hôtel Ermitage des Loges (££)

There's music on Wednesday and Thursday nights in the hotel bar; excellent restaurant.

✉ 11 avenue des Loges, 78100 Saint-Germain-en-Laye ☎ 01 39 21 50 90 🕐 All year

Pavillon Henri IV (££–£££)

Historic building (see panel this page) near the famous Grande Terrasse; great views.

✉ 19–21 rue Thiers, 78100 Saint-Germain-en-Laye ☎ 01 39 10 15 15 🕐 All year

Versailles

🚉 Gare Saint-Lazare to Versailles Rive Droite; RER C to Versailles Rive Gauche

Relais de Courlande (£)

Attractive converted 16th-century farmhouse; hydrotherapy facilities.

✉ 23 rue de la Division Leclerc, 78350 Les Loges-en-Josas ☎ 01 30 83 84 00
🕐 All year

Sofitel Château de Versailles (£££)

Luxury Château hotel next to Château de Versailles.

✉ 2bis avenue de Paris, 78000 Versailles ☎ 01 39 07 46 46
🕐 All year

Trianon Palace (£££)

This luxury establishment, on the edge of the Parc de Versailles, boasts an exclusive fitness club, two tennis courts and golf and riding facilities. It is one of the top palace hotels in France.

✉ 1 boulevard de la Reine, 78000 Versailles ☎ 01 30 84 50 00 🕐 All year

Drive through the Vallée De Chevreuse

Abbaye des Vaux de Cernay (££)

A 12th-century Cistercian abbey, the setting for an unforgettable stay in the Vallée de Chevreuse; in the grounds: swimming pool, fitness club, tennis; musical evenings, sons et lumières show.

✉ 78720 Cernay-la-Ville (14km northeast of Rambouillet)
☎ 01 34 85 23 00 and 01 34 85 11 59 🕐 All year

Auberge le Manet (£–££)

A hotel in a former building of the 13th-century Abbaye de Port-Royal; set in its own grounds.

✉ 61 avenue du Manet, 78180 Montigny-le-Bretonneux (just north of the D91, ➤ 90, Vallée de Chevreuse drive) ☎ 01 30 64 89 00 🕐 All year

Pavillon Henri IV

The lovely brick building of the Pavillon Henri IV, surmounted by a dome, is all that remains, together with another pavilion, of the Château Neuf erected at the beginning of the 17th century and demolished in the 18th century after being neglected for too long. King Louis XIV was actually born within its walls on 5 September 1638. The pavilion was turned into a hotel in 1836 and has subsequently attracted many famous guests.

Shopping in Paris

Opening Hours

Shops are usually open weekdays from 9–7. Some are closed on Mondays, others are open on Sundays. Smaller shops sometimes close for lunch. Food shops remain open later. Department stores close late on Thursdays (up to 10PM).

Duty-Free Shopping

Residents of non-EU countries are entitled to a VAT refund (about 14 per cent) if they spend over 182.94 euros in the same shop. Export receipts issued by shopkeepers must be presented on the day of departure to the Customs Officer, who may wish to see the goods. The refund will be credited within 30 days.

More information from: Cashback France SA, ✉ 68 rue de Paris, 93804 Epinay-sur-Seine Cédex ☎ 01 48 27 24 54

Department Stores

Bazar de l'Hôtel de Ville

Known as the BHV, this store is famous for its huge do-it-yourself department, which claims to be the place to find what you can't find anywhere else!
✉ 52–4 rue de Rivoli, 75001 Paris ☎ 01 42 74 90 00
🚇 Hôtel de Ville

Bon Marché Rive Gauche

The only department store on the Left Bank, and the first to open in Paris; famous for its Grande Epicerie, selling specialities from various countries and freshly prepared delicacies.
✉ 22 rue de Sèvres, 75007 Paris ☎ 01 44 39 80 00
🚇 Sèvres-Babylone

Galeries Lafayette

A few blocks away from the Printemps, with designer ready-to-wear fashion and lingerie. Under a giant glass dome there is an enticing display of everything a home and its inhabitants need.
✉ 40 boulevard Haussmann, 75009 Paris ☎ 01 42 82 34 56
🚇 Chaussée d'Antin

Monoprix

Chain of department stores for the budget-conscious. There is a large branch at the back of Au Printemps.
✉ 56 rue Caumartin, 75009 Paris ☎ 01 44 53 79 79
🚇 Havre-Caumartin

Au Printemps

Three stores in one: Le Printemps de la Mode, including ready-to-wear designer fashion, Le Printemps de la Maison, including elegant tableware and hi-fi, record and stationery department in the basement, and Brummell, devoted to men's wear.
✉ 64 boulevard Haussmann, 75009 Paris ☎ 01 42 82 50 00
🚇 Havre-Caumartin

Samaritaine

It lacks the stylishness of the boulevard Haussmann's stores but it offers a splendid view of Paris from the roof-top Toupary bistro.
✉ 19 rue de la Monnaie, 75001 Paris ☎ 01 40 41 20 20
🚇 Pont Neuf

Shopping Centres

Carrousel du Louvre

Elegant shopping centre located beneath the place du Carrousel and communicating with the Louvre; several boutiques connected with the arts, Virgin store and several bars serving food from different countries.
✉ 99 rue de Rivoli, 75001 Paris ☎ 01 43 16 47 15 🚇 Palais Royal

Drugstore Publicis

Unexpectedly situated at the top of the Champs-Elysées, a stone's throw from the Arc de Triomphe, this shopping mall has a restaurant and a selection of gift/souvenir shops.
✉ 133 avenue des Champs-Elysées, 75008 Paris ☎ 01 44 43 79 00 🚇 Charles de Gaulle-Etoile

Forum des Halles

Underground shopping centre on several floors including chain-store fashion boutiques and the new

Forum des Créateurs for young designers; also a huge FNAC store (▶107).
✉ 1–7 rue Pierre Lescot, 75001 Paris 🚇 Les Halles; RER Châtelet-Les Halles

Galeries Marchandes des Champs-Elysées
Several shopping malls link the Champs-Elysées and the parallel rue de Ponthieu between the Rond-Point des Champs-Elysées and the avenue George V; various boutiques including fashion and shoes.
✉ Avenue des Champs-Elysées, 75008 Paris 🚇 George V, Franklin-D Roosevelt

Marché Saint-Germain
Fashion and gift shops including clothes, shoes, leather goods, accessories, perfume, jewellery and gifts.
✉ Rue Clément, 75006 Paris 🚇 Mabillon

Trois Quartiers
Mainly traditional fashion boutiques in the exclusive Madeleine area.
✉ 23 boulevard de la Madeleine, 75001 Paris 🚇 01 42 97 80 12 🚇 Madeleine

Fashion – Haute Couture

Chanel
✉ 31 rue Cambon, 75001 Paris 🚇 01 42 86 28 00 🚇 Concorde

Christian Dior
✉ 30 avenue Montaigne, 75008 Paris 🚇 01 40 73 54 44 🚇 Champs-Elysées Clémenceau

Emmanuel Ungaro
✉ 2 avenue Montaigne, 75008 Paris 🚇 01 53 57 00 00 🚇 Alma-Marceau

Givenchy
✉ 3 avenue George V, 75008 Paris 🚇 01 44 31 50 23 🚇 Alma-Marceau

Pierre Cardin
✉ 27 avenue de Marigny, 75008 Paris 🚇 01 42 66 68 98 and 01 42 66 64 74 🚇 Champs-Elysées Clémenceau

Yves Saint-Laurent
✉ 5 avenue Marceau, 75016 Paris 🚇 01 44 31 64 00 🚇 Alma-Marceau

Fashion – Boutiques and Accessories

Hermès
Silk scarves, leather goods.
✉ 24 rue du Faubourg Saint-Honoré, 75008 Paris 🚇 01 40 17 47 17 🚇 Concorde

Jean-Paul Gaultier
Ready-to-wear fashion from this famous designer.
✉ 30 rue du Faubourg Saint-Antoine, 75012 Paris 🚇 01 44 68 84 84 🚇 Bastille

Madelios
Male fashion from city suits to casuals and accessories.
✉ 23 boulevard de la Madeleine, Paris 75001 🚇 01 53 45 00 00 🚇 Madeleine

Nina Jacob
Trendy fashion and accessories.
✉ 23 rue des Francs-Bourgeois, 75004 Paris 🚇 01 42 77 41 20 🚇 Saint-Paul

raoul et curly
Designer accessories, jewellery, perfumes, cosmetics, leather goods.
✉ 47 avenue de l'Opéra, 75002 Paris 🚇 01 47 42 50 10 🚇 Opéra

Fashion
Most top fashion houses are located in the Concorde/Champs-Elysées area, in particular, avenue Montaigne, avenue Marigny and rue du Faubourg Saint-Honoré. Fashion boutiques selling ready-to-wear designer clothes are to be found in place des Victoires, in the Marais district (rue des Francs-Bourgeois) in the Palais-Royal area (rue Saint-Honoré), and in and around Saint-Germain-des-Prés (rue Saint-Sulpice, rue Bonaparte, rue de Rennes, rue de Sèvres and rue de Grenelle).

Shopping Arcades

A number of the covered shopping arcades built at the end of the 18th and the beginning of the 19th centuries still survive, retaining their old-world charm. Lined with boutiques and tea-rooms, they offer a moment's respite from the city's bustle. The most attractively decorated are the Galerie Vivienne, Galerie Colbert and Galerie Véro-Dodat, near the Palais-Royal. Others, such as the Passage Jouffroy along the Grands Boulevards, have a more exotic flavour.

Walter Steiger

Luxury shoes for men and women.

✉ 83 rue du Faubourg Saint-Honoré, 75008 Paris ☎ 01 42 66 65 08 🚇 Miromesnil

Yohji Yamamoto

Ready-to-wear clothes by the Japanese designer.

✉ 22 rue de Sèvres, 75007 Paris ☎ 01 45 48 34 29 🚇 Saint-Germain-des-Prés

High-Class Jewellers

Boucheron

✉ 26 place Vendôme, 75001 Paris ☎ 01 42 61 58 16 🚇 Opéra

Cartier

✉ 13 rue de la Paix, 75002 Paris ☎ 01 42 61 58 56 🚇 Opéra

Chaumet

✉ 12 place Vendôme, 75001 Paris ☎ 01 44 77 24 00 🚇 Opéra

Miscellaneous Gifts

Affaire d'Homme

Designer gifts for men.

✉ 15 rue Bréa, 75006 Paris ☎ 01 46 34 69 33 🚇 Vavin

Agatha

Fashion jewellery shop.

✉ 97 rue de Rennes, 75006 Paris ☎ 01 45 48 81 30 🚇 Montparnasse-Bienvenüe

Lalique

Beautiful glass objects.

✉ 11 rue Royale, 75008 Paris ☎ 01 53 05 12 12 🚇 Concorde, Madeleine

Pallas

Designer luxury handbags.

✉ 21 rue St-Roch, 75001 Paris ☎ 01 53 45 00 00 🚇 Madeleine

Sic Amor

Fashion jewellery and accessories.

✉ 20 rue du Pont Louis-Philippe, 75004 Paris ☎ 01 42 76 02 37 🚇 Pont-Marie

Upla

Trendy gift shop.

✉ 5 rue St-Benoît, 75006 Paris ☎ 01 40 15 10 75 🚇 St-Germain des Prés

Art, Antiques and Handicrafts

Louvre des Antiquaires

This centre houses around 250 upmarket antique shops on three floors.

✉ 2 place du Palais-Royal, 75001 Paris ☎ 01 42 97 27 00 🚇 Palais-Royal

La Tuile à Loup

Handicrafts from various French regions.

✉ 35 rue Daubenton, 75005 Paris ☎ 01 47 07 28 90 🚇 Censier-Daubenton

Viaduc des Arts

Disused railway viaduct housing beneath its arches workshops and exhibition areas displaying contemporary art, handicrafts and decorative arts.

✉ 9–129 avenue Daumesnil, 75012 Paris ☎ Information: 01 44 75 80 66 🚇 Bastille, Ledru-Rollin, Reuilly-Diderot

Village Saint-Paul

A group of small antique dealers established between rue Saint-Paul and rue Charlemagne.

✉ Le Marais, 75004 Paris 🚇 Saint-Paul

Village Suisse

Very expensive antiques displayed in the former Swiss pavilions of the 1900 World Exhibition.

✉ 78 avenue de Suffren, 54 rue de la Motte-Picquet, 75017 Paris
🚇 La Motte Picquet, Grenelle

Books, CDs, Videotapes and Hi-Fi

The Abbey Bookshop

New and second-hand books from Britain, Canada and the USA.

✉ 29 rue de la Parcheminerie, 75005 Paris ☎ 01 46 33 16 24
🚇 Saint-Michel

FNAC

Books, hi-fi, videos, CDs, cameras, computers, on several floors.

✉ 28 avenue des Ternes, 75017 Paris (other branches in Montparnasse, Les Halles and Bastille) ☎ 01 44 09 19 02
🚇 Ternes

Gibert Joseph

Stationery, new and second-hand books, CDs and videos.

✉ 26–30 boulevard Saint-Michel, 75006 Paris ☎ 01 44 41 88 88 🚇 Odéon, Cluny-la-Sorbonne, Luxembourg

Shakespeare & Company

New and second-hand books in English.

✉ 37 rue de la Bûcherie, 75005 Paris ☎ 01 43 26 96 50
🚇 Maubert-Mutualité

Village Voice

English-language bookshop.

✉ 6 rue Princesse, 75006 Paris
☎ 01 46 33 36 47 🚇 Mabillon

W H Smith

Branch of the famous British chain-store; reference and children's books; guidebooks in English and French.

✉ 248 rue de Rivoli, 75001 Paris ☎ 01 44 77 88 99
🚇 Concorde

Children's Shops

Agnès B Enfant

Smart children's clothes by the fashionable designer.

✉ 2 rue du Jour, 75001 Paris
☎ 01 40 39 96 88
🚇 Les Halles

La Boutique de Floriane

Elegant children's clothes; other branches in rue de Sèvres, rue du Faubourg Saint-Honoré, rue de Grenelle, rue de Longchamp.

✉ 17 rue Tronchet, 75008 Paris
☎ 01 42 65 25 95
🚇 Madeleine

Chantelivre

Specialist bookshop dealing with all the subjects that interest children.

✉ 13 rue de Sèvres, 75006 Paris ☎ 01 45 48 87 90
🚇 Sèvres-Babylone

La Maison des Bonbons

Delicious sweets in all shapes.

✉ 14 rue Mouton Duvernet 75014 Paris ☎ 01 45 41 25 55
🚇 Mouton Duvernet

Le Nain Bleu

The most famous toy shop in Paris.

✉ 408 rue Saint-Honoré, 75008 Paris ☎ 01 42 60 39 01
🚇 Concorde, Madeleine

Food and Wines

Alain Dubois

This temple to an amazing range of cheese supplies Paris's top restaurants!

'Carré Rive Gauche'

The 'square' formed along the Left Bank by the quai Voltaire, rue de l'Université, rue du Bac and rue des Saints-Pères, which includes the rue de Verneuil, rue de Lille and rue de Beaune, is famous for its high concentration of antique dealers; every year in May, the area hosts the 'Cinq jours des objets extraordinaires', an exhibition of unusual antique objects.

Art and Antiques

Antique dealers and art galleries are often concentrated in the same area: in the Marais, stroll along rue Vieille-du-Temple, rue Debelleyme and rue Saint-Gilles. On the Left Bank, rue Jacob and rue des Saints-Pères are particularly interesting. You can't browse in the exclusive shops in the avenue Matignon and rue du Faubourg Saint-Honoré, since you need an appointment to see the dealers! The Bastille area is definitely avant-garde and artists often exhibit in their own studios.

Open Late

Some shops at the heart of the city are open until midnight or later every night, including Virgin Mégastore and Drugstore Publicis in the Champs-Elysées and the chain store Prisunic in rue de la Boétie near by.

✉ **80 rue de Tocqueville, 75017 Paris** ☎ **01 42 27 11 38**
🚇 **Malesherbes**

Berthillon
Mouth-watering ice cream in a wide range of flavours.
✉ **31 rue Saint-Louis-en-l'Ile, 75004 Paris** ☎ **01 43 54 31 61**
🕐 **Closed Mon and Tue**
🚇 **Pont-Marie**

Les Caves Augé
For serious wine lovers. This is the oldest wine shop in Paris.
✉ **116 boulevard Haussmann, 75008 Paris** ☎ **01 48 56 01 44**
🕐 **Closed one week in Aug**
🚇 **École-Militaire**

Fauchon and Hédiard
Strictly for gourmets! Two delicatessen shops with high-quality French regional products.
✉ **Fauchon at No 26, Hédiard at No 21 place de la Madeleine, 75008 Paris** ☎ **Fauchon: 01 47 42 90 10; Hédiard: 01 43 12 88 88**
🚇 **Madeleine**

Lenôtre
Succulent cakes that melt in the mouth!
✉ **15 bd. de Courcelles, 75008 Paris** ☎ **01 45 02 21 21**
🚇 **Villiers**

Lionel Poilâne
The most famous baker in Paris! Long queues form outside his shop for his bread prepared and baked in the traditional way.
✉ **8 rue du Cherche-Midi, 75006 Paris** ☎ **01 45 48 42 59**
🚇 **Sèvres-Babylone**

La Maison du Chocolat
High-quality chocolates.
✉ **8 bd. de la Madeleine, 75009 Paris** ☎ **01 47 42 28 44**
🚇 **Madeleine**

La Maison du Miel
Delicately flavoured honey from various regions of France.
✉ **24 rue Vignon, 75008 Paris** ☎ **01 47 42 26 70**
🚇 **Madeleine**

Nicolas
Chain-stores selling a wide range of good French wines; at least one store per *arrondissement*.
✉ **189 rue Saint-Honoré, 75001 Paris** ☎ **01 42 60 80 12**
🚇 **Palais-Royal**

Markets

Carreau du Temple
Covered market specialising in leather and second-hand clothes.
✉ **75003 Paris** 🕐 **Tue–Fri 9–1.30, Sat 9–6, Sun 9–2**
🚇 **Temple, Arts et Métiers**

Marché aux Fleurs
Picturesque daily market (8–7) that becomes a bird market on Sundays (9–7).
✉ **Place Louis Lépine, Ile de la Cité, 75004 Paris** 🚇 **Cité**

Marché aux Puces de Saint-Ouen
The largest flea market in Paris. Everything you can think of is for sale. Prices are often inflated, be prepared to bargain.
✉ **Between Porte de Saint-Ouen and Porte de Clignancourt, 75017 Paris** 🕐 **Sat, Sun and Mon 7:30–7** 🚇 **Porte de Clignancourt**

Marché aux Timbres
Stamp market for dealers and private collectors.
✉ **Rond-Point des Champs-Elysées, 75008 Paris** 🕐 **Thu, Sat and Sun 9–7** 🚇 **Franklin-D Roosevelt**

Shopping in the Ile de France

Meaux

Fromagerie de Meaux
Delicious Brie de Meaux and Coulommiers, two very tasty cheeses from Ile de France, made locally but famous nationwide.

✉ 4 rue du Général Leclerc, 77100 Meaux (11km north of Disneyland Paris) ☎ 01 64 34 22 82

Fontainebleau
🚇 Gare de Lyon to Fontainebleau-Avon, then 🚌 A or B

Librairie du Musée National de Fontainebleau
For history buffs fascinated by Napoleon I and European history at the beginning of the 19th century.

✉ Château de Fontainebleau, 77300 Fontainebleau ☎ 01 64 23 44 97

Drive in and Around the Forêt de Fontainebleau

Barbizon
Anabel's Galerie
Contemporary painting and sculpture.

✉ Le Bornage, 77630 Barbizon ☎ Fax: 01 60 69 23 96 ⏰ Weekends only

Galerie d'Art Castiglione
One of 18 art galleries to be found in this popular artists' village.

✉ Grande rue, 77630 Barbizon ☎ 01 60 66 40 40

Soisy-sur-Ecole
Verrerie d'Art de Soisy
The Verrerie d'Art de Soisy has demonstrations of glass-blowing by the traditional rod method. Visitors will also have an opportunity to purchase ornamental glassware.

✉ Le Moulin de Noues, 91840 Soisy-sur-Ecole ☎ 01 64 98 00 03 ⏰ Daily except Sun morning

Saint-Germain-en-Laye
🚇 RER Saint-Germain-en-Laye

Boutique du Musée des Antiquités Nationales
History books from prehistory to the early Middle Ages as well as reproductions of jewellery and various items from the museum's collections.

✉ Place du Château, 78100 Saint-Germain-en-Laye ☎ 01 39 10 13 22

Les Galeries de Saint-Germain
Close to the RER and the Château, 42 boutiques in les Galeries de Saint-Germain sell fashion, articles for the home and gifts; famous names include Chanel and Yves Saint-Laurent.

✉ 10 rue de la Salle, 78100 Saint-Germain-en-Laye ☎ 01 39 73 70 67 ⏰ Closed Mon

Versailles
🚇 Gare Saint-Lazare to Versailles Rive Droite; RER C to Versailles Rive Gauche

Librairie-Boutique de l'Ancienne Comédie
There are 2,000 titles connected with the castle, its gardens and its history, many with information on 17th-and 18th-century architecture.

✉ Château de Versailles, passage des Princes, 78000 Versailles ☎ 01 30 84 76 90

Street Markets
It is a tradition in France to buy food, and in particular fresh vegetables and fruit, from a market stall and Paris is no exception. Each *arrondissement* has its covered market, but open-air ones are much more colourful and lively and their higgledy-piggledy displays are definitely more picturesque. To get the feel of these typical Parisian attractions, go to the rue Mouffetard (🚇 Monge), the rue de Buci (🚇 Odéon) and the rue Lepic (🚇 Abbesses). They are open daily except on Mondays.

Paris and the Ile de France

Eating Out

Some chain restaurants offer set junior menus, often for less than 7 euros. Batifol, Bistro Romain, L'entrecôte, Hippopotamus, Pomme de Pain, Pizza Hut (in Paris), Chantegrill, Côte à Côte, Courtepaille, Pizza del Arte (outside Paris). Any good restaurant will always suggest a choice of dishes for your children.

Interactive Museums

Most major museums organise themed visits and workshops for children from an early age, on Wed and Sat; in addition to the museums listed here, there are also the Carnavalet, Cognacq-Jay, Louvre, Mode et Costume, Orsay, and Palais de la Découverte museums in Paris, and the Château de Saint-Germain-en-Laye and Château de Versailles, outside Paris.

Paris

Museums

Cité des Sciences et de l'Industrie

Cité des Enfants: for the 3–5 and 5–12 age groups. Book as soon as you arrive.
Techno cité: 11 years upwards.
Cinaxe: very effective simulator.

✉ 30 avenue Corentin-Cariou, 75019 Paris ☎ Information: 01 40 05 80 00 🕐 10–6; closed Mon 🚇 Porte de la Villette

Musée de la Curiosité et de la Magie

Fascinating demonstrations of magic; workshops during school holidays.

✉ 11 rue Saint-Paul, 75004 Paris ☎ 01 42 72 13 26 🕐 Wed, Sat and Sun 2–7 🚇 Saint-Paul

Musée Grévin

Five hundred wax figures of the famous, from Henry VIII to Michael Jackson and Arnold Schwarzeneger!

✉ 10 boulevard Montmartre, 75009 Paris ☎ 01 47 70 85 05 🕐 10–7 🚇 Rue Montmartre

Musée de la Marine

Shows for 8–12 year-olds, with titles such as *Treasure Island*, on Wednesdays.

✉ Palais de Chaillot, place du Trocadéro, 75016 Paris ☎ 01 53 65 69 69 🕐 Wed 3PM 🚇 Trocadéro

Musée National d'Histoire Naturelle

Spectacular procession of large and small animals in the Grande Galerie de l'Evolution.

✉ 57 rue Cuvier, 75005 Paris ☎ 01 40 79 30 00 🕐 10–6 (Thu 10PM); closed Tue 🚇 Jussieu, Gare d'Austerlitz

Musée d'Orsay

A tour and a workshop to initiate 5–10 year-olds to painting and sculpture.

✉ 62 rue de Lille, 75007 Paris ☎ 01 40 49 48 48 🕐 July and Aug Tue–Fri at 2PM 🚇 Solférino

Outdoor Activities

Aquaboulevard

Aqualand with slides, heated pool, waves, beaches etc.

✉ 4–6 rue Louis Armand, 75015 Paris ☎ 01 40 60 10 00 🕐 9AM–11PM (midnight on Fri and Sat) 🚇 Balard

Jardin d'Acclimatation

Adventure park at the heart of the Bois de Boulogne.

✉ Bois de Boulogne, 75016 Paris ☎ 01 40 67 90 82 🕐 10–6; small train from Porte Maillot on Wed, Sat, Sun, hols 1:30–6 🚇 Sablons, Porte Maillot

Jardin des Enfants aux Halles

An adventure ground for 7–11 year-olds.

✉ Forum des Halles, 105 rue Rambuteau, 75001 Paris ☎ 01 45 08 07 18 🕐 Oct–May 9–12 and 2–4 (Wed 10–4), closed Mon); Jul, Aug Tue–Thu, Sat and Sun 10–7, Fri 2–7 🚇 Les Halles

Parc des Buttes-Chaumont

Cave, waterfall, lake, island and suspended bridge stimulate imagination. Playgrounds for smaller children.

✉ 5 rue Botzaris, 75019 Paris ☎ 01 42 38 02 63 🕐 7AM–9PM 🚇 Buttes-Chaumont

Parc Zoologique de Paris

Located inside the Bois de Vincennes, this is much larger than the zoo of the Jardin des Plantes.

✉ 53 avenue de Saint-Maurice, 75012 Paris ☎ 01 44 75 20 10 (recorded information) ⏰ 9–6 (6:30 Sun and bank hols) Ⓜ Porte Dorée

Shows
Circus shows

They are seasonal but there are always several available at any time in and around Paris; information is available in the weekly publications *Pariscope* and *l'Officiel des Spectacles* both of which have a children's section.

Marionnettes du Champ-de-Mars

Indoor puppet show; two different shows every week.
✉ Champ-de-Mars (next to the Eiffel Tower), 75007 Paris ☎ 01 48 56 01 44 ⏰ 3.15 and 4.15; closed one week in Aug Ⓜ École-Militaire

Paris-story

Audio-visual show illustrating the history of Paris through its monuments.
✉ 11bis rue Scribe, 75009 Paris ☎ 01 42 66 62 06 ⏰ 9–6 on the hour Ⓜ Opéra

Ile de France
Outdoor Activities
Beach

There is a lovely beach at L'Isle-Adam on the banks of the Oise River.
✉ Plage de L'Isle-Adam, 95290 L'Isle-Adam (on the D922, ➤ 80) ☎ 01 34 69 01 68

Boat trips

Along the Oise, from Auvers and L'Isle-Adam.
✉ Tourisme Accueil Val d'Oise ☎ 01 30 29 51 00 ⏰ May–Sep

Fontainebleau

Rowing on the Etang des Carpes in the park; little train through the town and park; cycling through the forest (cycle hire at the station); riding (☎ 01 60 72 22 40).

✉ Office du Tourisme, 4 rue Royale, 77300 Fontainebleau ☎ 01 60 74 99 99 🚉 Gare de Lyon to Fontainebleau-Avon

Mer de Sable

Lots to do for children of all ages, as well as shows inspired by the American Far West, magic shows, and spectacular horse-riding shows in the sand dunes.
✉ 60950 Ermenonville, A1 motorway, exit No 7 Survilliers-Ermenonville-Saint-Witz (close to Parc Astérix) ☎ 03 44 54 00 96 ⏰ Apr–Sep 10:30–6:30 (variable, inquire beforehand) 🚉 RER Roissy-Aéroport Charles de Gaulle, then shuttle to Ermenonville

Theme parks (see the individual entries for Disneyland Paris ➤ 81 and Parc Astérix ➤ 84)

Versailles

Cycle through the magnificent park (cycle hire at the end of the Grand Canal) or take a ride in the little train (departure from the Bassin de Neptune).
✉ 78000 Versailles ☎ Information: 01 30 83 78 00 or 01 30 83 77 77 ⏰ 7–sunset 🚉 Gare Saint-Lazare-Versailles Rive Droite

Shows
Chantilly

Musée Vivant du Cheval: demonstration of dressage (daily) and horse show (1st Sun of every month).
✉ Grandes Ecuries, 60500 Chantilly ☎ 03 44 57 13 13 🚉 Gare du Nord to Chantilly-Gouvieux

Le Guignol du Parc de Saint-Cloud

Take a look at the puppet show in the park.
✉ Grille d'Orléans, route de Ville-d'Avray ☎ 01 48 21 75 37 ⏰ Wed, Sat 3 and 4, Sun 4 and 5 🚉 Gare Saint-Lazare to Sèvres/Ville d'Avray

Monuments

The following are among children's favourites: Arc de Triomphe, Conciergerie (older children), Grande Arche de la Défense, Notre-Dame (the towers), Tour Eiffel, Château de Chantilly (stables), Château de Fontainebleau and Château de Versailles.

Sea Life

Situated in the newly developed Val d'Europe complex, close to Disneyland Paris in Marne-la-Ville, this interactive marine-life centre includes some 30 aquariums displaying marine fauna and flora from around the world and offering an insight into endangered species schemes. Spectacular 360 degree tunnel!
✉ Centre Commercial International Val d'Europe, 14 cours du Danube, Serris, 77 Marne-la-Vallée. Take the A4 motorway towards Metz-Nancy, exit 14 ☎ 01 60 42 33 66 ⏰ 10–9

Entertainment in Paris

Nightlife News

Several brochures keep you up-to-date with events:

Weekly – *Pariscope* (including a *Time Out* selection in English) and *l'Officiel des Spectacles* issued Wednesday.

Monthly – *Paris Selection* from the Office de Tourisme de Paris.

Two-monthly – *What's On* (in English) highlights what's on in Paris and the provinces; available from English-language bookshops.

Three-monthly – *Time Out* free guide available from W H Smith.

At any time on the internet:
www.pariscope.fr

Changing Fashion

Hip clubs come and go and DJs move around from one to the other, but some things remain constant: nothing really starts before midnight, some clubs have an entry fee that includes one drink, others charge more for their drinks. It pays to be smartly dressed to get past the door people; jeans and trainers are out.

Concert Venues

Cité de la Musique

This new temple of classical music regularly sets new trends with special commissions.

✉ **221 avenue Jean Jaurès, 75019 Paris** ☎ **01 44 84 45 45**
Ⓜ **Porte de Pantin**

Salle Pleyel

Traditional concert hall, named after one of France's most famous piano-makers, recently refurbished, and home to the Orchestre de Paris.

✉ **252 rue du Faubourg Saint-Honoré, 75008 Paris** ☎ **01 45 61 53 00** Ⓜ **Ternes, Charles de Gaulle-Etoile**

Théâtre des Champs-Elysées

Paris's most prestigious classical concert venue with top international orchestras.

✉ **15 avenue Montaigne, 75008 Paris** ☎ **01 49 52 50 50**
Ⓜ **Alma-Marceau**

Théâtre du Châtelet

Classical concerts, opera performances, ballets and variety shows alternate in this 19th-century theatre that has welcomed great names such as Mahler and Diaghilev.

✉ **1 place du Châtelet, 75001 Paris** ☎ **01 40 28 28 40**
Ⓜ **Châtelet**

Zénith

This huge hall is the mecca of rock concerts, a privilege it shares with the Palais Omnisports de Paris Bercy (► 113).

✉ **211 avenue Jean Jaurès, 75019 Paris** ☎ **01 42 08 60 00**
Ⓜ **Porte de Pantin**

Cabaret and Music–Hall

Crazy Horse Saloon

One of the best shows in Paris with beautiful girls and striking colours and lights.

✉ **12 avenue George V, 75008 Paris** ☎ **01 47 23 32 32**
Ⓜ **Alma-Marceau**

Le Lido

The show put on by the famous Bluebell girls is mostly aimed at the tourists but it is still very effective. It is possible to have dinner on a *bateau-mouche* followed by a show at the Lido.

✉ **116bis avenue des Champs-Elysées, 75008 Paris** ☎ **01 40 76 56 10** Ⓜ **George V**

Moulin-Rouge

Undoubtedly the most famous of them all! The show still includes impressive displays of French can-can.

✉ **82 boulevard de Clichy, 75018 Paris** ☎ **01 53 09 82 82**
Ⓜ **Blanche**

Olympia

The most popular music-hall in France has been completely refurbished.

✉ **28 boulevard des Capucines, 75009 Paris** ☎ **01 47 42 25 49** Ⓜ **Opéra**

Jazz Clubs

Bilboquet

Select establishment at the heart of Saint-Germain-des-Prés for serious jazz fans.

✉ **13 rue Saint-Benoît, 75006 Paris** ☎ **01 45 48 81 84**
Ⓜ **Saint-Germain-des-Prés**

Caveau de la Huchette

Jazz and rock mania let loose in medieval cellars!

 5 rue de la Huchette, 75005 Paris ☎ 01 43 26 65 05
🚇 Saint-Michel

Nightclubs and Bars

Les Bains
Hip rendezvous of models and VIPs, with different styles of music.
 7 rue du Bourg-l'Abbé, 75003 Paris ☎ 01 48 87 01 80
🚇 Etienne Marcel

La Chapelle des Lombards
Salsa and Afro music; live shows mid-week.
 19 rue de Lappe, 75011 Paris
☎ 01 43 57 24 24 🚇 Bastille

La Casbah
Acid jazz and house alternate on different days with dance, disco music. Exotic décor.
 18–20 rue de la Forge-Royale, 75011 Paris ☎ 01 43 71 04 39 🚇 Faidherbe-Chaligny

Le Cithéa
Live music, disco, jazz, funk.
 114 rue Oberkampf, 75011 Paris ☎ 01 40 21 70 95

Divan du Monde
Jungle, Brazilian, trance, reggae, funk.
 75 rue des Martyrs, 75018 Paris ☎ 01 44 92 77 66
🚇 Pigalle

OPA
This bar/club offers house, reggae and trance as well as live concerts..
 9 rue Biscornet, 75012 Paris
☎ 01 49 28 97 16 🚇 Bastille

Rue Oberkampf
Still more music bars along this street, which teems with young Parisians during the summer evenings.
🚇 Parmentier

Sport

Piscine des Halles
Situated on Level 3 of Les Halles complex, this sports centre has a 50m-long underground swimming pool.
 10 place de la Rotonde, 75001 Paris ☎ 01 42 36 98 44
🚇 Les Halles

Piscine Pontoise Quartier Latin
Fitness club with swimming pool, squash court, sauna.
 19 rue de Pontoise, 75005 Paris ☎ 01 55 42 77 88
🚇 Maubert-Mutualité

Hippodrome d'Auteuil
Steeplechasing; Grand Steeplechase de Paris, mid-June.
 Bois de Boulogne, 75016 Paris ☎ 01 40 71 47 47
🚇 Porte d'Auteuil

Hippodrome de Longchamp
Flat-racing; Grand Prix de Paris in late June, Prix de l'Arc de Triomphe in October.
 Bois de Boulogne, 75016 Paris ☎ 01 44 30 75 00
🚇 Porte Maillot and 🚌 244

Hippodrome de Vincennes
Trotting races; Prix d'Amérique in late January.
 2 route de la Ferme, 75012 Paris ☎ 01 49 77 17 17
🚇 Château de Vincennes

Palais Omnisports de Paris Bercy (POPB)
Around 150 international sporting events every year.
 8 boulevard de Bercy, 75012 Paris ☎ 01 44 68 44 68
🚇 Bercy

Parc des Princes
The famous venue for national and international football and rugby matches.
 24 rue du Commandant-Guilbaud, 75016 Paris ☎ 01 42 30 03 60 🚇 Porte de Saint-Cloud

Roland Garros
Venue every year in late May and early June for the tennis tournament.
 2 avenue Gordon Bennett, 75016 Paris ☎ 01 47 43 48 00
🚇 Porte d'Auteuil

Free Concerts
The municipality of Paris organises free concerts in the city's parks and gardens between May and September (programmes from the Office de Tourisme de Paris). Organ concerts on the 3rd Sunday of every month in selected venues (☎ 01 42 76 67 00). Some church concerts are free, for instance in the Madeleine and the American Church on Sunday and in Saint-Merri on Saturday and Sunday. Concerts broadcast from La Maison de Radio-France are open to the public and the entrance is free (information and reservations ☎ 01 42 30 22 22).

Cinemas and Theatres
There are some 350 cinema screens in Paris. Most large cinemas show several films at once. On Friday and Saturday nights, there are long queues outside cinemas in the Champs-Elysées and the Grands Boulevards. Paris is also well stocked with theatres from the grand Comédie Française (☎ 01 44 58 15 15), where French classics are performed, to the tiny local theatre where contemporary plays either hit the limelight or flop into oblivion.

Entertainment in the Ile de France

Tourist Offices

For information about the Ile de France, contact the following:

Espace du Tourisme d'Ile-de-France
✉ Carrousel du Louvre, 99 rue de Rivoli, 75001 Paris ☎ 08 03 81 80 00 within France and 01 44 50 19 9 from abroad

Espace du Tourisme d'Ile-de-France et de Seine et Marne
✉ Festival Disney, 77705 Marne-la-Vallée cedex 4 ☎ As for Espace du Tourisme above and www.paris-ile-de-france.com

Comité Départemental du Tourisme des Yvelines
✉ 2 place André Mignot, 78012 Versailles cedex ☎ 01 39 07 71 22, www.cg78.fr

Office National des Forêts, Direction Régionale Ile-de-France
✉ Boulevard de Constance, 77300 Fontainebleau ☎ 01 60 74 92 40

La Haute Vallée de Chevreuse

The Parc Naturel Regional de la Haute Vallée de Chevreuse was created in 1984 on an area of 25,000 ha, including 12,000 ha of woodland. It is criss-crossed by footpaths offering many opportunities for walks of 1½ to 3 hours. Information and itineraries are available from the Maison du Parc in Chevreuse.

Outdoor Activities

Boat trips
Croisières sur l'Oise
River cruise through the beautiful countryside lying between L'Isle-Adam and Auvers-sur-Oise.
☎ 01 30 29 51 00 ⏰ Sun and holidays in summer

Golf
Disneyland Paris (27 holes)
Conveniently located near to the theme park and the Disneyland hotels.
✉ Allée de la Mare Houleuse, 77400 Magny le Hongre ☎ 01 60 45 68 90 🚇 RER to Marne-la-Vallée/Chessy

Fontainebleau (18 holes)
✉ Route d'Orléans, 77300 Fontainebleau ☎ 01 64 22 22 95 🚇 Gare de Lyon to Fontainebleau-Avon

Saint-Germain-en-Laye (27 holes)
Built in the Forêt de Saint-Germain by the Englishman Harry Colt.
✉ Route de Poissy, 78100 Saint-Germain-en-Laye ☎ 01 39 10 30 30 🚇 RER to Saint-Germain-en-Laye

Versailles: Golf de la Boulie (two 18-hole courses and one 9-hole course)
✉ Route du Pont Colbert, 78000 Versailles ☎ 01 39 50 59 41 🚇 Gare Saint-Lazare to Versailles Rive Droite

Hiking
Comité Régional de Randonnée Pédestre en Ile-de-France
Information on hiking in the seven *départements* of the Ile de France.
✉ 64 rue de Gergovie, 75014

Paris ☎ 01 43 95 61 62 🚇 Plaisance, Pernéty

Horse-Racing
Hippodrome de Chantilly
Prix du Jockey-Club and Prix de Diane-Hermès in June.
✉ 16 avenue du Général Leclerc, 60500 Chantilly ☎ 03 44 62 41 00 🚇 Gare du Nord to Chantilly-Gouvieux

Horse-Riding
Centre Equestre des Basses Masures
✉ Poigny-la-Forêt, 78120 Rambouillet (► 90) ☎ 01 34 84 70 29

Haras du Croc Marin
✉ Chemin rural des Trembleaux, 77690 Montigny-sur-Loing (► 83) ☎ 01 64 45 84 01

Leisure Parks
Saint-Quentin-en-Yvelines
Nature trails, a wide range of sporting activities, children's playground, cycle hire etc.
✉ D912, 78190 Trappes (7km west of Versailles) ☎ 01 30 62 20 12 🚇 RER C to Saint-Quentin-en-Yvelines (10-minute walk)

Torcy
Cycling, pony-trekking, windsurfing, canoeing etc.
✉ Route de Lagny, 77200 Torcy (9km west of Disneyland Paris) ☎ 01 64 80 50 75 🚇 RER to Torcy then 🚌 421

Mountain Bike Trails
Several itineraries through the Forêt de Fontainebleau.
Office du Tourisme ✉ 4 rue Royale, 77300 Fontainebleau ☎ 01 60 74 99 99 🚇 Gare de Lyon to Fontainebleau-Avon

Nature Park
Parc Naturel Régional de la Haute Vallée de Chevreuse
Themed nature trails: obtain

information from the Maison du Parc in Chevreuse.

✉ **La Maison du Parc, Château de la Madeleine, 78460 Chevreuse (➤ 90)** ☎ **01 30 52 09 09**

Concerts

Festival de Rambouillet
Concerts of classical music in June and July.

✉ **Palais du Roi de Rome, rue du Général-de-Gaulle, place de la Libération, 78120 Rambouillet** ☎ **01 34 57 34 57**

Saison Musicale de Royaumont
Concerts in the lovely 12th-century abbey from June to September.

✉ **Abbaye de Royaumont, 60500 Chantilly (➤ 80)** ☎ **01 30 35 59 00**

Soirées Musicales au Château de Versailles
Concerts of Baroque music on Thursdays and Saturdays, from November to June in the Opera house and the Royal Chapel. Information from the Centre de Musique Baroque de Versailles.

✉ **22 avenue de Paris, 78000 Versailles** ☎ **01 39 20 78 00**

Shows

Disneyland Paris
Buffalo Bill's Wild West Show
A fast moving dinner-show in the company of Buffalo Bill busy conquering the American wild West.

☎ **Bookings: 01 60 45 71 00**

Disney Village
Just outside the theme park, restaurants, clubs, bars and shops open late into the evening. There is a cinema

and even an aquatic circus!

✉ **Disneyland Paris, 77777 Marne-la-Vallée** ☎ **01 60 30 60 30**

Meaux (11km north of Disneyland Paris)
Spectacle Historique de Meaux
'Son et Lumière' show on a historical theme, lasting 1½ hours June–September. Information and bookings from Office de Tourisme de la Ville de Meaux.

✉ **2 rue St-Rémy, 77100 Meaux** ☎ **01 64 33 02 26**

Vaux-le-Vicomte
Visites aux Chandelles
Tours of the Château de Vaux-le-Vicomte by candlelight take place every Thursday and Saturday nights from May to mid-October.

✉ **Château de Vaux-le-Vicomte, 77950 Maincy** ☎ **01 64 14 41 90** 🚊 **Gare de Lyon to Melun then taxi**

Versailles
Grandes Eaux Musicales
There is a popular display of fountains with music held in the beautiful park of the Château de Versailles, every Sunday afternoon from May to October.

Grande Fête de Nuit
'Son et Lumière' show illustrating Louis XIV's life in the Château de Versailles and ending in a magnificent fireworks display; takes place seven times during the summer. Information is available from the Office de Tourisme.

✉ **Grande Écurie du Roy, 78000 Versailles** ☎ **01 30 83 78 88** 🚊 **Gare Saint-Lazare to Versailles Rive Droite**

Fountains in the Parc de Versailles
Louis XIV wanted all the fountains in the park to work simultaneously. In order to achieve this, Le Nôtre worked for ten years with several engineers, dug 60km of channels and laid 11km of underground piping linking 15 small lakes and eight artificial ones!

What's On When

Check First!

The venues of the events listed here are liable to change from one year to the next and in the case of major festivals, there is often more than one venue. Dates also vary slightly from year to year. Information and programmes are available from:

Office de Tourisme de Paris
✉ 127 avenue des Champs-Elysées, 75008 Paris ☎ 08 36 68 31 12, www.paris-touristoffice.com Ⓜ Charles de Gaulle-Etoile

Espace Régional du Tourisme Ile-de-France
✉ 99 rue de Rivoli, 75001 Paris ☎ 08 03 81 80 00, www.paris-ile-de-france.com Ⓜ Palais-Royal

Paris

June

Festival Foire Saint-Germain: Festival aimed at reviving traditions in the 'village of Saint-Germain-des-Prés'.
Fête de la Musique: On 21 June, Paris's squares, gardens, station halls and streets become alive with hundreds of musicians.

June–July

Festival d'orgue à Saint-Eustache: Classical music in this beautiful church.
La Villette Jazz Festival: Jazz in the Grande Halle and the Parc de la Villette.
14 July: Military parade down the Champs-Elysées, fireworks and popular ball to celebrate National Day.

July–August

Fête des Tuileries: Jardin des Tuileries becomes a fairground (begins end of June).
Paris, Quartier d'Eté: Open-air music, plays and dance.

July–September

Festival 'Musique en l'Ile': Classical music in the church of Saint-Louis-en-l'Ile and nearby Left Bank churches.
Biennale Internationale des Antiquaires: International antiques display, every other year (even years); last two weeks of September.

October

Foire Internationale d'Art Contemporain: Exhibition of contemporary art.
Mondial de l'Automobile: International motor-car show every two years (even years).

November–December

Salon nautique international: International boat show.

Ile-de-France

March

Salon des Antiquaires de Versailles: Antique fair.

May

Festival des Yvelines 'Musique et Architecture': Prestigious concerts at monuments within the *département*. Free.

May–July

Festival d'Auvers-sur-Oise: Singing, piano and chamber music with famous artists.

June–July

Festival de Saint-Denis: Symphonic concerts take place in Saint-Denis Basilica.

July–August

Fête des Loges de Saint-Germain-en-Laye: A fair held in Saint-Germain forest.

July–September

Festival de l'Orangerie de Sceaux: Chamber music festival in parc de Sceaux.

August

Fête de la Saint-Louis à Fontainebleau: An ancient royal tradition celebrated by fireworks at the Château.

September

Semaine de l'Elevage à Fontainebleau: A gathering of French horse-breeders.
Barbizon au temps des peintres...: Recalls 1848–70, when Forêt de Fontainebleau drew artists to Barbizon.

October

Festival de l'Abbaye des Vaux de Cernay: Classical music at historic sites in Vallée de Chevreuse.

Practical Matters

Before You Go   118
When You Are There   119–23
Language   124

Above: *Les Halles – old and new*
Right: *Egyptian obelisk, place de la Concorde*

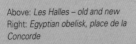

117

TIME DIFFERENCES

GMT 12 noon	France 1PM	Germany 1PM	USA (NY) 7AM	Netherlands 1PM	Spain 1PM

BEFORE YOU GO

WHAT YOU NEED

	UK	Germany	USA	Netherlands	Spain
Passport/National Identity Card	●	●	●	●	●
Visa	▲	▲	▲	▲	▲
Onward or Return Ticket	▲	▲	▲	▲	▲
Health Inoculations	▲	▲	▲	▲	▲
Health Documentation (➤ 123, Health)	●	●	●	●	●
Travel Insurance	○	○	○	○	○
Driving Licence (national)	●	●	●	●	●
Car Insurance Certificate (if own car)	●	●	●	●	●
Car Registration Document (if own car)	●	●	●	●	●

● Required
○ Suggested
▲ Not required

Some countries require a passport to remain valid for a minimum period (usually at least six months) beyond the date of entry – contact their consulate or embassy or your travel agent for details.

WHEN TO GO

Paris

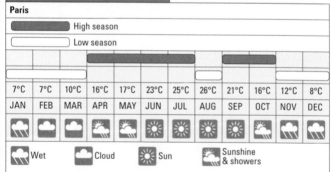

7°C	7°C	10°C	16°C	17°C	23°C	25°C	26°C	21°C	16°C	12°C	8°C
JAN	FEB	MAR	APR	MAY	JUN	JUL	AUG	SEP	OCT	NOV	DEC

High season
Low season

Wet Cloud Sun Sunshine & showers

TOURIST OFFICES

In the UK
French Tourist Office,
178 Piccadilly,
London W1V 0AL
☎ (0891) 244123
Fax: (020) 7493 6594

In the USA
French Government
Tourist Office,
444 Madison Avenue,
16th floor,
New York NY10022
☎ 212/838 7800
Fax: 212/838 7855

French Government
Tourist Office,
9454 Wilshire Boulevard,
Beverly Hills CA90212
☎ 310/271 6665
Fax: 310/276 2835

POLICE 17

FIRE 18

AMBULANCE 15

DOCTOR (24-hour call out) 01 47 07 77 77

WHEN YOU ARE THERE

ARRIVING

Paris has two main airports, Roissy-Charles-de-Gaulle (01 48 62 22 80), where most international flights arrive, and Orly (01 49 75 15 15). Eurostar trains, direct from London to Paris (☎ 0990 186 186 in Britain, ☎ 08 36 35 35 39 in France), take 3 hours.

Roissy/Charles-de-Gaulle Airport
Kilometres to city centre   **Journey times**

23 kilometres

🚌	45 minutes
🚆	50 minutes
🚗	30–60 minutes

Orly Airport
Kilometres to city centre   **Journey times**

14 kilometres

🚌	40 minutes
🚆	30 minutes
🚗	20–40 minutes

MONEY

The euro is the official currency of France. Euro banknotes and coins were introduced in January 2002. Banknotes are in denominations of 5, 10, 20, 50, 100, 200 and 500 euros and coins are in denominations of 1, 2, 5, 10, 20 and 50 cents, and 1 and 2 euros. Euro traveller's cheques are widely accepted, as are major credit cards. Credit and debit cards can also be used for withdrawing euro notes from cashpoint machines. Cashpoints are widely accessible throughout the city. France's former currency, the French franc, went out of circulation in early 2002.

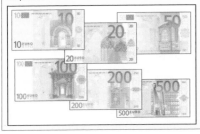

TIME

 France is on Central European Time (GMT+1). From late March, when clocks are put forward one hour, until late October, French summer time (GMT +2) operates.

CUSTOMS

 YES

From another EU country for personal use (guidelines):
800 cigarettes, 200 cigars, 1kg tobacco, 10 litres of spirits (over 22%), 20 litres of aperitifs, 90 litres of wine, of which 60 litres can be sparkling wine, 110 litres of beer.

From a non-EU country for personal use, the allowances are:
200 cigarettes OR 50 cigars OR 250kg tobacco, 1 litre spirits (over 22%), 2 litres jof intermediary products (eg sherry) and sparkling wine, 2 litres of still, wine, 50g perfume, 0.25 litres of eau de toilette. The value limit for goods is 175 euros.

Travellers under 17 years of age are not entitled to the tobacco and alcohol allowances.

 NO

Drugs, firearms, ammunition, offensive weapons, obscene material, unlicensed animals.

119

EMBASSIES

UK
☎ 01 44 51 31 00

Germany
☎ 01 53 83 45 00

USA
☎ 01 43 12 22 22

Netherlands
☎ 01 40 62 33 00

Spain
☎ 01 44 43 18 00

WHEN YOU ARE THERE

TOURIST OFFICES

Head Office
● Office de Tourisme de Paris
(Paris Tourism Bureau),
127 avenue des Champs-
Elysées, 75008 Paris
☎ 08 36 68 31 12
Fax: 01 49 52 53 00
www.paris-
touristoffice.com
🕐 Daily 9AM–8PM (Sun/pub
hols, Nov–Mar, 11AM–7PM)

Branches
● Gare de Lyon
🕐 Mon–Sat 8AM–8PM

● Tour Eiffel (Eiffel Tower)
🕐 May–Sep: daily
11AM–6:40PM

NATIONAL HOLIDAYS

J	F	M	A	M	J	J	A	S	O	N	D
1		(1)	(1)	3(4)	(1)	1	1			2	1

1 Jan	New Year's Day
Mar/Apr	Easter Sunday and Monday
1 May	Labour Day
8 May	VE Day
May	Ascension Day
May/Jun	Whit Sunday and Monday
14 July	Bastille Day
15 Aug	Assumption Day
1 Nov	All Saints' Day
11 Nov	Remembrance Day
25 Dec	Christmas Day

Banks, businesses, museums and most shops (except
boulangeries) are closed on these days.

OPENING HOURS

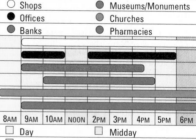

In addition to the times shown above, some shops
close between noon and 2PM and all day Sunday and
Monday. Large department stores open from 9:30AM
to 6:30PM and until 9 or 10PM one or two days a week.
Food shops open 7AM to 1:30PM and 4:30 to 8PM; some
open Sunday until noon. Some banks are open
extended hours, including Saturday morning but most
banks close weekends. Museum and monument
opening times vary but national museums close
Tuesday (except the Musée d'Orsay, Versailles and
the Trianon Palace which close Monday), while most
other city museums usually close Monday.

DRIVE ON THE RIGHT

TOILETS CHARGE

PUBLIC TRANSPORT

Internal Flights Air Inter Europe is the leading domestic airline – information via Air France (☎ 08 20 82 08 20). Daily departures from Orly and Roissy/Charles-de-Gaulle airports connect Paris with major French cities/towns in an average flight time of one hour.

RER The RER (pronounced 'ehr-oo-ehr') is the fast suburban rail service, which also serves the city centre. There are four lines (*lignes*): A, B, C and D, and it is connected with the métro and SNCF suburban network. Services run 5:30AM to midnight, with trains every 12 minutes.

Métro Paris's underground with over 300 stations ensures you are never more than 500m from a métro stop. Lines are numbered 1 to 14 and are known by the names of the stations at each end. Follow the orange *correspondance* signs to change lines. The métro runs daily 5:30AM to 12:45AM.

Buses Buses are a good way of seeing Paris (especially route 24), although traffic can be very heavy. Bus stops show the numbers of buses that stop there. Buses run 6:30AM to 8:30PM with a reduced service on Sunday and after 8:30PM. Bus tickets are the same as those for the métro.

Boat The Batobus river shuttle (☎ 01 44 11 33 99) that plies the Seine from April to September provides an unusual view of Paris. It stops at the Eiffel Tower, Musée d'Orsay, the Louvre, Notre-Dame and the Hôtel de Ville; every 35 minutes, 10AM to 7PM (flat fare or all-day unlimited travel ticket).

CAR RENTAL

Car-rental companies have desks at Roissy/ Charles-de-Gaulle and Orly airports, and in Paris itself. Car hire is expensive but airlines and tour operators offer fly-drive, and French Railways (SNCF) – train/car, packages that are cheaper than hiring locally.

TAXIS

Taxis can be hailed if you see one with its roof light on. Taxis are metered with a surcharge for luggage, journeys after 10PM and before 6:30AM, and for going from and to stations and airports. Queues can be vast, particularly at railway stations.

DRIVING

Speed limits on toll motorways (*autoroutes*) **130kph** (**110kph** when wet). Non-toll motorways and dual carriageways: **110kph** (**100kph** when wet). Paris ring road (*périphérique*): **80kph**.

Speed limits on country roads: **90kph** (**80kph** when wet)

Speed limits on urban roads: **50kph**

Must be worn in front seats at all times and in rear seats where fitted.

Random breath-testing frequent. Limit: 0.05 per cent alcohol in blood.

Leaded petrol is sold as *essence super* (98 octane). Unleaded is available in two grades: *essence sans plomb* (95 octane) and *essence super sans plomb* (98 octane). Diesel (*Gasoil* or *Gazole*) is also readily available. In Paris filling stations can be hard to spot, often consisting of little more than a few kerb-side pumps.

If your car breaks down in Paris, contact the 24-hour repair service (☎ 01 43 31 14 14). On motorways (*autoroutes*) use the orange-coloured emergency phones (located every 2km) to contact the breakdown service.

PERSONAL SAFETY

Petty crime, particularly theft of wallets and handbags is fairly common in Paris. Be aware of innocent, scruffy-looking children, they may be working the streets in gangs, fleecing unwary tourists. Report any loss or theft to the *Police Municipale* (blue uniforms). To be safe:

- Watch your bag on the métro, in busy tourist areas like Beaubourg and the Champs-Elysées and in museum queues.
- Cars should be well-secured.
- Keep valuables in your hotel safe.

Police assistance:
☎ **17** from any call box

TELEPHONES

Gare Montparnasse

All telephone numbers in France comprise ten digits. Paris and Ile de France numbers all begin with 01. There are no area codes, simply dial the number. Most public phones use a phone-card (*télécarte*) sold in units of 50 or 120 from France Telecom shops, post offices, tobacconists and railway stations. Cafés have phones that take coins.

International Dialling Codes

From France to:

UK:	**00 44**
Germany:	**00 49**
USA:	**00 1**
Netherlands:	**00 31**
Spain:	**00 34**

POST

LA POSTE

Post offices
Post offices are identified by a yellow or brown 'La Poste' or 'PTT' sign. Paris's main post office at 52 rue du Louvre is open 24 hours.
☎ 01 40 28 20 00
The branch at 71 avenue des Champs-Elysées opens 8AM–10PM (Sun 10AM–8PM).
Other branches:
🕐 8–7 (12 Sat); closed Sun

ELECTRICITY

The power supply in Paris is: 220 volts

Sockets accept two-round-pin (or increasingly three-round-pin) plugs, so an adaptor is needed for most non-Continental appliances and a voltage transformer for appliances operating on 100–120 volts.

TIPS/GRATUITIES

Yes ✓ No ✗		
Hotels (service included)	✓	(change)
Restaurants (service included)	✓	(change)
Cafés (service included)	✓	(change)
Taxis	✓	(1euro)
Tour guides	✓	(1 euro)
Porters	✓	(1 euro)
Usherettes	✓	(30c)
Hairdressers	✓	(1 euro)
Cloakroom attendants	✓	(15–30c)
Toilets	✓	(change)

PHOTOGRAPHY

What to photograph: Paris's monumental buildings and animated Parisians drinking in pavement cafés.

Where you need permission to photograph: certain museums will allow you to photograph inside. In churches with mural paintings and icons where flashlight is required permission must be sought first.

Where to buy film: shops and photo laboratories sell the most popular brands and types of film. Rapid film development is possible but quite expensive.

HEALTH

Insurance

Nationals of EU countries can obtain medical treatment at reduced cost in France with the relevant documentation (Form E111 for Britons), although private medical insurance is still advised and is essential for all other visitors.

Dental Services

As for general medical treatment (see above, **Insurance**), nationals of EU countries can obtain dental treatment at reduced cost. Around 70 per cent of standard dentists' fees are refunded. Still, private medical insurance is advised for all.

Sun Advice

July and August (when most Parisians leave the city) are the sunniest (and hottest) months. If 'doing the sights' cover up or apply a sunscreen and take on plenty of fluids. To escape the sun altogether spend the day visiting a museum.

Drugs

Pharmacies – recognised by their green cross sign – possess highly qualified staff able to offer medical advice, provide first-aid and prescribe a wide range of drugs, though some are available by prescription (*ordonnance*) only.

Safe Water

It is quite safe to drink tap water in Paris and all over France, but never drink from a tap marked *eau non potable* (not drinking water). Many prefer the taste of mineral water, which is fairly cheap and widely available in several brands.

CONCESSIONS

Students/Youths Holders of an International Student Identity Card (ISIC) are entitled to half-price admission to museums and sights and discounted air and ferry tickets, plus cheap meals in some student cafeterias. Those under 26, but not a student, with the International Youth Travel Card (or GO 25 Card) qualify for similar discounts as ISIC holders.

Senior Citizens Visitors over 60 can get discounts (up to 50 per cent) in museums, on public transport and in places of entertainment. Discounts apply to holders of the *Carte Vermeil*, which can be purchased from the *Abonnement* office of any main railway station. Without the card, show your passport and you may still get the discount.

CLOTHING SIZES

France	UK	Rest of Europe	USA	
46	36	46	36	
48	38	48	38	
50	40	50	40	Suits
52	42	52	42	
54	44	54	44	
56	46	56	46	
41	7	41	8	
42	7.5	42	8.5	
43	8.5	43	9.5	
44	9.5	44	10.5	Shoes
45	10.5	45	11.5	
46	11	46	12	
37	14.5	37	14.5	
38	15	38	15	
39/40	15.5	39/40	15.5	Shirts
41	16	41	16	
42	16.5	42	16.5	
43	17	43	17	
36	8	34	6	
38	10	36	8	
40	12	38	10	Dresses
42	14	40	12	
44	16	42	14	
46	18	44	16	
38	4.5	38	6	
38	5	38	6.5	
39	5.5	39	7	Shoes
39	6	39	7.5	
40	6.5	40	8	
41	7	41	8.5	

WHEN DEPARTING

- Contact the airport or airline on the day prior to leaving to ensure flight details are unchanged.
- It is advisable to arrive at the airport two hours before the flight is due to take off.
- Check the duty-free limits of the country you are entering before departure.

LANGUAGE

You will usually hear well-enunciated French in Paris, spoken quite quickly and in a myriad of accents as many Parisians come from the provinces. English is spoken by those involved in the tourist trade and by many in the centre of Paris – less so in the outskirts. However, attempts to speak French will always be appreciated. Below is a list of a few words that may be helpful. The gender of words is indicated by (m) or (f) for masculine and feminine. More extensive coverage can be found in the AA's *Essential French Phrase Book* which lists over 2,000 phrases and 2,000 words.

hotel	*hôtel (m)*	rate	*tarif (m)*
room	*chambre (f)*	breakfast	*petit déjeuner (m)*
..single/double	*une personne /deux personnes (f)*	toilet	*toilette (f)*
		bathroom	*salle de bain (f)*
...one/two nights	*une/deux nuits (f)*	shower	*douche (f)*
...per person/per room	*par personne/par chambre*	balcony	*balcon (m)*
		key	*clef/clé (f)*
reservation	*réservation (f)*	room service	*service de chambre*

bank	*banque (f)*	English pound	*livre sterling (f)*
exchange office	*bureau de change (m)*	American dollar	*dollar (m)*
post office	*poste (f)*	banknote	*billet (m)*
cashier	*caissier (m)*	coin	*pièce (f)*
foreign exchange	*change (m)*	credit card	*carte de crédit (f)*
		traveller's cheque	*chèque de voyage (m)*
currency	*monnaie (f)*	giro cheque	*chèque postal (m)*

restaurant	*restaurant (m)*	starter	*hors d'oeuvres (m)*
café	*café (m)*	main course	*plat principal (m)*
table	*table (f)*	dish of the day	*plat du jour (m)*
menu	*carte (f)*	dessert	*dessert (m)*
set menu	*menu (m)*	drink	*boisson (f)*
wine list	*carte des vins (f)*	waiter	*garçon (m)*
lunch	*déjeuner (m)*	waitress	*serveuse (f)*
dinner	*dîner (m)*	the bill	*addition (f)*

aeroplane	*avion (m)*	...first/second class	*première/deuxième classe (f)*
airport	*aéroport (m)*		
train	*train (m)*	ticket office	*guichet (m)*
...station	*gare (f)*	timetable	*horaire des départs et des arrivées (m)*
bus	*l'autobus (m)*		
...station	*gare routière (f)*		
ferry	*bateau (m)*	seat	*place (f)*
...port	*port (m)*	non-smoking	*non-fumeurs*
ticket	*billet (m)*	reserved	*réservée*
...single/return	*simple/retour (m)*	taxi!	*taxi! (m)*

yes	*oui*	help!	*au secours!*
no	*non*	today	*aujourd'hui*
please	*s'il vous-plaît*	tomorrow	*demain*
thank you	*merci*	yesterday	*hier*
hello	*bonjour*	how much?	*combien?*
goodbye	*au revoir*	expensive	*cher*
goodnight	*bonsoir*	closed	*fermé*
sorry	*pardon*	open	*ouvert*

INDEX

Académie Française 53
accommodation 100–3
Alexandre III, pont 32
amusement parks 110–11
André-Citroën, parc 13
Antiquités Nationales, Musée des 86
Aquaboulevard 110
Arc de Triomphe 32
Arènes de Lutèce 12
Armée, Musée de l' 19
arrondissements 7, 31
art and antiques shops 106–7, 108
Art Moderne, Musée National d' 16
Art Moderne de la Ville de Paris, Musée d' 33
Arts Asiatiques-Guimet, Musée National des 33
Arts Décoratifs, Musée des 33
Arts et Métiers-Techniques, Musée National des 33
Assemblée Nationale Palais-Bourbon 34
Au Lapin Agile 61
Auberge de la Bonne Franquette 61
Auberge Ganne 83
Auvers-sur-Oise, Château d' 80

Baccarat, Musée 34
Balzac, Maison de 34
banks 120
banlieue 7
Barbizon 83
Bastille 35
Bateau-Lavoir 58–9, 61
beach 110
Bibliothèque Mazarine 53
Bibliothèque Nationale de France 38
Billettes, Eglise des 57
bistros 6, 92
boat trips 9, 111, 114
Bois de Boulogne 13
Bois de Vincennes 13
buses 121
Buttes-Chaumont, parc des 13, 110

cabaret and music-hall 112
Cabinet des Médailles et des Antiques 38
Café les Deux Magots 9, 71
cafés 6, 51, 92
car rental 121
Carnavalet, Musée 39
Centre Georges Pompidou 16
Cernuschi, Musée 39
Chaillot, Palais de 40
Chantilly, Château de 81
Charles-de-Gaulle, place 50
Chasse et de la Nature, Musée de la 56

Châtelet, place du 43
Chevreuse 90
children's attractions 110–11
Chinatown 31
Chirac, Jacques 14
Cinéma-Henri Langlois, Musée du 40
cinemas and theatres 113
circus shows 111
Cité, Ile de la 41, 43
Cité de la Musique 26, 112
Cité des Sciences et de l'Industrie 26, 110
climate 118, 123
clothing sizes 123
Cluny, Musée de 7, 62
Cognacq-Jay, Musée 44
Colline de l'Automobile 18
Comédie-Française 65
concert venues 112, 113, 115
concessions 123
La Conciergerie 44
Concorde, place de la 9, 45
Condé, Musée 81
Courances, Château de 83
Curiosité et de la Magie, Musée de la 110
customs regulations 119
cycle tours 51

Dampierre, Château de 90
Découverte, Palais de la 48
departure information 124
Disneyland Paris 81, 115
Dôme, Eglise du 19
drinking water 123
drives
    Fontainebleau 83
    in the painters' footsteps 80
    Vallée de Chevreuse 90
driving 118, 121
duty-free shopping 104

eating out 37, 50, 92–9, 110
Ecouen, Château d' 82
electricity 122
Elysée, Palais de l' 47
embassies 120
emergency telephone numbers 119, 122
entertainment 112–16
Equipages, Musée des 87
Eugène Delacroix, Musée National 45

famous Parisians 14
fashion shopping 105–6
Faubourg St-Germain 31, 46
Faubourg St-Honoré 47
festivals and events 116
Floral de Paris, parc 51
Fontaine de Médicis 12
Fontaine des Quatre Saisons 46
Fontainebleau 83, 111
Fontainebleau, Château de 82
food and drink 36–7
Fragonard, Musée 47
France, Ile de 78–90

France Miniature 84
funicular 9, 61

Gobelins, Manufacture Nationale des 48
Grand Palais 48
La Grande Arche de la Défense 18
grands boulevards 49
Granges de Port-Royal, Musée National des 90
Grévin, Musée 110

Les Halles 52
Haussmann, Baron 14
health 118, 123
helicopter rides 51
Histoire de France, Musee de l' 56
Histoire Naturelle, Musée National d' 68, 110
history 10–11
Homme, Musée de l' 40
hot-air ballooning 51
Hôtel de Ville 53

Ile de France 78–90
Institut de France 53
Institut du Monde Arabe 54
insurance 118, 123
Les Invalides 19
L'Isle-Adam 80, 111

Jacquemart-André, Musée 54
jazz clubs 112–13
Jeu de Paume, Galerie Nationale du 54
Jewish quarter 56, 57

language 124
Le Nôtre, André 14, 83, 85, 87
Left Bank 24, 69
Le Louvre 20–1
Luxembourg, Jardin du 9, 12, 69

Madeleine, Eglise de la 55
Maillol, Musee 55
Malmaison, Château de 84
maps
    arrondissements 31
    metro 76–7
    Paris 28–9
Le Marais 50, 56, 57
La Mare au Diable 99
Marine, Musée de la 40, 110
markets 43, 108, 109
Marmottan-Monet, Musée 58
Meaux 115
Milly-la-Forêt 83
Mode et du Costume, Musée de la 58
Molière 14, 66
Monceau, parc 13
money 119
Montmartre 31, 58–9, 61
Montmartre, Musée de 59
Montmartre vineyard 59, 61

Montparnasse 31, 62
Moulin de la Galette 59
Moulin-Rouge 9, 58, 112
Moyen-Age, Musée National du 62
museums 120
Musique, Musée de la 63

Napoléon I, Musée 82
national holidays 120
Neuf, pont 7, 43
nightclubs and bars 112, 113
Nissim de Camondo, Musée 63
Notre-Dame 22

Obelisk 45
opening hours 120
Opéra Garnier 64
Opéra National de Paris-Bastille 35
Orangerie, Musee National de l' 64
Orsay, Musée d' 23, 110

Palais-Royal 65
Palais-Royal, Jardin du 13
Panthéon 66
Panthéon Bouddhique 33
Parc Astérix 85
Parc Naturel Régional de la Haute Vallée de Chevreuse 90, 114
Le Parvis 18
passports and visas 118
Pavillon Cassan 80
Pavillon de l'Arsenal 66
Pavillon Henri IV 103
Père-Lachaise, Cimetière du 66
personal safety 122
Petit Palais, Musée du 67
pharmacies 120, 123
photography 123
Picasso, Musée 67
Pissarro, Musée 80
Plans-Reliefs, Musée des 19

Plantes, Jardin des 68
police 122
Pontoise 80
population 7
Port-Royal-des-Champs, Abbaye de 90
postal services 122
public transport 121
puppet shows 111

les quais 9, 24
Quartier Latin 31, 43, 68, 69

Rambouillet, Château de 90
Renaissance, Musée National de la 82
Right Bank 24
Rodin, Musée 70
Royaumont, Abbaye de 80

Sacré-Coeur, Basilique du 9, 70
Sainte-Chapelle 73
Saint-Cloud, parc de 85
Saint-Denis, Basilique 86
St-Etienne-du-Mont 68, 69
St-Eustache, Eglise 52
Saint-Germain-en-Laye 86
St-Germain-des-Prés (church) 7, 71
St-Germain-des-Prés (district) 31, 69
St-Gervais-St-Protais, Eglise 53
Saint-Louis, Ile 43, 72
St-Louis-des-Invalides 19
St-Séverin 43
St-Sulpice, place 72
Sceaux, Château de 87
senior citizens 123
Serrure, Musée de la 57
Sèvres, Musée National de la Céramique de 87
shopping 104–9, 120
Sorbonne 68

sport and leisure 51, 113–15
students 123

taxis 121
telephones 122
theme parks 81, 85
time 118, 119
tipping 122
La Tour Eiffel 9, 25
toilets 121
Tour Montparnasse 62
Tour St-Jacques 53
tourist offices 114, 118, 120
Tournelle, pont de la 9
trains 121
Tuileries, Jardin des 74

Vallée de Chevreuse 90
Van Gogh, Maison de 80
Vaux-le-Vicomte, Château de 87, 115
Vendôme, place 74
Versailles, Château de 88–9, 111, 115
Vert Galant, square du 12
Viaduc des Arts 35
Victoires, place des 65
Victor Hugo, Maison de 75
views of Paris 51
La Villette 26
Vin, Musée du 36, 37
Vincennes, Château de 89
Vivant du Cheval, Musee 81, 111
Viviani, square 12
Vosges, place des 57, 75

walks
along the Seine and on the islands 43
Le Marais 57
Montmartre 61
Quartier Latin and St-Germain-des-Prés 69

zoos 68, 110–11

Acknowledgements

The Automobile Association wishes to thank the following photographers, libraries and associations for their assistance in the preparation of this book: DACS *Femmes a Leur Toilette*, Pablo Picasso, © Succession Picasso/DACS 1997 67; **HULTON GETTY** 10b; **MARY EVANS** 10a, 14a, 14b, 35b; **PARC ASTERIX** 85; **SPECTRUM COLOUR LIBRARY** 122b; www.euro.ecb.int/ 119 (euro notes).

The remaining photographs are held in the Association's own library (**AA PHOTO LIBRARY**) with contributions from: P ENTICNAP f/cover e (Eiffel Tower), b/cover, 20, 60, 61; P KENWOOD f/cover c (sign), 27, 34, 35a, 45a, 45b, 53b, 54, 55; E MEACHER 31c; R MOSS 83, 122c; D NOBLE 78, 79, 80, 81, 82, 86, 87, 88/9, 89a, 90; K PATERSON 5a, 6a, 9a, 9b, 12, 13a, 16, 18, 19, 24, 25, 28, 39, 40, 49, 50b, 51b, 52, 53a, 57, 62, 64, 65a, 66, 71, 75a, 89b, 91b, 122a; B RIEGER f/cover a (Notre-Dame) 5b, 7, 8b, 13b, 37a, 37d, 43, 47, 48, 63, 84a, 84b; C SAWYER f/cover d (waitress); A SOUTER f/cover h (Metro sign), 6 ,6b, 15a, 15b, 17a, 22, 26, 31, 32, 33a, 33b, 36, 37b, 41, 42, 44, 46, 50a, 51a, 56, 58, 59, 65b, 67, 68, 69, 70b, 72, 74, 76/7, 91a; JA TIMS f/cover b (sculpture), f (gold statue), g (Arc de Triumphe), i (Louvre), bottom (Eiffel Tower), 21, 75b; W VOYSEY 17b, 70a, 117b

Author's Acknowledgements

The author would like to thank Mairie de Paris, Office de Tourisme de Paris, and Comité Régional du Tourisme d'Ile de France.

Contributors
Updated by Elizabeth Morris   Managing editor: Hilary Weston
Page Layout: Design 23   Indexer: Marie Lorimer

Dear Essential Traveller

Your comments, opinions and recommendations are very important to us. So please help us to improve our travel guides by taking a few minutes to complete this simple questionnaire.

You do not need a stamp (unless posted outside the UK). If you do not want to cut this page from your guide, then photocopy it or write your answers on a plain sheet of paper.

Send to: **The Editor, AA World Travel Guides, FREEPOST SCE 4598, Basingstoke RG21 4GY.**

Your recommendations...

We always encourage readers' recommendations for restaurants, nightlife or shopping – if your recommendation is used in the next edition of the guide, we will send you a *FREE* AA *Essential* Guide of your choice. Please state below the establishment name, location and your reasons for recommending it.

_____

_____ —

_____

_____

Please send me **AA *Essential*** _____
(*see list of titles inside the front cover*)

About this guide...

Which title did you buy?
AA *Essential* _____
Where did you buy it? _____
When? m̲ m̲ / y̲ y̲

Why did you choose an AA *Essential* Guide? _____

_____

_____

_____

_____

Did this guide meet your expectations?
Exceeded ☐ Met all ☐ Met most ☐ Fell below ☐
Please give your reasons_____

_____

_____

_____

continued on next page...

Were there any aspects of this guide that you particularly liked? _____
_____
_____
_____

Is there anything we could have done better? _____
_____
_____
_____
_____

About you...

Name (*Mr/Mrs/Ms*) _____
   Address _____
_____
_____ Postcode _____
   Daytime tel nos _____

Which age group are you in?
   Under 25 ☐ 25–34 ☐ 35–44 ☐ 45–54 ☐ 55–64 ☐ 65+ ☐

How many trips do you make a year?
   Less than one ☐ One ☐ Two ☐ Three or more ☐

Are you an AA member? Yes ☐ No ☐

About your trip...

When did you book? m m / y y   When did you travel? m m / y y
How long did you stay? _____
Was it for business or leisure? _____
Did you buy any other travel guides for your trip?
   If yes, which ones? _____
_____

Thank you for taking the time to complete this questionnaire. Please send
   it to us as soon as possible, and remember, you do not need a stamp
   (*unless posted outside the UK*).

Happy Holidays!

AA All In One

French
Phrasebook

AA Publishing

Contents

Introduction   5

Pronunciation guide   6

1 Useful lists   7–16

1.1 Today or tomorrow?   8
1.2 Bank holidays   9
1.3 What time is it?   9
1.4 One, two, three ...   10
1.5 The weather   12
1.6 Here, there ...   13
1.7 What does that
     sign say?   15
1.8 Telephone alphabet   15
1.9 Personal details   16

2 Courtesies   17–23

2.1 Greetings   18
2.2 How to ask a question   19
2.3 How to reply   20
2.4 Thank you   21
2.5 Sorry   22
2.6 What do you think?   22

3 Conversation   24–32

3.1 I beg your pardon?   25
3.2 Introductions   26
3.3 Starting/ending a
     conversation   28
3.4 Congratulations and
     condolences   28
3.5 A chat about the
     weather   28
3.6 Hobbies   29
3.7 Being the host(ess)   29
3.8 Invitations   29

3.9 Paying a compliment   30
3.10 Chatting someone up   31
3.11 Arrangements   32
3.12 Saying goodbye   32

4 Eating out   33–42

4.1 On arrival   34
4.2 Ordering   35
4.3 The bill   37
4.4 Complaints   38
4.5 Paying a compliment   39
4.6 The menu   39
4.7 Alphabetical list of
     drinks and dishes   39

5 On the road   43–56

5.1 Asking for directions   44
5.2 Customs   45
5.3 Luggage   46
5.4 Traffic signs   47
5.5 The car   48
     The parts of a car   50–51
5.6 The petrol station   48
5.7 Breakdown and repairs   49
5.8 The bicycle/moped   52
     The parts of a
     bicycle   54–55
5.9 Renting a vehicle   53
5.10 Hitchhiking   56

6 Public
        transport   57–64

6.1 In general   58
6.2 Questions to
     passengers   59
6.3 Tickets   60

6.4	**I**nformation	61
6.5	**A**eroplanes	63
6.6	**T**rains	63
6.7	**T**axis	63

7 **O**vernight accommodation **65–73**

7.1	**G**eneral	66
7.2	**C**amping	67
	Camping	
	equipment	68–69
7.3	**H**otel/B&B/apartment/	
	holiday house	70
7.4	**C**omplaints	72
7.5	**D**eparture	73

8 **M**oney matters **74–76**

8.1	**B**anks	75
8.2	**S**ettling the bill	76

9 **P**ost and telephone **77–81**

9.1	**P**ost	78
9.2	**T**elephone	79

10 **S**hopping **82–90**

10.1	**S**hopping	
	conversations	83
10.2	**F**ood	85
10.3	**C**lothing and shoes	86
10.4	**P**hotographs and video	87
10.5	**A**t the hairdresser's	89

11 **A**t the Tourist Information Centre **91–96**

11.1	**P**laces of interest	92
11.2	**G**oing out	94
11.3	**B**ooking tickets	95

12 **S**ports **97–100**

12.1	**S**porting questions	98
12.2	**B**y the waterfront	98
12.3	**I**n the snow	99

13 **S**ickness **101–107**

13.1	**C**all (fetch) the doctor	102
13.2	**P**atient's ailments	102
13.3	**T**he consultation	103
13.4	**M**edication and	
	prescriptions	105
13.5	**A**t the dentist's	106

14 **I**n trouble **108–113**

14.1	**A**sking for help	109
14.2	**L**oss	110
14.3	**A**ccidents	110
14.4	**T**heft	111
14.5	**M**issing person	111
14.6	**T**he police	112

15 **W**ord list **114–153**

Basic grammar	154

Introduction

● **Welcome to the AA's French Phrasebook,
which contains everything you'd expect from a
comprehensive language guide. It's concise, accessible
and easy to understand, and you'll find it
indispensable on your trip abroad.**

This guide is divided into 15 themed sections and
starts with a pronunciation table which explains the
phonetic pronunciation to all the words and phrases
you'll need to know for your trip, while at the back of
the book is an extensive word list and grammar guide
which will help you construct basic sentences in
French.

Throughout the book you'll come across coloured
boxes with a 🐾 beside them. These are designed to
help you if you can't understand what your listener is
saying to you. Hand the book over to them and
encourage them to point to the appropriate answer to
the question you are asking.

Other coloured boxes in the book - this time without
the symbol - give alphabetical listings of themed words
with their English translations beside them.

For extra clarity, we have put all English words and
phrases in black, foreign language terms in red and
their phonetic pronunciation in italic.

This phrasebook covers all subjects you are likely to
come across during the course of your visit, from
reserving a room for the night to ordering food and
drink at a restaurant and what to do if your car breaks
down or you lose your traveller's cheques and money.
With over 2,000 commonly used words and essential
phrases at your fingertips you can rest assured that
you will be able to get by in all situations, so let the
AA's French Phrasebook become your passport to a
secure and enjoyable trip!

Pronunciation guide

The pronunciation provided should be read as if it were English, bearing in mind the following main points:

Vowels

a, à or â	a in man	ah	table	tahbl
é	like a in make	ay	été	aytay
è, ê, e	like ai in air	eh	rêve	rehv
e	sometimes	uh	le, ne, je, me	luh, nuh,
	like u in fluff			jhuh, muh
i	like ee in seen	ee	si	see
ô	like o in foam	oa	hôtel	oatehl
o	like o in John	o	homme	om
	sometimes like ô	oa	arroser	ahroasay
u	between ee and ew	ew	tu	tew

Combinations of letters which represent vowel sounds:

ez, er	similar to é	ay	louer	looay
ais, ait	the eh sound	eh	fait	feh
au, eau	similar to ô	oa	beau	boa
ail	like i in side	ahy	travail	trahvahy
ei	similar to è	eh	Seine	sehn
eille	eh + y as in yes	ehy	bouteille	bootehy
eu	similar to e above	uh	feu	fuh
iè	ye as in yes	yeh	siècle	syehkl
ié, ier, iez	y + the ay sound	yay	janvier	jhohnvyay
ille	ee + y as in yes	eey	famille	fameey
oi, oy	combines w + a	wah	moi	mwah
ou, oû	oo as in hoot	oo	vous	voo
ui	combines w and ee	wee	cuir	kweer

Consonants

ch	like sh in shine	sh	chaud	shoa
ç	like s in some	s	garçon	gahrsawn
g	before e, i and y			
	like s in leisure	jh	nager	nahjhay
	before a, o and u			
	like g in got	g	gâteau	gahtoa
gn	like ny in canyon	ny	agneau	ahnyoa
h	silent			
j	like s in leisure	jh	jour	jhoor
qu	like k in kind	k	que	kuh
r	rolled at the back of the throat			
w	like v in vine	v	wagonlit	vahgawnlee

Nasal sounds

Nasal sounds are written in French by adding an n to a vowel or a combination of vowels pronounced as the English ng:

an/am, en/em	a little like song	ohn	français, lentement	frohnseh, lohntmohn
in/im, ain, aim, ein	a little like bang	ahn	instant, faim	ahnstohn, fahn
on/om	a nasal form of awn	awn	non	nawn
un/um	a little like rung	uhn	un	uhn
ien	y + the ahn sound	yahn	bien	byahn

Useful lists

1.1 **T**oday or tomorrow? 8

1.2 **B**ank holidays 9

1.3 **W**hat time is it? 9

1.4 **O**ne, two, three... 10

1.5 **T**he weather 12

1.6 **H**ere, there... 13

1.7 **W**hat does that sign say? 15

1.8 **T**elephone alphabet 15

1.9 **P**ersonal details 16

Useful lists

Useful lists

1 .1 **T**oday or tomorrow?

What day is it today? _____ C'est quel jour aujourd'hui?
seh kehl jhoor oajhoordwee?

Today's Monday_____ Aujourd'hui c'est lundi
oajhoordwee seh luhndee

– Tuesday_____ Aujourd'hui c'est mardi
oajhoordwee seh mahrdee

– Wednesday _____ Aujourd'hui c'est mercredi
oajhoordwee seh mehrkruhdee

– Thursday_____ Aujourd'hui c'est jeudi
oajhoordwee seh jhuhdee

– Friday_____ Aujourd'hui c'est vendredi
oajhoordwee seh vohndruhdee

– Saturday _____ Aujourd'hui c'est samedi
oajhoordwee seh sahmdee

– Sunday _____ Aujourd'hui c'est dimanche
oajhoordwee seh deemohnsh

in January _____ en janvier
ohn jhohnvyay

since February _____ depuis février
duhpwee fayvryay

in spring_____ au printemps
oa prahntohn

in summer_____ en été; l'été
ohn naytay; laytay

in autumn _____ en automne
ohn noatonn

in winter_____ en hiver; l'hiver
ohn neevehr; leevehr

1998_____ mille neuf cent quatre-vingt-dix-huit
meel nuhf sohn kahtr vahn dee zweet

the twentieth century _____ le vingtième siècle
luh vahntyehm syehkl

What's the date today? ____ Quelle est la date aujourd'hui?
kehl eh lah daht oajhoordwee?

Today's the 24th_____ Aujourd'hui on est le vingt-quatre
oajhoordwee awn neh luh vahnkahtr

Monday 3 November _____ lundi, le trois novembre 1997
1997 *luhndee, luh trwah novohnbr meel nuhf sohn
kahtr vahn dee seht*

in the morning _____ le matin
luh mahtahn

in the afternoon_____ l'après-midi
lahpreh meedee

in the evening _____ le soir
luh swahr

at night_____ la nuit
lah nwee

this morning_____ ce matin
suh mahtahn

this afternoon_____ cet après-midi
seht ahpreh meedee

this evening	ce soir
	suh swahr
tonight	ce soir
	suh swahr
last night	hier soir
	yehr swahr
this week	cette semaine
	seht suhmehn
next month	le mois prochain
	luh mwah proshahn
last year	l'année passée
	lahnay pahsay
next...	prochain/prochaine
	proshahn/proshehn
in...days/weeks/ months/years	dans...jours/semaines/mois/ans
	dohn...jhoor/suhmehn/mwah/ohn
...weeks ago	il y a...semaines
	eel ee ah...suhmehn
day off	jour de congé
	jhoor duh kawnjhay

.2 Bank holidays

● **The most important** Bank holidays in France are the following:

January 1	Le Jour de l'An (New Year's Day)
March/April	Pâques, (Easter)
	le lundi de Pâques (Easter Monday)
May 1	La Fête du Travail (May Day; Labour Day)
May 8	Le Jour de la Libération (Liberation Day)
May/June	L'Ascension; la Pentecôte (Ascension; Whit Sunday)
July 14	La Fête Nationale (Bastille Day)
August 15	L'Assomption (Assumption)
November 1	La Toussaint (All Saints' Day)
November 11	L'Armistice (Armistice Day)
December 25	Noël (Christmas)

Most shops, banks and government institutions are closed on these days. Banks close the afternoon before a Bank holiday and some banks close on Mondays in the provinces. Good Friday and Boxing Day are not Bank Holidays.

.3 What time is it?

What time is it?	Quelle heure est-il?
	kehl uhr eh teel?
It's nine o'clock	Il est neuf heures
	eel eh nuh vuhr
– five past ten	Il est dix heures cinq
	eel eh dee zuhr sahnk
– a quarter past eleven	Il est onze heures et quart
	eel eh tawnz uhr ay kahr
– twenty past twelve	Il est douze heures vingt
	eel eh dooz uhr vahn
– half past one	Il est une heure et demie
	eel eh tewn uhr ay duhmee
– twenty–five to three	Il est trois heures moins vingt-cinq
	eel eh trwah zuhr mwahn vahn sahnk

– a quarter to four	Il est quatre heures moins le quart
	eel eh kahtr uhr mwahn luh kahr
– ten to five	Il est cinq heures moins dix
	eel eh sahnk uhr mwahn dees
– twelve noon	Il est midi
	eel eh meedee
– midnight	Il est minuit
	eel eh meenwee
half an hour	une demi-heure
	ewn duhmee uhr
What time?	A quelle heure?
	ah kehl uhr?
What time can I come round?	A quelle heure puis-je venir?
	ah kehl uhr pwee jhuh vuhneer?
At...	A...
	ah...
After...	Après...
	ahpreh...
Before...	Avant...
	ahvohn...
Between...and...	Entre...et...
	ohntr...ay...
From...to...	De...à...
	duh...ah...
In...minutes	Dans...minutes
	dohn...meenewt
– an hour	Dans une heure
	dohn zewn uhr
– ...hours	Dans...heures
	dohn...uhr
– a quarter of an hour	Dans un quart d'heure
	dohn zuhn kahr duhr
– three quarters of an hour	Dans trois quarts d'heure
	dohn trwah kahr duhr
early/late	trop tôt/tard
	troa toa/tahr
on time	à temps
	ah tohn
summertime	l'heure d'été
	luhr daytay
wintertime	l'heure d'hiver
	luhr deevehr

1 .4 One, two, three...

0	zéro	*zayroa*
1	un	*uhn*
2	deux	*duh*
3	trois	*trwah*
4	quatre	*kahtr*
5	cinq	*sahnk*
6	six	*sees*
7	sept	*seht*
8	huit	*weet*
9	neuf	*nuhf*
10	dix	*dees*

11	_____	onze	*awnz*
12	_____	douze	*dooz*
13	_____	treize	*trehz*
14	_____	quatorze	*kahtorz*
15	_____	quinze	*kahnz*
16	_____	seize	*sehz*
17	_____	dix-sept	*dee seht*
18	_____	dix-huit	*dee zweet*
19	_____	dix-neuf	*deez nuhf*
20	_____	vingt	*vahn*
21	_____	vingt et un	*vahn tay uhn*
22	_____	vingt-deux	*vahn duh*
30	_____	trente	*trohnt*
31	_____	trente et un	*trohn tay uhn*
32	_____	trente-deux	*trohnt duh*
40	_____	quarante	*kahrohnt*
50	_____	cinquante	*sahnkohnt*
60	_____	soixante	*swahssohnt*
70	_____	soixante-dix	*swahssohnt dees*
80	_____	quatre-vingts	*kahtr vahn*
90	_____	quatre-vingt-dix	*kahtr vahn dees*
100	_____	cent	*sohn*
101	_____	cent un	*sohn uhn*
110	_____	cent dix	*sohn dees*
120	_____	cent vingt	*sohn vahn*
200	_____	deux cents	*duh sohn*
300	_____	trois cents	*trwah sohn*
400	_____	quatre cents	*kahtr sohn*
500	_____	cinq cents	*sahnk sohn*
600	_____	six cents	*see sohn*
700	_____	sept cents	*seht sohn*
800	_____	huit cents	*wee sohn*
900	_____	neuf cents	*nuhf sohn*
1,000	_____	mille	*meel*
1,100	_____	mille cent	*meel sohn*
2,000	_____	deux mille	*duh meel*
10,000	_____	dix mille	*dee meel*
100,000	_____	cent mille	*sohn meel*
1,000,000	_____	un million	*uhn meelyawn*
1st	_____	le premier	*luh pruhmyay*
2nd	_____	le deuxième	*luh duhzyehm*
3rd	_____	le troisième	*luh trwahzyehm*
4th	_____	le quatrième	*luh kahtryehm*
5th	_____	le cinquième	*luh sahnkyehm*
6th	_____	le sixième	*luh seezyehm*
7th	_____	le septième	*luh sehtyehm*
8th	_____	le huitième	*luh weetyehm*
9th	_____	le neuvième	*luh nuhvyehm*
10th	_____	le dixième	*luh deezyehm*
11th	_____	le onzième	*luh awnzyehm*
12th	_____	le douzième	*luh doozyehm*
13th	_____	le treizième	*luh trehzyehm*
14th	_____	le quatorzième	*luh kahtorzyehm*
15th	_____	le quinzième	*luh kahnzyehm*

16th _____	le seizième	*luh sehzyehm*
17th _____	le dix-septième	*luh dee sehtyehm*
18th _____	le dix-huitième	*luh dee zweetyehm*
19th _____	le dix-neuvième	*luh deez nuhvyehm*
20th _____	le vingtième	*luh vahntyehm*
21st _____	le vingt et unième	*luh vahn tay-ewnyehm*
22nd _____	le vingt-deuxième	*luh vahn duhzyehm*
30th _____	le trentième	*luh trohntyehm*
100th _____	le centième	*luh sohntyehm*
1,000th _____	le millième	*luh meelyehm*
once _____	une fois	*ewn fwah*
twice _____	deux fois	*duh fwah*
double _____	le double	*luh doobl*
triple _____	le triple	*luh treepl*
half _____	la moitié	*lah mwahtyay*
a quarter _____	un quart	*uhn kahr*
a third _____	un tiers	*uhn tyehr*

a couple, a few, some _____ quelques, un nombre de, quelques
kehlkuh, uhn nawnbr duh, kehlkuh

2 + 4 = 6 _____ deux plus quatre égalent six
duh plews kahtr aygahl sees

4 - 2 = 2 _____ quatre moins deux égalent deux
kahtr mwahn duh aygahl duh

2 x 4 = 8 _____ deux fois quatre égalent huit
duh fwah kahtr aygahl weet

4 ÷ 2 = 2 _____ quatre divisé par deux égalent deux
kahtr deeveezay pahr duh aygahl duh

odd/even _____ impair/pair
ahnpehr/pehr

total _____ (au) total
(oa) totahl

6 x 9 _____ six fois neuf
see fwah nuhf

1.5 The weather

Is the weather going to be good/bad?	Va-t-il faire beau/mauvais? *vah teel fehr boa/moaveh?*	
Is it going to get colder/hotter?	Va-t-il faire plus froid/plus chaud? *vah teel fehr plew frwah/plew shoa?*	
What temperature is it going to be?	Quelle température va-t-il faire? *Kehl tohnpayrahtewr vah teel fehr?*	
Is it going to rain?	Va-t-il pleuvoir? *vah teel pluhvwahr?*	
Is there going to be a storm?	Va-t-il faire de la tempête? *vah teel fehr duh lah tohnpeht?*	
Is it going to snow?	Va-t-il neiger? *vah teel nehjhay?*	
Is it going to freeze?	Va-t-il geler? *vah teel jhuhlay?*	
Is the thaw setting in?	Va-t-il dégeler? *vah teel dayjhuhlay?*	
Is it going to be foggy?	Y aura-t-il du brouillard? *ee oarah teel dew brooy-yahr?*	

English	Va-t-il faire de l'orage?
Is there going to be a _____ thunderstorm?	Va-t-il faire de l'orage? *vah teel fehr duh lorahjh?*
The weather's _____ changing	Le temps change *luh tohn shohnjh*
It's cooling down _____	Ça se rafraîchit *sah suh rahfrehshee*
What's the weather_____ going to be like today/ tomorrow?	Quel temps va-t-il faire aujourd'hui/demain? *kehl tohn vah teel fehr oajhoordwee/duhmahn?*

nuageux **cloudy**	pluvieux **raining**	les rafales de vent **squalls**
beau **fine**	la canicule **scorching hot**	l'ouragan (m.) **hurricane**
chaud **hot**	la grêle **hail**	lourd **muggy**
...degrés (au-dessous/au- dessus de zéro) **...degrees (below/ above zero)**	la neige **snow** la pluie **rain**	l'orage (m.) **thunderstorm** orageux **stormy**
couvert **overcast**	la vague de chaleur **heatwave**	pénétrant **bleak**
le crachin **drizzle**	l'averse (f.) **shower**	ciel dégagé **clear**
doux **mild**	le brouillard **fog**	brumeux **misty**
ensoleillé **sunny**	le gel **ice**	vent faible/ modéré/fort
frais **chilly**	le vent **wind**	**light/moderate/ strong wind**
froid **cold**	le verglas **black ice**	venteux **windy**
humide **damp**	les nuages **clouds**	

1 .6 Here, there...

See also 5.1 Asking for directions

here/there _____	ici/là *eesee/lah*
somewhere/nowhere _____	quelque part/nulle part *kehlkuh pahr/newl pahr*
everywhere _____	partout *pahrtoo*
far away/nearby _____	loin/à côté *lwahn/ah koatay*
right/left _____	la droite/la gauche *lah drwaht/lah goash*
to the right/left of _____	à droite de/à gauche de *ah drwaht duh/ah goash duh*
straight ahead _____	tout droit *too drwah*

via _____	par	*pahr*
in _____	dans	*dohn*
on _____	sur	*sewr*
under _____	sous	*soo*
against _____	contre	*kawntr*
opposite _____	en face de	*ohn fahs duh*
next to _____	à côté de	*ah koatay duh*
near _____	près de	*preh duh*
in front of _____	devant	*devohn*
in the centre _____	au milieu de	*oa meelyuh duh*
forward _____	en avant	*ohn nahvohn*
down _____	en bas	*ohn bah*
up _____	en haut	*ohn oa*
inside _____	à l'intérieur	*ah lahntayryuhr*
outside _____	à l'extérieur	*ah lehxtayryuhr*
behind _____	derrière	*dehryehr*
at the front _____	à l'avant	*ah lahvohn*
at the back _____	à l'arrière	*ah lahryehr*
in the north _____	au nord	*oa nor*
to the south _____	vers le sud	*vehr luh sewd*
from the west _____	venant de l'ouest	*vuhnohn duh lwehst*
from the east _____	venant de l'est	*vuhnohn duh lehst*

14

See 5.4 Traffic signs

à louer	entrée gratuite	ne pas déranger s'il
for hire	**admission free**	vous plaît
à vendre	entrée interdite	**do not disturb please**
for sale	**no entry**	ouvert/fermé
accueil	escalier roulant	**open/closed**
reception	**escalator**	peinture fraîche
animaux interdits	escalier	**wet paint**
no pets allowed	**stairs**	pelouse interdite
ascenseur	escalier de secours	**keep off the grass**
lift	**fire escape**	premiers soins
attention à la marche	...étage	**first aid**
mind the step	**...floor**	propriété privée
attention chien	frein de secours	**private (property)**
méchant	**emergency brake**	renseignements
beware of the dog	haute tension	**information**
caisse	**high voltage**	réservé
pay here	heures d'ouverture	**reserved**
complet	**opening hours**	risque d'incendie
full	interdit d'allumer un	**fire hazard**
dames	feu	soldes
ladies	**no open fires**	**sale**
danger	interdit de fumer	sortie
danger	**no smoking**	**exit**
défense de toucher	interdit de	sortie de secours
please do not touch	photographier	**emergency exit**
eau non potable	**no photographs**	pousser/tirer
no drinking water	liquidation de stock	**push/pull**
en panne	**closing-down sale**	toilettes, wc
out of order	messieurs	**toilets**
entrée	**gents/gentlemen**	
entrance		

.8 Telephone alphabet

a	_____ *ah*	comme Anatole	*kom ahnnahtol*
b	_____ *bay*	comme Berthe	*kom behrt*
c	_____ *say*	comme Célestin	*kom saylehstahn*
d	_____ *day*	comme Désiré	*kom dayzeeray*
e	_____ *uh*	comme Eugène	*kom uhjhehn*
f	_____ *ehf*	comme François	*kom frohnswah*
g	_____ *jhay*	comme Gaston	*kom gahstawn*
h	_____ *ash*	comme Henri	*kom ohnree*
i	_____ *ee*	comme Irma	*kom eermah*
j	_____ *jhee*	comme Joseph	*kom jhosehf*
k	_____ *kah*	comme Kléber	*kom klaybehr*
l	_____ *ehl*	comme Louis	*kom looee*
m	_____ *ehm*	comme Marcel	*kom mahrsehl*
n	_____ *ehn*	comme Nicolas	*kom neekolah*
o	_____ *oh*	comme Oscar	*kom oskahr*
p	_____ *pay*	comme Pierre	*kom pyehr*
q	_____ *kew*	comme Quintal	*kom kahntahl*

Useful lists

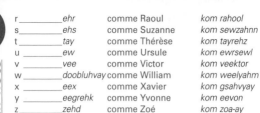

r _____ehr	comme Raoul	*kom rahool*
s_____ehs	comme Suzanne	*kom sewzahnn*
t _____tay	comme Thérèse	*kom tayrehz*
u _____ew	comme Ursule	*kom ewrsewl*
v _____vee	comme Victor	*kom veektor*
w _____doobluhvay	comme William	*kom weelyahm*
x _____eex	comme Xavier	*kom gsahvyay*
y _____eegrehk	comme Yvonne	*kom eevon*
z_____zehd	comme Zoé	*kom zoa-ay*

1 .9 Personal details

surname_____	nom
	nawn
christian name(s)_____	prénom(s)
	praynawn
initials_____	initiales
	eeneesyahl
address (street/number) ___	adresse (rue/numéro)
	ahdrehs (rew/newmayroa)
post code/town _____	code postal/ville
	kod postahl/veel
sex (male/female) _____	sexe (m/f)
	sehx (ehm/ehf)
nationality _____	nationalité
	nahsyonahleetay
date of birth _____	date de naissance
	daht duh nehsohns
place of birth _____	lieu de naissance
	lyuh duh nehsohns
occupation_____	profession
	profehsyawn
married/single/divorced____	marié(e) /célibataire/divorcé(e)
	mahreeay/sayleebahtehr/deevorsay
widowed _____	veuf/veuve
	vuhf/vuhv
(number of) children _____	(nombre d')enfants
	(nawnbr d)ohnfohn
identity card/passport/_____	numéro de carte d'identité/
driving licence number	passeport/permis de conduire
	newmayroa duh kahrt deedohnteetay/
	pahspor/pehrmee duh kawndweer
place and date of issue ____	lieu et date de délivrance
	lyuh ay daht duh dayleevrohns

2

Courtesies

2.1 Greetings 18

2.2 How to ask a question 19

2.3 How to reply 20

2.4 Thank you 21

2.5 Sorry 22

2.6 What do you think? 22

2 Courtesies

● **It is usual in France** to shake hands on meeting and parting company. Female friends and relatives may kiss each other on both cheeks when meeting and parting company. With men this varies according to the region. It is also polite to say monsieur and madame quite systematically as part of a greeting, i.e. Bonjour, monsieur; au revoir, madame.

● **The English** 'you' is expressed in French by either 'tu' or 'vous'. 'Tu' is the more familiar form of address, used to talk to someone close or used between young people or when adults are talking to young children. 'Vous' is the more formal and polite form of address. 'On' is the generalised form of 'nous' meaning people in general ('one' and 'we' in English).

2 .1 Greetings

Hello, Mr Smith _____	Bonjour monsieur Smith
	bawnjhoor muhsyuh dewpawn
Hello, Mrs Jones _____	Bonjour madame Jones
	bawnjhoor mahdahm dewrohn
Hello, Peter _____	Salut, Pierre
	sahlew, pyehr
Hi, Helen _____	Ça va, Hélène?
	sah vah, aylehn?
Good morning, madam___	Bonjour madame
	bawnjhoor mahdahm
Good afternoon, sir _____	Bonjour monsieur
	bawnjhoor muhsyuh
Good evening_____	Bonsoir
	bawhnswahr
How are you? _____	Comment allez-vous?
	komohn tahlay voo?
Fine, thank you, _____ and you?	Très bien et vous?
	treh byahn ay voo?
Very well _____	Très bien
	treh byahn
Not very well _____	Pas très bien
	pah treh byahn
Not too bad_____	Ça va
	sah vah
I'd better be going_____	Je m'en vais
	jhuh mohn veh
I have to be going _____	Je dois partir
	jhuh dwah pahrteer
Someone's waiting for me	On m'attend
	awn mahtohn
Bye!_____	Salut!
	sahlew!
Goodbye _____	Au revoir
	oa ruhvwahr
See you soon _____	A bientôt
	ah byahntoa
See you later _____	A tout à l'heure
	ah too tah luhr

See you in a little while	A tout de suite
	ah toot sweet
Sleep well	Dormez bien/dors bien
	dormay byahn, dor byahn
Good night	Bonne nuit
	bon nwee
Have fun	Amuse-toi bien
	ahmewz twah byahn
Good luck	Bonne chance
	bon shahns
Have a nice holiday	Bonnes vacances
	bon vahkohns
Have a good trip	Bon voyage
	bawn vwahyahjh
Thank you, you too	Merci, de même
	mehrsee, duh mehm
Say hello to...for me	Mes amitiés à...
	may zahmeetyay ah...

.2 How to ask a question

Who?	Qui?
	kee?
Who's that?	Qui est-ce?
	kee ehs?
What?	Quoi?
	kwah?
What's there to see here?	Qu'est-ce qu'on peut voir ici?
	kehsk awn puh vwahr eesee?
What kind of hotel is that?	C'est quelle sorte d'hôtel?
	seh kehl sort doatehl?
Where?	Où?
	oo?
Where's the toilet?	Où sont les toilettes?
	oo sawn lay twahleht?
Where are you going?	Où allez-vous?
	oo ahlay voo?
Where are you from?	D'où venez-vous?
	doo vuhnay voo?
How?	Comment?
	komohn?
How far is that?	C'est loin?
	seh lwahn?
How long does that take?	Combien de temps faut-il?
	kawnbyahn duh tohn foa teel?
How long is the trip?	Combien de temps dure le voyage?
	kawnbyahn duh tohn dewr luh vwahyahjh?
How much?	Combien?
	kawnbyahn?
How much is this?	C'est combien?
	seh kawnbyahn?
What time is it?	Quelle heure est-il?
	kehl uhr eh teel?
Which?	Quel? Quels?/Quelle? Quelles?
	kehl?
Which glass is mine?	Quel est mon verre?
	kehl eh mawn vehr?

When?	Quand?
	kohn?
When are you leaving?	Quand partez-vous?
	kohn pahrtay voo?
Why?	Pourquoi?
	poorkwah?
Could you...me?	Pouvez-vous me...?
	poovay voo muh...?
Could you help me, please?	Pouvez-vous m'aider s'il vous plaît?
	poovay voo mayday seel voo pleh?
Could you point that out to me?	Pouvez-vous me l'indiquer?
	poovay voo muh lahndeekay?
Could you come with me, please?	Pouvez-vous m'accompagner s'il vous plaît?
	poovay voo mahkawnpahnnyay seel voo pleh?
Could you...?	Voulez-vous...?
	voolay voo...?
Could you reserve some tickets for me, please?	Voulez-vous me réserver des places s'il vous plaît?
	voolay voo muh rayzehrvay day plahs seel voo pleh?
Do you know...?	Connaissez-vous...?
	konehssay voo...?
Do you know another hotel, please?	Vous connaissez peut-être un autre hôtel?
	voo konehssay puh tehtr uhn noatr oatehl?
Do you know whether...?	Savez-vous si...?
	sahvay voo see...?
Do you have a...?	Avez-vous un...?
	ahvay voo zuhn...?
Do you have a vegetarian dish, please?	Vous avez peut-être un plat sans viande?
	voo zahvay puh tehtr uhn plah sohn vyohnd?
I'd like...	Je voudrais...
	jhuh voodreh...
I'd like a kilo of apples, please	Je voudrais un kilo de pommes
	jhuh voodreh zuhn keeloa duh pom
Can I...?	Puis-je...?
	pwee jhuh...?
Can I take this?	Puis-je prendre ceci?
	pwee jhuh prohndr suhsee?
Can I smoke here?	Puis-je fumer ici?
	pwee jhuh fewmay eesee?
Could I ask you something?	Puis-je vous demander quelque chose?
	pwee jhuh voo duhmohnday kehlkuh shoaz?

2 .3 How to reply

Yes, of course	Oui, bien sûr
	wee, byahn sewr
No, I'm sorry	Non, je suis désolé
	nawn, jhuh swee dayzolay
Yes, what can I do for you?	Oui, que puis-je faire pour vous?
	wee, kuh pwee jhuh fehr poor voo?
Just a moment, please	Un moment s'il vous plaît
	uhn momohn seel voo pleh

2

No, I don't have _____ time now	Non, je n'ai pas le temps en ce moment
	nawn, jhuh nay pah luh tohn ohn suh momohn
No, that's impossible _____	Non, c'est impossible
	nawn, seh tahnposseebl
I think so _____	Je le crois bien
	jhuh luh krwah byahn
I agree_____	Je le pense aussi
	jhuh luh pohns oasee
I hope so too_____	Je l'espère aussi
	jhuh lehspehr oasee
No, not at all_____	Non, absolument pas
	nawn, ahbsolewmohn pah
No, no-one _____	Non, personne
	nawn, pehrson
No, nothing_____	Non, rien
	nawn, ryahn
That's (not) right _____	C'est (ce n'est pas) exact
	seht (suh neh pahz) ehgzah
I (don't) agree_____	Je suis (je ne suis pas) d'accord avec vous
	jhuh swee (jhuh nuh swee pah) dahkor ahvehk voo
All right _____	C'est bien
	seh byahn
Okay _____	D'accord
	dahkor
Perhaps _____	Peut-être
	puh tehtr
I don't know _____	Je ne sais pas
	jhuh nuh seh pah

.4 Thank you

Thank you _____	Merci/merci bien
	mehrsee/mehrsee byahn
You're welcome_____	De rien/avec plaisir
	duh ryahn/ahvehk playzeer
Thank you very much _____	Merci beaucoup
	mehrsee boakoo
Very kind of you_____	C'est aimable de votre part
	seh taymahbl duh votr pahr
I enjoyed it very much _____	C'était un réel plaisir
	sayteh tuhn rayehl playzeer
Thank you for your _____ trouble	Je vous remercie pour la peine
	jhuh voo ruhmehrsee poor lah pehn
You shouldn't have _____	Vous n'auriez pas dû
	voo noaryay pah dew
That's all right _____	Pas de problème
	pah duh problehm

.5 Sorry

Excuse me_____	Excusez-moi
	ehxkewzay mwah
Sorry! _____	Pardon!
	pahrdawn!
I'm sorry, I didn't know...___	Pardon, je ne savais pas que...
	pahrdawn jhuh nuh sahveh pah kuh...
I do apologise_____	Excusez-moi
	ehxkewzay mwah
I'm sorry_____	Je suis désolé
	jhuh swee dayzolay
I didn't do it on purpose, it was an accident	Je ne l'ai pas fait exprès, c'était un accident
	jhuh ne lay pah feh ehxpreh, sayteh tuhn nahxeedohn
That's all right _____	Ce n'est pas grave
	suh neh pah grahv
Never mind _____	Ça ne fait rien
	sah nuh feh ryahn
It could've happened to anyone	Ça peut arriver à tout le monde
	sah puh ahreevay ah too luh mawnd

.6 What do you think?

Which do you prefer?_____	Qu'est-ce que vous préférez?
	kehs kuh voo prayfayray?
What do you think?_____	Qu'en penses-tu?
	kohn pohns tew?
Don't you like dancing? ____	Tu n'aimes pas danser?
	tew nehm pah dohnsay?
I don't mind_____	Ça m'est égal
	sah meh taygahl
Well done!_____	Très bien!
	treh byahn!
Not bad!_____	Pas mal!
	pah mahl!
Great! _____	Génial!
	jhaynyahl!
Wonderful! _____	Super!
	sewpehr!
It's really nice here! _____	C'est drôlement agréable ici!
	seh droalmohn ahgrayahbl eesee!
How nice! _____	Pas mal, chouette!
	pah mahl, shweht!
How nice for you! _____	C'est formidable!
	seh formeedahbl!
I'm (not) very happy with...	Je suis (ne suis pas) très satisfait(e) de...
	jhuh swee (nuh swee pah) treh sahteesfeh(t) duh...
I'm glad..._____	Je suis content(e) que...
	jhuh swee kawntohn(t) kuh...
I'm having a great time ____	Je m'amuse beaucoup
	jhuh mahmewz boakoo

22

I'm looking forward to it	Je m'en réjouis
	jhuh mohn rayjhwee
I hope it'll work out	J'espère que cela réussira
	jhehspehr kuh suhlah rayewseerah
That's ridiculous!	C'est nul!
	seh newl!
That's terrible!	Quelle horreur!
	kehl oruhr!
What a pity!	C'est dommage!
	seh domahjh!
That's filthy!	C'est dégoûtant!
	seh daygootohn!
What a load of rubbish!	C'est ridicule/C'est absurde!
	seh reedeekewl/seh tahbsewrd!
I don't like...	Je n'aime pas...
	jhuh nehm pah...
I'm bored to death	Je m'ennuie à mourir
	jhuh mohnnwee ah mooreer
I've had enough	J'en ai assez/ras le bol
	jhon nay ahsay/rahl bol
This is no good	Ce n'est pas possible
	suh neh pah posseebl
I was expecting something completely different	Je m'attendais à quelque chose de très différent
	jhuh mahtohndeh ah kehlkuh shoaz duh treh deefayrohn

Conversation

3.1 I beg your pardon? 25

3.2 Introductions 26

3.3 Starting/ending a conversation 28

3.4 Congratulations and condolences 28

3.5 A chat about the weather 28

3.6 Hobbies 29

3.7 Being the host(ess) 29

3.8 Invitations 29

3.9 Paying a compliment 30

3.10 Chatting someone up 31

3.11 Arrangements 32

3.12 Saying goodbye 32

Conversation

3.1 I beg your pardon?

I don't speak any/ _____ I speak a little...	Je ne parle pas/je parle un peu... *jhuh nuh pahrl pah/jhuh pahrl uhn puh..*
I'm English _____	Je suis anglais/anglaise *jhuh swee zohngleh/zohnglehz*
I'm Scottish _____	Je suis écossais/écossaise *jhuh swee zaykosseh/zaykossehz*
I'm Irish _____	Je suis irlandais/irlandaise *jhuh swee zeerlohndeh/zeerlohndehz*
I'm Welsh _____	Je suis gallois/galloise *jhuh swee gahlwah/gahlwahz*
Do you speak _____ English/French/German?	Parlez-vous anglais/français/allemand? *pahrlay voo ohngleh/ frohnseh/ahlmohn?*
Is there anyone who _____ speaks...?	Y a-t-il quelqu'un qui parle...? *ee yah teel kehlkuhn kee pahrl...?*
I beg your pardon? _____	Que dites-vous? *kuh deet voo?*
I (don't) understand _____	Je (ne) comprends (pas) *jhuh (nuh) kawnprohn (pah)*
Do you understand me? ___	Me comprenez-vous? *me kawnpruhnay voo?*
Could you repeat that, _____ please?	Voulez-vous répéter s'il vous plaît? *voolay voo raypaytay seel voo pleh?*
Could you speak more _____ slowly, please?	Pouvez-vous parler plus lentement? *poovay voo pahrlay plew lohntmohn?*
What does that word _____ mean?	Qu'est-ce que ce mot veut dire? *kehs kuh suh moa vuh deer?*
Is that similar to/the _____ same as...?	Est-ce (environ) la même chose que...? *ehs (ohnveerawn) lah mehm shoaz kuh...?*
Could you write that _____ down for me, please?	Pouvez-vous me l'écrire? *poovay voo muh laykreer?*
Could you spell that _____ for me, please?	Pouvez-vous me l'épeler? *poovay voo muh laypuhlay?*

(See 1.8 Telephone alphabet)

Could you point that _____ out in this phrase book, please?	Pouvez-vous me le montrer dans ce guide de conversation? *poovay voo muh luh mawntray dohn suh gueed duh kawnvehrsahsyawn?*
One moment, please, _____ I have to look it up	Un moment, je dois le chercher *uhn momohn, jhuh dwah luh shehrshay*
I can't find the word/the ___ sentence	Je ne trouve pas le mot/la phrase *jhuh nuh troov pah luh moa/lah frahz*
How do you say _____ that in...?	Comment dites-vous cela en...? *komohn deet voo suhlah ohn...?*
How do you pronounce _____ that?	Comment prononcez-vous cela? *komohn pronawnsay voo suhlah?*

3

Conversation

May I introduce myself?	Puis-je me présenter?
	pwee jhuh muh prayzohntay?
My name's...	Je m'appelle...
	jhuh mahpehl...
I'm...	Je suis...
	jhuh swee...
What's your name?	Comment vous appelez-vous?
	komohn voo zahpuhlay voo?
May I introduce...?	Puis-je vous présenter?
	pwee jhuh voo prayzohntay?
This is my wife/ daughter/mother/ girlfriend	Voici ma femme/fille/mère/mon amie
	vwahsee mah fahm/feey/mehr/mawn nahmee
– my husband/son/ father/boyfriend	Voici mon mari/fils/père/ami
	vwahsee mawn mahree/fees/pehr/ahmee
How do you do	Enchanté(e).
	ohnshohntay
Pleased to meet you	Je suis heureux(se) de faire votre connaissance
	jhuh swee zuhruh(z) duh fehr votr kohnehssohns
Where are you from?	D'où venez-vous?
	doo vuhnay voo?
I'm from England/Scotland/ Ireland/Wales	Je viens d'Angleterre/d'Ecosse/d'Irlande/du pays de Galles
	jhuh vyahn dohngluhtehr/daykos/deerlohnd/ dew payee duh gahl
What city do you live in?	Vous habitez dans quelle ville?
	voo zahbeetay dohn kehl veel?
In..., It's near...	A...C'est à côté de...
	ah...seh tah koatay duh...
Have you been here long?	Etes-vous ici depuis longtemps?
	eht voo zeesee duhpwee lawntohn?
A few days	Depuis quelques jours
	depwee kehlkuh jhoor
How long are you staying here?	Combien de temps restez-vous ici?
	kawnbyahn duh tohn rehstay voo zeesee?
We're (probably) leaving tomorrow/in two weeks	Nous partirons (probablement) demain/dans quinze jours
	noo pahrteerawn (probahbluhmohn) duhmahn/dohn kahnz jhoor
Where are you staying?	Où logez-vous?
	oo lojhay voo?
In a hotel/an apartment	Dans un hôtel/appartement
	dohn zuhn noatehl/ahpahrtuhmohn
On a camp site	Dans un camping
	dohn zuhn kohnpeeng
With friends/relatives	Chez des amis/chez de la famille
	shay day zahmee/shay duh lah fahmeey
Are you here on your own/with your family?	Etes-vous ici seul/avec votre famille?
	eht voo zeesee suhl/ahvehk votr fahmeey?
I'm on my own	Je suis seul(e)
	jhuh swee suhl

I'm with my_____ partner/wife/husband	Je suis avec mon ami(e)/ma femme/mon mari
	jhuh swee zahvehk mawn nahmee/mah fahm/mawn mahreey
– with my family _____	Je suis avec ma famille
	jhuh swee zahvehk mah fahmeey
– with relatives_____	Je suis avec de la famille
	jhuh swee zahvehk duh lah fahmeey
– with a friend/friends _____	Je suis avec un ami/une amie /des amis
	jhuh swee zahvehk uhn nahmee/ewn ahmee/day zahmee
Are you married? _____	Etes-vous marié(e)?
	eht voo mahreeay?
Do you have a steady _____ boyfriend/girlfriend?	As-tu un petit ami (une petite amie)?
	ah tew uhn puhtee tahmee (ewn puhteet ahmee)?
That's none of your_____ business	Cela ne vous regarde pas
	suhlah nuh voo ruhgahrd pah
I'm married _____	Je suis marié(e)
	jhuh swee mahreeay
– single_____	Je suis célibataire
	jhuh swee sayleebahtehr
– separated _____	Je suis séparé(e)
	jhuh swee saypahray
– divorced _____	Je suis divorcé(e)
	jhuh swee deevorsay
– a widow/widower_____	Je suis veuf/veuve
	jhuh swee vuhf/vuhv
I live alone/with _____ someone	J'habite tout(e) seul(e)/avec quelqu'un
	jhahbeet too suhl(toot suhl)/ahvehk kehlkuhn
Do you have any _____ children/grandchildren?	Avez-vous des enfants/petits-enfants?
	ahvay voo day zohnfohn/puhtee zohnfohn?
How old are you? _____	Quel âge avez-vous?
	kehl ahjh ahvay voo?
How old is he/she? _____	Quel âge a-t-il/a-t-elle?
	kehl ahjh ah teel/ah tehl?
I'm...years old_____	J'ai...ans
	jhay...ohn
He's/she's...years old _____	Il/elle a...ans
	eel/ehl ah...ohn
What do you do for a_____ living?	Quel est votre métier?
	kehl eh votr maytyay?
I work in an office _____	Je travaille dans un bureau
	jhuh trahvahy dohn zuhn bewroa
I'm a student/ _____ I'm at school	Je fais des études/je vais à l'école
	jhuh feh day zaytewd/jhuh veh zah laykol
I'm unemployed_____	Je suis au chômage
	jhuh swee zoa shoamajh
I'm retired _____	Je suis retraité(e)
	jhuh swee ruhtrehtay
I'm on a disability _____ pension	Je suis en invalidité
	jhuh swee zohn nahnvahleedeetay
I'm a housewife _____	Je suis femme au foyer
	jhuh swee fahm oa fwahyay
Do you like your job? _____	Votre travail vous plaît?
	votr trahvahy voo pleh?

Most of the time	Ça dépend
	sah daypohn
I prefer holidays	J'aime mieux les vacances
	Jhehm myuh lay vahkohns

3.3 Starting/ending a conversation

Could I ask you something?	Puis-je vous poser une question?
	pwee jhuh voo poazay ewn kehstyawn?
Excuse me	Excusez-moi
	ehxkewsay mwah
Excuse me, could you help me?	Pardon, pouvez-vous m'aider?
	pahrdawn, poovay voo mayday?
Yes, what's the problem?	Oui, qu'est-ce qui se passe?
	wee, kehs kee suh pahss?
What can I do for you?	Que puis-je faire pour vous?
	kuh pwee jhuh fehr poor voo?
Sorry, I don't have time now	Excusez-moi, je n'ai pas le temps maintenant
	ehxkewsay mwah, jhuh nay pah luh tohn mahntuhnohn
Do you have a light?	Vous avez du feu?
	voo zahvay dew fuh?
May I join you?	Puis-je m'asseoir à côté de vous?
	pwee jhuh mahsswahr ah koatay duh voo?
Could you take a picture of me/us? Press this button.	Voulez-vous me/nous prendre en photo? Appuyez sur ce bouton.
	voolay voo muh/noo prohndr ohn foatoa? ahpweeyay sewr suh bootawn
Leave me alone	Laissez-moi tranquille
	laysay mwah trohnkeey
Get lost	Fichez le camp
	feeshay luh kohn
Go away or I'll scream	Si vous ne partez pas, je crie
	see voo nuh pahrtay pah, jhuh kree

3.4 Congratulations and condolences

Happy birthday/many happy returns	Bon anniversaire/bonne fête
	bohn nahnneevehrsehr/bon feht
Please accept my condolences	Mes condoléances
	may kawndolayohns
I'm very sorry for you	Cela me peine beaucoup pour vous
	suhlah muh pehn boakoo poor voo

3.5 A chat about the weather

See also 1.5 The weather

It's so hot/cold today!	Qu'est-ce qu'il fait chaud/froid aujourd'hui!
	kehs keel feh shoa/frwah oajhoordwee!
Nice weather, isn't it?	Il fait beau, n'est-ce pas?
	eel feh boa, nehs pah?
What a wind/storm!	Quel vent/orage!
	kehl vohn/orahjh!

All that rain/snow! _____	Quelle pluie/neige!
	kehl plwee/nehjh!
All that fog! _____	Quel brouillard!
	kehl brooy-yahr!
Has the weather been _____ like this for long here?	Fait-il ce temps-là depuis longtemps?
	feh teel suh tohn lah duhpwee lawntohn?
Is it always this hot/cold ___ here?	Fait-il toujours aussi chaud/froid ici?
	feh teel toojhoor oasee shoa/frwah eesee?
Is it always this dry/wet_____ here?	Fait-il toujours aussi sec/humide ici?
	feh teel toojhoor oasee sehk/ewmeed eesee?

.6 Hobbies

Do you have any _____ hobbies?	Avez-vous des passe-temps?
	ahvay voo day pahs tohn?
I like painting/_____ reading/photography/ DIY	J'aime peindre/lire/la photo/le bricolage
	jhehm pahndr/leer/lah foatoa/luh breekolahjh
I like music _____	J'aime la musique
	jhehm lah mewzeek
I like playing the _____ guitar/piano	J'aime jouer de la guitare/du piano
	jhehm jhooay duh lah gueetahr/dew pyahnoa
I like going to the _____ movies	J'aime aller au cinéma
	jhehm ahlay oa seenaymah
I like travelling/_____ sport/fishing/walking	J'aime voyager/faire du sport/la pêche/me promener
	jhehm vvwahyahjhay/fehr dew spor/lah pehsh/ muh promuhnay

.7 Being the host(ess)

See also 4 Eating out

Can I offer you a drink? _____	Puis-je vous offrir quelque chose à boire?
	pwee jhuh voo zofreer kehlkuh shoaz ah bwahr?
What would you like_____ to drink?	Que désires-tu boire?
	kuh dayzeer tew bwahr?
Something non-_____ alcoholic, please.	De préférence quelque chose sans alcool
	duh prayfayrohns kehlkuh shoaz sohn zahlkol
Would you like a _____ cigarette/cigar/to roll your own?	Voulez-vous une cigarette/un cigare/rouler une cigarette?
	voolay voo zewn seegahreht/uhn seegahr/roolay ewn seegahreht?
I don't smoke _____	Je ne fume pas
	jhuh nuh fewm pah

.8 Invitations

Are you doing anything_____ tonight?	Faites-vous quelque chose ce soir?
	feht voo kehlkuh shoaz suh swahr?
Do you have any plans _____ for today/this afternoon/tonight?	Avez-vous déjà fait des projets pour aujourd'hui/cet après-midi/ce soir?
	ahvay voo dayjhah feh day projheh poor oa-jhoordwee/seht ahpreh meedee/suh swahr?
Would you like to go _____ out with me?	Aimeriez-vous sortir avec moi?
	aymuhryay voo sorteer ahvehk mwah?

Would you like to go ____ dancing with me?	Aimeriez-vous aller danser avec moi? *aymuhryay voo zahlay dohnsay ahvehk mwah?*
Would you like to have ____ lunch/dinner with me?	Aimeriez-vous déjeuner/dîner avec moi? *aymuhryay voo dayjhuhnay/deenay ahvehk mwah?*
Would you like to come____ to the beach with me?	Aimeriez-vous aller à la plage avec moi? *aymuhryay voo zahlay ah lah plahjh ahvehk mwah?*
Would you like to come____ into town with us?	Aimeriez-vous aller en ville avec nous? *aymuhryay voo zahlay ohn veel ahvehk noo?*
Would you like to come____ and see some friends with us?	Aimeriez-vous aller chez des amis avec nous? *aymuhryay voo zahlay shay day zahmee ahvehk noo?*
Shall we dance?____	On danse? *awn dohns?*
– sit at the bar? ____	On va s'asseoir au bar? *awn vah saswahr oa bahr?*
– get something to drink? __	On va boire quelque chose? *awn vah bwahr kehlkuh shoaz?*
– go for a walk/drive?____	On va marcher un peu/on va faire un tour en voiture? *awn vah mahrshay uhn puh/awn vah fehr uhn toor ohn vwahtewr?*
Yes, all right ____	Oui, d'accord *wee, dahkor*
Good idea ____	Bonne idée *bon eeday*
No (thank you) ____	Non (merci) *nawn (mehrsee)*
Maybe later____	Peut-être tout à l'heure *puh tehtr too tah luhr*
I don't feel like it ____	Je n'en ai pas envie *jhuh nohn nay pah zohnvee*
I don't have time ____	Je n'ai pas le temps *jhuh nay pah luh tohn*
I already have a date ____	J'ai déjà un autre rendez-vous *jhay dayjhah uhn noatr rohnday voo*
I'm not very good at____ dancing/volleyball/ swimming	Je ne sais pas danser/jouer au volley/nager *jhuh nuh seh pah dohnsay/jhooay oa volay/nahjhay*

3 .9 Paying a compliment

You look wonderful! ____	Vous avez l'air en pleine forme! *voo zahvay lehr ohn plehn form!*
I like your car! ____	Quelle belle voiture! *kehl behl vwahtewr!*
I like your ski outfit! ____	Quelle belle combinaison de ski! *kehl behl kawnbeenehzawn duh skee!*
You're a nice boy/girl ____	Tu es un garçon/une fille sympathique *tew eh zuhn gahrsohn/ewn feey sahnpahteek*
What a sweet child! ____	Quel adorable enfant! *kehl ahdorahbl ohnfohn!*

You're a wonderful _____ dancer!	Vous dansez très bien!
	voo dohnsay treh byahn!
You're a wonderful _____ cook!	Vous faites très bien la cuisine!
	voo feht treh byahn lah kweezeen!
You're a terrific soccer _____ player!	Vous jouez très bien au football!
	voo jhooay treh byahn oa footbol!

3.10 Chatting someone up

I like being with you _____	J'aime bien être près de toi
	jhehm byahn ehtr preh duh twah
I've missed you so much ___	Tu m'as beaucoup manqué
	tew mah boakoo mohnkay
I dreamt about you _____	J'ai rêvé de toi
	jhay rehvay duh twah
I think about you all day ___	Je pense à toi toute la journée
	jhuh pohns ah twah toot lah jhoornay
You have such a sweet ____ smile	Tu souris si gentiment
	tew sooree see jhohnteemohn
You have such beautiful ___ eyes	Tu as de si jolis yeux
	tew ah duh see jhoalee zyuh
I'm in love with you _____	Je suis amoureux/se de toi
	jhuh swee zahmooruh(z) duh twah
I'm in love with you too ___	Moi aussi de toi
	mwah oasee duh twah
I love you _____	Je t'aime
	jhuh tehm
I love you too _____	Je t'aime aussi
	jhuh tehm oasee
I don't feel as strongly _____ about you	Je n'ai pas d'aussi forts sentiments pour toi
	jhuh nay pah doasee for sohnteemohn poor twah
I already have a _____ boyfriend/girlfriend	J'ai déjà un ami/une amie
	jhay dayjhah uhn nahmee/ewn ahmee
I'm not ready for that _____	Je n'en suis pas encore là
	jhuh nohn swee pah zohnkor lah
This is going too fast _____ for me.	Ça va un peu trop vite
	sah vah uhn puh troa veet
Take your hands off me ____	Ne me touche pas
	nuh muh toosh pah
Okay, no problem _____	D'accord, pas de problème
	dahkor, pah duh problehm
Will you stay with me _____ tonight?	Tu restes avec moi cette nuit?
	tew rehst ahvehk mwah seht nwee?
I'd like to go to bed _____ with you	J'aimerais coucher avec toi
	jhehmuhreh kooshay ahvehk twah
Only if we use a _____ condom	Seulement en utilisant un préservatif
	suhlmohn ohn newteeleezohn uhn prayzehrvahteef
We have to be careful ____ about AIDS	Il faut être prudent à cause du sida
	eel foa tehtr prewdohn ah koaz dew seedah
That's what they all say ____	Ils disent tous pareil
	eel deez toos pahrehy
We shouldn't take any ____ risks	Ne prenons aucun risque
	nuh pruhnawn zoakuhn reesk

31

Do you have a condom? ___	Tu as un préservatif?
	tew ah zuhn prayzehrvahteef?
No? In that case we _____ won't do it	Non? Alors je ne veux pas
	nawn? ahlor jhuh nuh vuh pah

3.11 Arrangements

When will I see _____ you again?	Quand est-ce que je te revois?
	kohn tehs kuh jhuh tuh ruhvwah?
Are you free over the _____ weekend?	Vous êtes/tu es libre ce week-end?
	voozeht/tew eh leebr suh week-ehnd?
What shall we arrange? ____	Que décidons-nous?
	kuh dayseedawn noo?
Where shall we meet? _____	Où nous retrouvons-nous?
	oo noo ruhtroovawn noo?
Will you pick me/us up? ___	Vous venez me/nous chercher?
	voo vuhnay muh/noo shehrshay?
Shall I pick you up? _____	Je viens vous/te chercher?
	jhuh vyahn voo/tuh shehrshay?
I have to be home by... ____	Je dois être à la maison à...heures
	jhuh dwah zehtr ah lah mehzawn ah...uhr

3.12 Saying goodbye

I don't want to see _____ you anymore	Je ne veux plus vous revoir
	jhuh nuh vuh plew voo ruhvwahr
Can I take you home? _____	Puis-je vous raccompagner à la maison?
	pwee jhuh voo rahkawnpahnyay ah lah mehzawn?
Can I write/call you? _____	Puis-je vous écrire/téléphoner?
	pwee jhuh voo zaykreer/taylayfonay?
Will you write/call me? _____	M'écrirez-vous/me téléphonerez-vous?
	maykreeray voo/muh taylayfonuhray voo?
Can I have your _____ address/phone number?	Puis-je avoir votre adresse/numéro de téléphone?
	pwee jhahvwahr votr ahdrehs/newmayroa duh taylayfon?
Thanks for everything _____	Merci pour tout
	mehrsee poor too
It was very nice _____	C'était très agréable
	sayteh treh zahgrayahbl
Say hello to... _____	Présentez mes amitiés à...
	prayzohntay may zahmeetyay ah...
Good luck _____	Bonne chance
	bon shohns
When will you be back? ___	Quand est-ce que tu reviens?
	kohn tehs kuh tew ruhvyahn?
I'll be waiting for you _____	Je t'attendrai
	jhuh tahtohndray
I'd like to see you again ____	J'aimerais te revoir
	jhehmuhreh tuh ruhvwahr
I hope we meet _____ again soon	J'espère que nous nous reverrons bientôt
	jhehspehr kuh noo noo ruhvehrawn byahntoa
You are welcome _____	Vous êtes le/la bienvenu(e)
	voozeht luh/lah byahnvuhnew

Eating out

4.1 **O**n arrival 34

4.2 **O**rdering 35

4.3 **T**he bill 37

4.4 **C**omplaints 38

4.5 **P**aying a compliment 39

4.6 **T**he menu 39

4.7 **A**lphabetical list of drinks
and dishes 39

4 Eating out

● **In France** people usually have three meals:

1 *Le petit déjeuner* (breakfast) approx. between 7.30 and 10am. Breakfast is light and consists of *café au lait* (white coffee) or lemon tea, a croissant, or slices of baguette (French bread), with butter and jam.

2 *Le déjeuner* (lunch) approx. between midday and 2pm. Lunch always includes a hot dish and is the most important meal of the day. Offices and shops often close and lunch is taken at home, in a restaurant or canteen (in some factories and schools). It usually consists of four courses:
– starter
– main course
– cheese
– dessert

3 *Le dîner* (dinner) between 7.30 and 9pm. Dinner is a light hot meal, usually taken with the family.

At around 5pm, a special snack (*le goûter*) is served to children, usually a roll or slices of baguette and biscuits with some chocolate.

 .1 On arrival

I'd like to book a table for seven o'clock, please?	Puis-je réserver une table pour sept heures?
	pwee jhuh rayzehrvay ewn tahbl poor seht uhr?
I'd like a table for two, please	Une table pour deux personnes s'il vous plaît
	ewn tahbl poor duh pehrson seel voo pleh
We've/we haven't booked	Nous (n')avons (pas) réservé
	noo zahvawn/noo nahvawn pah rayzehrvay
Is the restaurant open yet?	Le restaurant est déjà ouvert?
	luh rehstoarohn eh dayjhah oovehr?
What time does the restaurant open/close?	A quelle heure ouvre/ferme le restaurant?
	ah kehl uhr oovr/fehrm luh rehstoarohn?
Can we wait for a table?	Pouvons-nous attendre qu'une table soit libre?
	poovawn noo zahtohndr kewn tahbl swah leebr?
Do we have to wait long?	Devons-nous attendre longtemps?
	devawn noo zahtohndr lawntohn?

Vous avez réservé?	Do you have a reservation?
A quel nom?	What name, please?
Par ici, s'il vous plaît.	This way, please
Cette table est réservée.	This table is reserved
Nous aurons une table de libre dans un quart d'heure.	We'll have a table free in fifteen minutes.
Voulez-vous patienter (au bar)?	Would you like to wait (at the bar)?

Is this seat taken? _____	Est-ce que cette place est libre?
	ehs kuh seht plahs eh leebr?
Could we sit here/there? ___	Pouvons-nous nous asseoir ici/là-bas?
	poovawn noo noo zahswahr eesee/lahbah?
Can we sit by the_____	Pouvons-nous nous asseoir près de la
window?	fenêtre?
	poovawn noo noo zahswahr preh duh lah
	fuhnehtr?
Can we eat outside? _____	Pouvons-nous aussi manger dehors?
	poovawn noo zoasee mohnjhay duh-ohr?
Do you have another _____	Avez-vous encore une chaise?
chair for us?	*ahvay voo zohnkor ewn shehz?*
Do you have a highchair? __	Avez-vous une chaise haute?
	ahvay voo zewn shehz oat?
Is there a socket for _____	Y a-t-il une prise pour ce chauffe-biberon?
this bottle-warmer?	*ee ya teel ewn preez poor suh shoaf*
	beebuhrawn?
Could you warm up _____	Pouvez-vous me réchauffer ce biberon/ce
this bottle/jar for me?	petit pot?
	poovay voo muh rayshoafay suh
	beebuhrawn/suh puhtee poa?
Not too hot, please _____	Pas trop chaud s'il vous plaît
	pah troa shoa seel voo pleh
Is there somewhere I _____	Y a-t-il ici une pièce où je peux m'occuper
can change the baby's	du bébé?
nappy?	*ee ya teel eesee ewn pyehs oo jhuh puh*
	mokewpay dew baybay?
Where are the toilets? _____	Où sont les toilettes?
	oo sawn lay twahleht?

4 .2 Ordering

Waiter! _____	Garçon!
	gahrsawn!
Madam! _____	Madame!
	mahdahm!
Sir!_____	Monsieur!
	muhsyuh!
We'd like something to ___	Nous aimerions manger/boire quelque
eat/a drink	chose
	noo zaymuhryawn mohnjhay/bwahr kehlkuh
	shoaz
Could I have a quick_____	Puis-je rapidement manger quelque
meal?	chose?
	pwee jhuh rahpeedmohn mohnjhay kehlkuh
	shoaz?
We don't have much _____	Nous avons peu de temps
time	*noo zavawn puh duh tohn*
We'd like to have a _____	Nous voulons d'abord boire quelque
drink first	chose
	noo voolawn dahbor bwahr kehlkuh shoaz
Could we see the_____	Pouvons-nous avoir la carte/la carte des
menu/wine list, please?	vins?
	poovawn noo zahvwahr lah kahrt/lah kahrt
	day vahn?
Do you have a menu _____	Vous avez un menu en anglais?
in English?	*voo zahvay zuhn muhnew ohn nohngleh?*

Do you have a dish of the day?	Vous avez un plat du jour?
	voo zahvay zuhn plah dew jhoor?
We haven't made a choice yet	Nous n'avons pas encore choisi
	noo nahvawn pah zohnkor shwahzee
What do you recommend?	Qu'est-ce que vous nous conseillez?
	kehs kuh voo noo kawnsayay?
What are the specialities of the region/house?	Quelles sont les spécialités de cette région/de la maison?
	kehl sawn lay spaysyahleetay duh seht rayjhyawn/duh lah mehzawn?
I like strawberries/olives	J'aime les fraises/les olives
	jhehm lay frehz/lay zoleev
I don't like meat/fish/...	Je n'aime pas la viande/le poisson/...
	jhuh nehm pah lah vyohnd/luh pwahssawn/...
What's this?	Qu'est-ce que c'est?
	kehs kuh seh?
Does it have...in it?	Y a-t-il du/de la/des...dedans?
	ee ya teel dew/duh lah/day...duhdohn?
What does it taste like?	A quoi cela ressemble-t-il?
	ah kwah suhlah ruhsohnbluh teel?
Is this a hot or a cold dish?	Ce plat, est-il chaud ou froid?
	suh plah, eh teel shoa oo frwah?
Is this sweet?	Ce plat, est-il sucré?
	suh plah, eh teel sewkray?
Is this spicy?	Ce plat, est-il épicé?
	suh plah, eh teel aypeesay?
Do you have anything else, please?	Vous avez peut-être autre chose?
	voo zahvay puh tehtr oatr shoaz?
I'm on a salt-free diet	Le sel m'est interdit
	luh sehl meh tahntehrdee
I can't eat pork	La viande de porc m'est interdite
	lah vyohnd duh por meh tahntehrdeet
– sugar	Le sucre m'est interdit
	luh sewkr meh tahntehrdee
– fatty foods	Le gras m'est interdit
	luh grah meh tahntehrdee
– (hot) spices	Les épices (fortes) me sont interdites
	lay zaypees (fort) muh sawn tahntehrdeet

Vous désirez prendre un apéritif?	Would you like a drink first?
Vous avez déjà fait votre choix?	Have you decided?
Que désirez-vous boire?	What would you like to drink?
Bon appétit	Enjoy your meal
Vous désirez votre viande saignante, à point ou bien cuite?	Would you like your steak rare, medium or well done?
Vous désirez un dessert/du café?	Would you like a dessert/coffee?

I'll have what those people are having	J'aimerais la même chose que ces personnes-là
	jhehmuhreh lah mehm shoaz kuh say pehrson lah
I'd like... _____	J'aimerais...
	jhehmuhreh...
We're not having a _____ starter	Nous ne prenons pas d'entrée
	noo nuh pruhnawn pah dohntray
The child will share_____ what we're having	L'enfant partagera notre menu
	lohnfohn pahrtahjhuhrah notr muhnew
Could I have some _____ more bread, please?	Encore du pain s'il vous plaît
	ohnkor dew pahn seel voo pleh
– a bottle of water/wine_____	Une autre bouteille d'eau/de vin
	ewn oatr bootehy doa/duh vahn
– another helping of... _____	Une autre portion de...
	ewn oatr porsyawn duh...
– some salt and pepper_____	Pouvez-vous apporter du sel et du poivre?
	poovay voo zahportay dew sehl ay dew pwahvr?
– a napkin _____	Pouvez-vous apporter une serviette?
	poovay voo zahportay ewn sehrvyeht?
– a spoon_____	Pouvez-vous apporter une cuillère?
	poovay voo zahportay ewn kweeyehr?
– an ashtray _____	Pouvez-vous apporter un cendrier?
	poovay voo zahportay uhn sohndryay?
– some matches_____	Pouvez-vous apporter des allumettes?
	poovay voo zahportay day zahlewmeht?
– some toothpicks _____	Pouvez-vous apporter des cure-dents?
	poovay voo zahportay day kewr dohn?
– a glass of water _____	Pouvez-vous apporter un verre d'eau?
	poovay voo zahportay uhn vehr doa?
– a straw (for the child) ___	Pouvez-vous apporter une paille (pour l'enfant)?
	poovay voo zahportay ewn paheey (poor lohnfohn)?
Enjoy your meal!_____	Bon appétit!
	bohn nahpaytee!
You too! _____	De même vous aussi
	duh mehm voo zoasee
Cheers!_____	Santé!
	sohntay!
The next round's on me ___	La prochaine tournée est pour moi
	lah proshehn toornay eh poor mwah
Could we have a doggy_____ bag, please?	Pouvons-nous emporter les restes pour notre chien?
	poovawn noo zohnportay lay rehst poor notr shyahn?

.3 The bill

See also 8.2 Settling the bill

How much is this dish? ____	Quel est le prix de ce plat?
	kehl eh luh pree duh suh plah?
Could I have the bill, _____ please?	L'addition s'il vous plaît
	lahdeesyawn seel voo pleh

All together _____	Tout ensemble
	too tohnsohnbl
Everyone pays separately _	Chacun paye pour soi
	shahkuhn pehy poor swah
Could we have the menu __ again, please?	Pouvons-nous revoir la carte?
	poovawn noo ruhvwahr lah kahrt?
The...is not on the bill _____	Le...n'est pas sur l'addition
	luh...neh pah sewr lahdeesyawn

It's taking a very_____ long time	C'est bien long
	seh byahn lawn
We've been here an _____ hour already.	Nous sommes ici depuis une heure
	noo som zeesee duhpwee zewn uhr
This must be a mistake ____	Cela doit être une erreur
	suhlah dwah tehtr ewn ehruhr
This is not what I_____ ordered.	Ce n'est pas ce que j'ai commandé
	suh neh pah suh kuh jhay komohnday
I ordered..._____	J'ai commandé un...
	jhay komohnday uhn...
There's a dish missing _____	Il manque un plat
	eel mohnk uhn plah
This is broken/not clean ___	C'est cassé/ce n'est pas propre
	seh kahssay/suh neh pah propr
The food's cold _____	Le plat est froid
	luh plah eh frwah
– not fresh _____	Le plat n'est pas frais
	luh plah neh pah freh
– too salty/sweet/spicy_____	Le plat est trop salé/sucré/épicé
	luh plah eh troa sahlay/sewkray/aypeesay
The meat's not done_____	La viande n'est pas cuite
	lah vyohnd neh pah kweet
– overdone _____	La viande est trop cuite
	lah vyohnd eh troa kweet
– tough _____	La viande est dure
	lah vyohnd eh dewr
– off_____	La viande est avariée
	lah vyohnd eh tahvahryay
Could I have something ___ else instead of this?	Vous pouvez me donner autre chose à la place?
	voo poovay muh donay oatr shoaz ah lah plahs?
The bill/this amount is _____ not right	L'addition/cette somme n'est pas exacte
	lahdeesyawn/seht som neh pah zehgzahkt
We didn't have this_____	Ceci nous ne l'avons pas eu
	suhsee noo nuh lahvawn pah zew
There's no paper in the ___ toilet	Il n'y a plus de papier hygiénique dans les toilettes
	eel nee yah plew duh pahpyay eejhyayneek dohn lay twahleht
Do you have a _____ complaints book?	Avez-vous un registre de réclamations?
	ahvay voo zuhn ruhjheestr duh rayklahmahsyawn?
Will you call the_____ manager, please?	Voulez-vous appeler le directeur s'il vous plaît?
	voolay voo zahpuhlay luh deerehktuhr seel voo pleh?

4 .5 Paying a compliment

That was a wonderful _____ meal	Nous avons très bien mangé
	noo zahvawn treh byahn mohnjhay
The food was excellent _____	Le repas était succulent
	luh ruhpah ayteh sewkewlohn
The...in particular was _____ delicious	Le...surtout était délicieux
	luh...sewrtoo ayteh dayleesyuh

4 .6 The menu

apéritifs	gibier	plat principal
aperitifs	**game**	**main course**
boissons alcoolisées	hors d'oeuvres	potages
alcoholic beverages	**starters**	**soups**
boissons chaudes	légumes	service compris
hot beverages	**vegetables**	**service included**
carte des vins	plats chauds	spécialités
wine list	**hot dishes**	régionales
coquillages	plats froids	**regional specialities**
shellfish	**cold dishes**	viandes
desserts	plat du jour	**meat dishes**
sweets	**dish of the day**	volailles
fromages	pâtisserie	**poultry**
cheese	**pastry**	

4 .7 Alphabetical list of drinks and dishes

agneau	beurre	caille
lamb	**butter**	**quail**
ail	biftec	calmar
garlic	**steak**	**squid**
amandes	bière (bière	canard
almonds	pression)	**duck**
ananas	**beer (draught beer)**	câpres
pineapple	biscuit	**capers**
anchois	**biscuit**	carpe
anchovy	boeuf	**carp**
anguille	**beef**	carte des vins
eel	boissons alcoolisées	**wine list**
anis	**alcoholic beverages**	céleri
aniseed	boissons chaudes/	**celery**
apéritif	froides	cerises
aperitif	**hot/cold beverages**	**cherries**
artichaut	boudin noir/blanc	champignons
artichoke	**black/white pudding**	**mushrooms**
asperge	brochet	crème chantilly
asparagus	**pike**	**cream (whipped)**
baguette	cabillaud	châtaigne
french stick	**cod**	**chestnut**
banane	café (noir/au lait)	chausson aux
banana	**coffee (black/white)**	pommes
		apple turnover

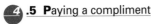

chou-fleur	croque monsieur	fines herbes
cauliflower	**toasted ham and**	**herbs**
choucroute	**cheese sandwich**	foie gras
sauerkraut	cru	**goose liver**
chou	**raw**	fraises
cabbage	crustacés	**strawberries**
choux de Bruxelles	**seafood**	framboises
Brussels sprouts	cuisses de	**raspberries**
citron	grenouilles	frit
lemon	**frog's legs**	**fried**
civet de lièvre	cuit(à l'eau)	friture
jugged hare	**boiled**	**deep-fried**
clou de girofle	dattes	fromage
clove	**dates**	**cheese**
cocktails	daurade	fruit de la passion
cocktails	**sea bream**	**passion fruit**
cognac	dessert	fruits de la saison
brandy	**sweet**	**seasonal fruits**
concombre	eau minérale	gaufres
cucumber	gazeuse/non	**waffles**
confiture	gazeuse	gigot d'agneau
jam	**sparkling/still**	**leg of lamb**
consommé	**mineral water**	glace
broth	échalote	**ice cream**
coquillages	**shallot**	glaçons
shellfish	écrevisse	**ice cubes**
coquilles	**crayfish**	grillé
Saint-Jacques	endives	**grilled**
scallops	**chicory**	groseilles
cornichon	entrecôte	**redcurrants**
gherkin	**sirloin steak**	hareng
côte/côtelette	entrées	**herring**
chop	**first course**	haricots blancs
côte de boeuf	épices	**haricot beans**
T-bone steak	**spices**	haricots verts
côte de porc	épinards	**french beans**
pork chop	**spinach**	homard
côtelette d'agneau	escargots	**lobster**
lamb chop	**snails**	hors d'oeuvre
côtelettes dans	farine	**starters**
l'échine	**flour**	huîtres
spare rib	fenouil	**oysters**
couvert	**fennel**	jambon
cutlery	fèves	blanc/cru/fumé
crabe	**broad beans**	**ham(cooked/Parma**
crab	figues	**style)/smoked)**
crêpes	**figs**	jus de citron
pancakes	filet de boeuf	**lemon juice**
crevettes grises	**fillet**	jus de fruits
shrimps	filet mignon	**fruit juice**
crevettes roses	**fillet steak**	jus d'orange
prawns	filet de porc	**orange juice**
croissant	**tenderloin**	
croissant		

lait/demi-écrémé/ entier	oignon	pruneaux
milk/semi-skimmed/ full-cream	onion	prunes
langouste	olives	queue de boeuf
crayfish	olives	oxtail
langoustine	omelette	ragoût
scampi	omelette	stew
langue	origan	ris de veau
tongue	oregano	sweetbread
lapin	pain au chocolat	riz
rabbit	chocolate bun	rice
légumes	part	rôti de boeuf (rosbif)
vegetables	portion	roast beef
lentilles	pastis	rouget
lentils	pastis	red mullet
liqueur	pâtisserie	saignant
liqueur	pastry	rare
lotte	pêche	salade verte
monkfish	peach	lettuce
loup de mer	petite friture	salé/sucré
sea bass	fried fish(whitebait or similar)	salted/sweet
macaron	petits (biscuits) salés	sandwich
macaroon	savoury biscuits	sandwich
maïs	petit pain	saumon
sweetcorn	roll	salmon
épis de maïs	petits pois	sel
corn (on the cob)	green peas	salt
marron	pigeon	service compris/non compris
chestnut	pigeon	service (not) included
melon	pintade	sole
melon	guinea fowl	sole
menu du jour/à la carte	plat du jour	soupe
menu of the day/à la carte	dish of the day	soup
morilles	plats froids/chauds	soupe à l'oignon
morels	cold/hot courses	onion soup
moules	poire	spécialités régionales
mussels	pear	regional specialities
mousse au chocolat	pois chiches	sucre
chocolate mousse	chick peas	sugar
moutarde	poisson	thon
mustard	fish	tuna
myrtilles	poivre	thym
bilberries	pepper	thyme
noisette	poivron	tripes
hazelnut	green/red pepper	tripe
noix	pomme	truffes
walnut	apple	truffles
noix de veau	pommes de terre	truite
fillet of veal	potatoes	trout
oeuf à la coque/dur/au plat	pommes frites	truite saumonée
egg soft/hard boiled/fried	chips	salmon trout
	poulet(blanc)	turbot
	chicken(breast)	turbot
	prune	
	plum	

vapeur (à la)	vin blanc	vinaigre
steamed	white wine	vinegar
venaison	vin rosé	xérès
venison	rosé wine	sherry
viande hachée	vin rouge	
minced meat/mince	red wine	

5 **O**n the road

5.1 **A**sking for directions 44

5.2 **C**ustoms 45

5.3 **L**uggage 46

5.4 **T**raffic signs 47

5.5 **T**he car 48
The parts of a car 50–51

5.6 **T**he petrol station 48

5.7 **B**reakdown and repairs 49

5.8 **T**he bicycle/moped 52
The parts of a bicycle 54–55

5.9 **R**enting a vehicle 53

5.10 **H**itchhiking 56

5.1 **A**sking for directions

Excuse me, could I ask you something?	Pardon, puis-je vous demander quelque chose? *pahrdawn, pwee jhuh voo duhmohnday kehlkuh shoaz?*
I've lost my way	Je me suis égaré(e) *jhuh muh swee zaygahray*
Is there an... around here?	Connaissez-vous un...dans les environs? *konehssay voo zuhn... dohn lay zohnveerawn?*
Is this the way to...?	Est-ce la route vers...? *ehs lah root vehr...?*
Could you tell me how to get to...?	Pouvez-vous me dire comment aller à...? *poovay voo muh deer komohn tahlay ah...?*
What's the quickest way to...?	Comment puis-je arriver le plus vite possible à...? *komohn pwee jhuh ahreevay luh plew veet pohseebl ah...?*
How many kilometres is it to...?	Il y a encore combien de kilomètres jusqu'à...? *eel ee yah ohnkor kohnbyahn duh keeloamehtr jhewskah...?*
Could you point it out on the map?	Pouvez-vous me l'indiquer sur la carte? *poovay voo muh lahndeekay sewr lah kahrt?*

Je ne sais pas, je ne suis pas d'ici	I don't know, I don't know my way around here
Vous vous êtes trompé	You're going the wrong way
Vous devez retourner à...	You have to go back to...
Là-bas les panneaux vous indiqueront la route	From there on just follow the signs
Là-bas vous demanderez à nouveau votre route	When you get there, ask again

tout droit **straight ahead**	le carrefour **the intersection**	l'immeuble **the building**
à gauche **left**	la rue **the street**	à l'angle, au coin **at the corner**
à droite **right**	le feu (de signalisation) **the traffic light**	la rivière, le fleuve **the river**
tourner **turn**	le tunnel **the tunnel**	l'autopont **the fly-over**
suivre **follow**	le panneau `cédez la priorité' **the `give way' sign**	le pont **the bridge**
traverser **cross**		le passage à niveau **the level crossing**

| la barrière | le panneau direction... | la flèche |
| boom | the sign pointing to... | the arrow |

5 .2 Customs

● **Border documents** (France, Belgium, Luxembourg): valid passport, visa. For car and motorbike: valid UK driving licence and registration document, insurance document, green card, UK registration plate. Caravan: must be entered on the green card and driven with the same registration number. A warning triangle, headlamp convertors and extra headlamp bulbs must be carried. Insurance should also be upgraded.

Import and export specifications:

– Foreign currency: no restrictions

– Alcohol (aged 17 and above): 10 litres of spirits and 90 litres of wine.

– Tobacco (aged 17 and above): 800 cigarettes, 200 cigars or a kilo of tobacco. Restricted to personal consumption only.

Votre passeport s'il vous plaît _____	Your passport, please
La carte verte s'il vous plaît _____	Your green card, please
La carte grise s'il vous plaît _____	Your vehicle documents, please
Votre visa s'il vous plaît _____	Your visa, please
Où allez-vous? _____	Where are you heading?
Combien de temps pensez-vous rester?	How long are you planning to stay?
Avez-vous quelque chose à déclarer? ___	Do you have anything to declare?
Voulez-vous l'ouvrir? _____	Open this, please

My children are entered _____ on this passport
Mes enfants sont inscrits dans ce passeport
may zohnfohn sawn tahnskree dohn suh pahspor

I'm travelling through _____
Je suis de passage
jhuh swee duh pahsahjh

I'm going on holiday to... __
Je vais en vacances en...
jhuh veh zohn vahkohns ohn...

I'm on a business trip _____
Je suis en voyage d'affaires
jhuh swee zohn vwahyahjh dahfehr

I don't know how long _____ I'll be staying yet
Je ne sais pas encore combien de temps je reste
jhuh nuh seh pah zohnkor kawnbyahn duh tohn jhuh rehst

I'll be staying here for _____ a weekend
Je reste un week-end ici
jhuh rehst uhn weekehnd eesee

– for a few days _____
Je reste quelques jours ici
jhuh rehst kehlkuh jhoor eesee

– for a week _____
Je reste une semaine ici
jhuh rehst ewn suhmehn eesee

On the road

–for two weeks _____	Je reste quinze jours ici
	jhuh rehst kahnz jhoor eesee
I've got nothing to _____ declare	Je n'ai rien à déclarer
	jhuh nay ryahn nah dayklahray
I've got...with me _____	J'ai... avec moi
	jhay... ahvehk mwah
– ...cartons of cigarettes ___	J'ai des cartouches de cigarettes
	jhay day kahrtoosh duh seegahreht
– ...bottles of... _____	J'ai des bouteilles de...
	jhay day bootehy duh...
– some souvenirs _____	J'ai quelques souvenirs
	jhay kehlkuh soovneer
These are personal _____ effects	Ce sont des affaires personnelles
	suh sawn day zahfehr pehrsonehl
These are not new _____	Ces affaires ne sont pas neuves
	say zahfehr nuh sawn pah nuhv
Here's the receipt _____	Voici la facture
	vwahsee lah fahktewr
This is for private use _____	C'est pour usage personnel
	seh poor ewzahjh pehrsonehl
How much import duty ____ do I have to pay?	Combien de droits d'importation dois-je payer?
	kawnbyahn duh drwah dahnpohrtasyawn dwah jhuh payay?
Can I go now? _____	Puis-je partir maintenant?
	pwee jhuh pahrteer mahntuhnohn?

🔵 .3 Luggage

Porter! _____	Porteur!
	portuhr!
Could you take this _____ luggage to...?	Voulez-vous porter ces bagages à... s'il vous plaît?
	voolay voo portay say bahgahjh ah... seel voo pleh?
How much do I _____ owe you?	Combien vous dois-je?
	kawnbyahn voo dwah jhuh?
Where can I find a _____ luggage trolley?	Où puis-je trouver un chariot pour les bagages?
	oo pwee jhuh troovay uhn shahryoa poor lay bahgahjh?
Could you store this _____ luggage for me?	Puis-je mettre ces bagages en consigne?
	pwee jhuh mehtr say bahgahjh ohn kawnseenyuh?
Where are the luggage ____ lockers?	Où est la consigne automatique?
	oo eh lah kawnseenyuh oatoamahteek?
I can't get the locker _____ open	Je n'arrive pas à ouvrir la consigne
	jhuh nahreev pah zah oovreer lah kawnseenyuh
How much is it per item ___ per day?	Combien cela coûte-t-il par bagage par jour?
	kawnbyahn suhlah koot-uh teel pahr bahgahjh pahr jhoor?
This is not my bag/ _____ suitcase	Ce n'est pas mon sac/ma valise
	suh neh pah mawn sahk/mah vahleez

There's one item/bag/ ____ suitcase missing still	Il manque encore une chose/un sac/une valise	
	eel mohnk ohnkor ewn shoaz/uhn sahk/ewn vahleez	
My suitcase is damaged ___	Ma valise est abîmée	
	mah vahleez eh tahbeemay	

.4 Traffic signs

accès interdit à tous les véhicules	déviation	sens unique
no entry	**diversion**	**one-way traffic**
accotement non stabilisé	fin de...	serrez à droite
soft verge	**end of...**	**keep right**
allumez vos feux	fin d'allumage des feux	sortie
switch on lights	**end of need for lights**	**exit**
autoroute		sortie de camions
motorway	fin de chantier	**factory/works exit**
barrière de dégel	**end of road works**	interdiction de stationner
road closed	interdiction de dépasser	**no parking**
bison fûté	**no overtaking**	taxis
recommended route	interdiction de klaxonner	**taxi rank**
brouillard fréquent	**no horns**	travaux (sur...km)
beware fog	interdiction sauf riverains	**roadworks ahead**
cédez le passage	**access only**	véhicules lents
give way	limite de vitesse	**slow traffic**
chaussée à gravillons	**speed limit**	véhicules transportant des matières dangereuses
loose chippings	passage à niveau	
chaussée déformée	**level crossing**	**vehicles transporting dangerous substances**
uneven road surface	passage d'animaux	
chaussée glissante	**animals crossing**	verglas fréquent
slippery road	passage pour piétons	**ice on road**
circulation alternée	**pedestrian crossing**	virages sur...km
alternate priority	péage	**bends for...km**
danger	**toll**	vitesse limite
danger	poids lourds	**maximum speed**
carrefour dangereux	**heavy goods vehicles**	zone bleue
dangerous crossing	rappel	**parking disc required**
danger priorité à droite	**reminder**	zone piétonne
priority to vehicles from right	remorques et semi-remorques	**pedestrian zone**
descente dangereuse	**lorries and articulated lorries**	
steep hill		

.5 The car

See the diagram on page 51.

● **Particular traffic regulations:**
– maximum speed for cars:
  130km/h on toll roads
  110km/h on other motorways
  90km/h outside town centres
  60km/h in town centres
– give way: all traffic from the right has the right of way, including slow
  vehicles, except for major roads.

.6 The petrol station

● **Petrol is more expensive** in France so it is advisable to fill up
before leaving the UK.

How many kilometres to the next petrol station, please?	Il y a combien de kilomètres jusqu'à la prochaine station-service?
	eel ee yah kawnbyahn duh keeloamehtr jhewskah lah proshehn stasyawn sehrvees?
I would like...litres of..., please	Je voudrais ... litres
	jhuh voodreh ... leetr
– 4-star	Je voudrais ... litres de super
	jhuh voodreh ... leetr duh sewpehr
– leaded	Je voudrais ... litres d'essence ordinaire
	jhuh voodreh ... leetr dehssohns ohrdeenehr
– unleaded	Je voudrais ... litres d'essence sans plomb
	jhuh voodreh ... leetr dehssohns sohn plawn
– diesel	Je voudrais ... litres de gazoil
	jhuh voodreh ... leetr duh gahzwahl
I would like...francs worth of petrol, please.	Je voudrais pour ... francs d'essence s'il vous plaît
	jhuh voodreh poor ... frohn dehssohns seel voo pleh
Fill it up, please	Le plein s'il vous plaît
	luh plahn seel voo pleh
Could you check...?	Vous voulez contrôler...?
	voo voolay kawntroalay...?
– the oil level	Vous voulez contrôler le niveau d'huile?
	voo voolay kawntroalay luh neevoa dweel?
– the tyre pressure	Vous voulez contrôler la pression des pneus?
	voo voolay kawntroalay lah prehsyawn day pnuh?
Could you change the oil, please?	Vous pouvez changer l'huile?
	voo poovay shohnjhay lweel?
Could you clean the windows/the windscreen, please?	Vous pouvez nettoyer les vitres/le pare-brise?
	voo poovay nehtwahyay lay veetr/luh pahrbreez?
Could you give the car a wash, please?	Vous pouvez faire laver la voiture?
	voo poovay fehr lahvay lah vwahtewr?

On the road

5

48

I'm having car trouble. Could you give me a hand?	Je suis en panne. Vous pouvez m'aider? *jhuh swee zohn pahnn. voo poovay mayday?*
I've run out of petrol	Je n'ai plus d'essence *jhuh neh plew dehssohns*
I've locked the keys in the car	J'ai laissé les clefs dans la voiture fermée *jhay layssay lay klay dohn lah vwahtewr fehrmay*
The car/motorbike/ moped won't start	La voiture/la moto/le vélomoteur ne démarre pas *lah vwahtewr/lah moatoa/luh vayloamotuhr nuh daymahr pah*
Could you contact the recovery service for me, please?	Vous pouvez m'appeler l'assistance routière? *voo poovay mahpuhlay lahseestohns rootyehr?*
Could you call a garage for me, please?	Vous pouvez m'appeler un garage? *voo poovay mahpuhlay uhn gahrahjh?*
Could you give me a lift to...?	Puis-je aller avec vous jusqu'à ...? *pwee jhahlay ahvehk voo jhewskah ...?*
– a garage/into town?	Puis-je aller avec vous jusqu'à un garage/la ville? *pwee jhahlay ahvehk voo jhewskah uhn gahrahjh/lah veel?*
– a phone booth?	Puis-je aller avec vous jusqu'à une cabine téléphonique? *pwee jhahlay ahvehk voo jhewskah ewn kahbeen taylayfoneek?*
– an emergency phone?	Puis-je aller avec vous jusqu'à un téléphone d'urgence? *pwee jhalay ahvehk voo jhewskah uhn taylayfon dewrjhohns?*
Can we take my bicycle/moped?	Est-ce que vous pouvez également prendre mon vélo(moteur)? *ehs kuh voo poovay aygahlmohn prohndr mawn vayloa(motuhr)?*
Could you tow me to a garage?	Vous pouvez me remorquer jusqu'à un garage? *voo poovay muh ruhmorkay jhewskah uhn gahrahjh?*
There's probably something wrong with...(See page 50)	Le ... a certainement quelque chose de défectueux *luh ... ah sehrtehnemohn kehlkuh shoaz duh dayfehktewuh*
Can you fix it?	Vous pouvez le réparer? *voo poovay luh raypahray?*
Could you fix my tyre?	Vous pouvez réparer mon pneu? *voo poovay raypahray mawn pnuh?*
Could you change this wheel?	Vous pouvez changer cette roue? *voo poovay shohnjhay seht roo?*
Can you fix it so it'll get me to...?	Vous pouvez le réparer pour que je puisse rouler jusqu'à...? *voo poovay luh raypahray poor kuh jhuh pwees roolay jhewskah...?*

The parts of a car
(the diagram shows the numbered parts)

1	battery	la batterie	*lah bahtree*
2	rear light	le feu arrière	*luh fuh ahryehr*
3	rear-view mirror	le rétroviseur	*luh raytroaveezuhr*
	reversing light	le phare de recul	*luh fahr duh ruhkewl*
4	aerial	l'antenne(f.)	*lohntehn*
	car radio	l'autoradio(m.)	*loatoarahdyoa*
5	petrol tank	le réservoir d'essence	*luh rayzehrvwahr dehssohns*
	inside mirror	le rétroviseur intérieur	*luh raytroaveezuhr ahntayryuhr*
6	sparking plugs	les bougies(f.)	*lay boojhee*
	fuel filter/pump	le filtre à carburant	*luh feeltr ah kahrbewrohn*
		la pompe à carburant	*lah pawnp ah kahrbewrohn*
7	wing mirror	le rétroviseur de côté	*luh raytroaveezuhr duh koatay*
8	bumper	le pare-chocs	*luh pahr shok*
	carburettor	le carburateur	*luh kahrbewrahtuhr*
	crankcase	le carter	*luh kahrtehr*
	cylinder	le cylindre	*luh seelahndr*
	ignition	l'allumage	*l'ahlewmahjh*
	warning light	la lampe témoin	*lah lohnp taymwahn*
	dynamo	la dynamo	*lah deenahmoa*
	accelerator	l'accélérateur	*lahksaylayrahtuhr*
	handbrake	le frein à main	*luh frahn ah mahn*
	valve	la soupape	*lah soopahp*
9	silencer	le silencieux	*luh seelohnsyuh*
10	boot	le coffre	*luh kofr*
11	headlight	le phare	*luh fahr*
	crank shaft	le vilebrequin	*luh veelbruhkahn*
12	air filter	le filtre à air	*luh feeltr ah ehr*
	fog lamp	le phare anti-brouillard	*luh fahr ohntee brooy-yahr*
13	engine block	le bloc moteur	*luh blok motuhr*
	camshaft	l'arbre à cames	*lahrbr ah kahm*
	oil filter/pump	le filtre à huile	*luh feeltr ah weel*
		la pompe à huile	*lah pawnp ah weel*
	dipstick	la jauge du niveau d'huile	*lah jhoajh dew neevoa dweel*
	pedal	la pédale	*lah paydahl*
14	door	la portière	*lah portyehr*
15	radiator	le radiateur	*luh rahdyahtuhr*
16	disc brake	le frein à disque	*luh frahn ah deesk*
	spare wheel	la roue de secours	*lah roo duh suhkoor*
17	indicator	le clignotant	*luh kleenyohtohn*
18	windscreen wiper	l'essuie-glace(m.)	*lehswee glahs*
19	shock absorbers	les amortisseurs(m.)	*lay zahmorteesuhr*
	sunroof	le toit ouvrant	*luh twah oovrohn*
	starter motor	le démarreur	*luh daymahruhr*
20	steering column	la colonne de direction	*lah kolon duh deerehksyawn*
	steering wheel	le volant	*luh volohn*

On the road

5

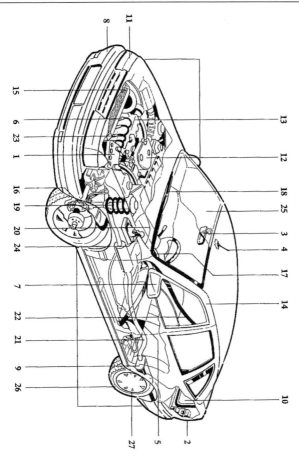

21	exhaust pipe	le tuyau d'échappement	*luh tweeyoa dayshahpmohn*
22	seat belt	la ceinture de sécurité	*lah sahntewr duh saykewreetay*
	fan	le ventilateur	*luh vohnteelahtuhr*
23	distributor cable	le câble distributeur	*luh kahbl deestreebewtuhr*
24	gear lever	le levier de vitesses	*luh luhvyay duh veetehs*
25	windscreen	le pare-brise	*luh pahrbreez*
	water pump	la pompe à eau	*lah pawnp ah oa*
26	wheel	la roue	*lah roo*
27	hubcap	l'enjoliveur	*lohnjholeevuhr*
	piston	le piston	*luh peestawn*

Which garage can _____ help me?	Quel garage pourrait m'aider?
	kehl gahrahjh pooreh mayday?
When will my car/bicycle __ be ready?	Quand est-ce que ma voiture/ma bicyclette sera prête?
	kohn tehs kuh mah vwahtewr/mah beeseekleht suhrah preht?
Can I wait for it here?_____	Je peux l'attendre ici?
	jhuh puh lahtohndr eesee?
How much will it cost? ____	Combien cela va coûter?
	kawnbyahn suhlah vah kootay?
Could you itemise _____ the bill?	Vous pouvez me détailler la note?
	voo poovay muh daytahyay lah not?
Can I have a receipt for ____ the insurance?	Puis-je avoir un reçu pour l'assurance?
	pwee jhahvwahr uhn ruhsew poor lahsewrohns?

 .8 The bicycle/moped

See the diagram on page 55.

● **Cycle paths** are rare in France. Bikes can be hired at tourist centres (*vélo tout terrain* = mountain bike). Not much consideration for bikes should be expected on the roads. The maximum speed for mopeds is 45km/h both inside and outside town centres. A helmet is compulsory.

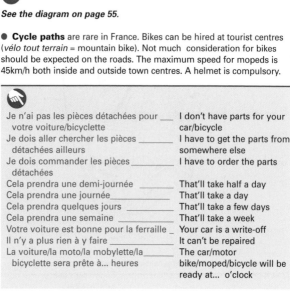

Je n'ai pas les pièces détachées pour ___ votre voiture/bicyclette	I don't have parts for your car/bicycle
Je dois aller chercher les pièces _____ détachées ailleurs	I have to get the parts from somewhere else
Je dois commander les pièces_____ détachées	I have to order the parts
Cela prendra une demi-journée _____	That'll take half a day
Cela prendra une journée_____	That'll take a day
Cela prendra quelques jours _____	That'll take a few days
Cela prendra une semaine _____	That'll take a week
Votre voiture est bonne pour la ferraille _	Your car is a write-off
Il n'y a plus rien à y faire _____	It can't be repaired
La voiture/la moto/la mobylette/la_____ bicyclette sera prête à... heures	The car/motor bike/moped/bicycle will be ready at... o'clock

I'd like to rent a...	J'aimerais louer un...
	jhehmuhreh looay uhn...
Do I need a (special) licence for that?	Me faut-il un permis spécial?
	muh foa teel uhn pehrmee spaysyal?
I'd like to rent the...for...	Je voudrais louer le/la...pour
	jhuh voodreh looay luh/lah...poor
– one day	Je voudrais louer le/la...pour une journée
	jhuh voodreh looay luh/lah...poor ewn jhoornay
– two days	Je voodreh louer le/la...pour deux jours
	jhuh voodreh looay luh/lah...poor duh jhoor
How much is that per day/week?	C'est combien par jour/semaine?
	seh kawnbyahn pahr jhoor/suhmehn?
How much is the deposit?	De combien est la caution?
	duh kawnbyahn eh lah koasyawn?
Could I have a receipt for the deposit?	Puis-je avoir un reçu pour la caution?
	pwee jhahvwahr uhn ruhsew poor lah koasyawn?
How much is the surcharge per kilometre?	Quel est le supplément par kilomètre?
	kehl eh luh sewplaymohn pahr keeloamehtr?
Does that include petrol?	Est-ce que l'essence est incluse?
	ehs kuh lehsohns eh tahnklewz?
Does that include insurance?	Est-ce que l'assurance est incluse?
	ehs kuh lahsewrohns eh tahnklewz?
What time can I pick the...up tomorrow?	Demain, à quelle heure puis-je venir chercher la...?
	duhmahn ah kehl uhr pwee jhuh vuhneer shehrshay lah...?
When does the...have to be back?	Quand dois-je rapporter la...?
	kohn dwah jhuh rahportay lah...?
Where's the petrol tank?	Où est le réservoir?
	oo eh luh rayzehrvwahr?
What sort of fuel does it take?	Quel carburant faut-il utiliser?
	kehl kahrbewrohn foa teel ewteeleezay?

The parts of a bicycle
(the diagram shows the numbered parts)

1 rear lamp	le feu arrière	*luh fuh ahryehr*
2 rear wheel	la roue arrière	*lah roo ahryehr*
3 (luggage) carrier	le porte-bagages	*luh port bahgahjh*
4 bicycle fork	la tête de fourche	*lah teht duh foorsh*
5 bell	la sonnette	*lah sohneht*
inner tube	la chambre à air	*lah shohnbr ah ehr*
tyre	le pneu	*luh pnuh*
6 crank	le pédalier	*luh paydahlyay*
7 gear change	le changement de vitesse	*luh shohnjhmohn duh veetehs*
wire	le fil (électrique)	*luh feel (aylehktreek)*
dynamo	la dynamo	*lah deenahmoa*
bicycle trailer	la remorque de bicyclette	*lah ruhmork duh beeseekleht*
frame	le cadre	*luh kahdr*
8 dress guard	le protège-jupe	*luh protehjh jhewp*
9 chain	la chaîne	*lah shehn*
chainguard	le carter	*luh kahrtehr*
padlock	l'antivol(m.)	*lohnteevol*
milometer	le compteur kilométrique	*luh kawntuhr keeloamaytreek*
child's seat	le siège-enfant	*luh syehjh ohnfohn*
10 headlamp	le phare	*luh fahr*
bulb	l'ampoule(f.)	*lohnpool*
11 pedal	la pédale	*lah paydahl*
12 pump	la pompe	*lah pawnp*
13 reflector	le réflecteur	*luh rayflehktuhr*
14 break blocks	les patins	*lay pahtahn*
15 brake cable	le câble de frein	*luh kahbl duh frahn*
16 wheel lock	le cadenas pour bicyclette	*lah kaduhnah poor beeseekleht*
17 carrier straps	le tendeur	*luh tohnduhr*
tachometer	le compteur de vitesse	*luh kawntuhr duh veetehs*
18 spoke	le rayon	*luh rayawn*
19 mudguard	le garde-boue	*luh gahrd boo*
20 handlebar	le guidon	*luh gueedawn*
21 chain wheel	le pignon	*luh peenyawn*
toe clip	le câle-pied	*luh kahl pyay*
22 crank axle	l'axe du pédalier(m.)	*lahx dew paydahlyay*
drum brake	le frein à tambour	*luh frahn ah tohnboor*
rim	la jante	*lah jhohnt*
23 valve	la valve	*lah vahlv*
24 valve tube	le raccord souple de la valve	*luh rahkor soopl duh lah vahlv*
25 gear cable	la chaîne du dérailleur	*lah shehn dew dayrahyuhr*
26 fork	la fourche	*lah foorsh*
27 front wheel	la roue avant	*lah roo ahvohn*
28 saddle	la selle	*lah sehl*

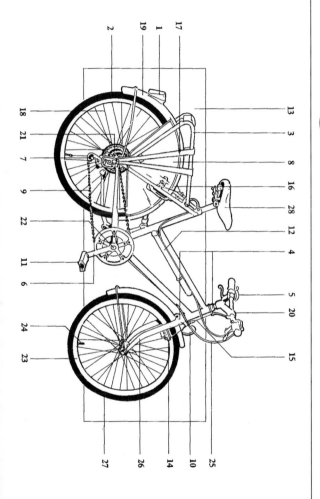

Where are you heading?	Où allez-vous?
	oo ahlay voo?
Can I come along?	Pouvez-vous m'emmener en voiture?
	poovay voo momuhnay ohn vwahtewr?
Can my boyfriend/ girlfriend come too?	Mon ami(e), peut-il/peut-elle venir avec nous?
	mawn nahmee, puh teel/puh tehl vuhneer ahvehk noo?
I'm trying to get to...	Je dois aller à...
	jhuh dwah zahlay ah...
Is that on the way to...?	C'est sur la route de...?
	seh sewr lah root duh...?
Could you drop me off...?	Vous pouvez me déposer...?
	voo poovay muh daypoazay...?
– here?	Vous pouvez me déposer ici?
	voo poovay muh daypoazay eesee?
– at the...exit?	Vous pouvez me déposer à la sortie vers...?
	voo poovay muh daypoazay ah lah sohrtee vehr...?
– in the centre?	Vous pouvez me déposer dans le centre?
	voo poovay muh daypoazay dohn luh sohntr?
– at the next roundabout?	Vous pouvez me déposer au prochain rond-point?
	voo poovay muh daypoazay oa proshahn rawnpwahn?
Could you stop here, please?	Voulez-vous arrêter ici s'il vous plaît?
	voolay voo zahrehtay eesee seel voo pleh?
I'd like to get out here	Je voudrais descendre ici
	jhuh voodreh duhsohndr eesee
Thanks for the lift	Merci pour la route
	mehrsee poor lah root

Public transport

6.1 In general 58

6.2 Questions to passengers 59

6.3 Tickets 60

6.4 Information 61

6.5 Aeroplanes 63

6.6 Trains 63

6.7 Taxis 63

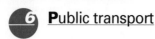

Public transport

6.1 In general

● **You can check** departure times by telephone or minitel - a computerised information system widely available in France (for example in many post offices). Tickets for buses and the *métro* (Paris, Lyon and Marseille) are cheaper when bought in a *carnet* (book of ten), available at kiosks near some bus stops, at newsagents and in *métro* stations.

Announcements

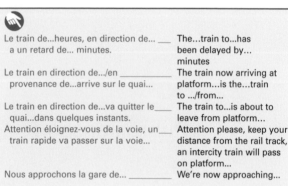

Le train de...heures, en direction de... a un retard de... minutes.	The...train to...has been delayed by... minutes
Le train en direction de.../en provenance de...arrive sur le quai...	The train now arriving at platform...is the...train to .../from...
Le train en direction de...va quitter le quai...dans quelques instants.	The train to...is about to leave from platform...
Attention éloignez-vous de la voie, un train rapide va passer sur la voie...	Attention please, keep your distance from the rail track, an intercity train will pass on platform...
Nous approchons la gare de...	We're now approaching...

Where does this train go to?	Où va ce train? *oo vah suh trahn?*
Does this boat go to...?	Ce bateau, va-t-il à...? *suh bahtoa, vah teel ah...?*
Can I take this bus to...?	Puis-je prendre ce bus pour aller à...? *pwee jhuh prondr suh bews poor ahlay ah...?*
Does this train stop at...?	Ce train s'arrête-t-il à...? *suh trahn sahreht-uh-teel ah...?*
Is this seat taken/free/reserved?	Est-ce que cette place est occupée/libre/réservée? *ehs kuh seht plahs eh tokewpay/leebr/rayzehrvay?*
I've booked...	J'ai réservé... *jhay rayzehrvay...*
Could you tell me where I have to get off for... ?	Voulez-vous me dire où descendre pour...? *voolay voo muh deer oo duhsohndr poor...?*
Could you let me know when we get to...?	Voulez-me prévenir lorsque nous serons à...? *voolay voo muh prayvuhneer lorskuh noo suhrawn zah...?*
Could you stop at the next stop, please?	Voulez-vous vous arrêter au prochain arrêt s'il vous plaît? *voolay voo voo zahrehtay oa proshahn nahreht seel voo pleh?*

Where are we now? _____	Où sommes-nous ici?
	oo som noo zeesee?
Do I have to get off _____ here?	Dois-je descendre ici?
	dwah jhuh duhsohndr eesee?
Have we already _____ passed...?	Avons-nous déjà dépassé...?
	ahvawn noo dayjhah daypahsay...?
How long have I been _____ asleep?	Combien de temps ai-je dormi?
	kawnbyahn duh tohn ay jhuh dormee?
How long does... _____ stop here?	Combien de temps...reste ici?
	kawnbyahn duh tohn...rehst eesee?
Can I come back on the ___ same ticket?	Puis-je revenir avec ce billet?
	pwee jhuh ruhvuhneer ahvehk suh beeyeh?
Can I change on this _____ ticket?	Puis-je prendre une correspondance avec ce billet?
	pwee jhuh prondr ewn korehspawndohns ahvehk suh beeyeh?
How long is this ticket _____ valid for?	Combien de temps ce billet reste-t-il valable?
	kawnbyahn duh tohn suh beeyeh rehst-uh-teel vahlahbl?
How much is the _____ supplement for the TGV (high speed train)?	Combien coûte le supplément pour le TGV?
	kawnbyahn koot luh sewplaymohn poor luh tayjhayvay?

6.2 Questions to passengers

Ticket types

Première classe ou deuxième classe? ___	First or second class?
Aller simple ou retour?_____	Single or return?
Fumeurs ou non fumeurs?_____	Smoking or non-smoking?
Côté fenêtre ou côté couloir? _____	Window or aisle?
A l'avant ou à l'arrière?_____	Front or back?
Place assise ou couchette? _____	Seat or couchette?
Au-dessus, au milieu ou au-dessous? ___	Top, middle or bottom?
Classe touriste ou classe affaires?_____	Tourist class or business class?
Une cabine ou un fauteuil? _____	Cabin or seat?
Une personne ou deux personnes? _____	Single or double?
Vous êtes combien de personnes à_____ voyager?	How many are travelling?

Destination

Où allez-vous?_____	Where are you travelling?
Quand partez-vous?_____	When are you leaving?
Votre...part à..._____	Your...leaves at...
Vous devez prendre une_____ correspondance	You have to change trains
Vous devez descendre à... _____	You have to get off at...

Vous devez passer par... _____	You have to travel via...
L'aller est le... _____	The outward journey is on...
Le retour est le... _____	The return journey is on...
Vous devez être à bord au plus tard à... _____	You have to be on board by...

On board

Votre billet s'il vous plaît _____	Your ticket, please
Votre réservation s'il vous plaît _____	Your reservation, please
Votre passeport s'il vous plaît _____	Your passport, please
Vous n'êtes pas à la bonne place _____	You're in the wrong seat
Vous êtes dans le mauvais... _____	You're on/in the wrong...
Cette place est réservée _____	This seat is reserved
Vous devez payer un supplément _____	You'll have to pay a supplement
Le...a un retard de...minutes _____	The...has been delayed by...minutes

6 .3 Tickets

Where can I...? _____	Où puis-je...?
	oo pwee jhuh...?
– buy a ticket? _____	Où puis-je acheter un billet?
	oo pwee jhahshtay uhn beeyeh?
– make a reservation? _____	Où puis-je réserver une place?
	oo pwee jhuh rayzehrvay ewn plahs?
– book a flight? _____	Où puis-je réserver un vol?
	oo pwee jhuh rayzehrvay uhn vol?
Could I have a...to...., please? _____	Puis-je avoir...en direction de...?
	pwee jhahvwahr...ohn deerehksyawn duh...?
– a single _____	Puis-je avoir un aller simple?
	pwee jhahvwahr uhn nahlay sahnpl?
– a return _____	Puis-je avoir un aller-retour?
	pwee jhahvwahr uhn nahlay ruhtoor?
first class _____	première classe
	pruhmyehr klahs
second class _____	deuxième classe
	duhzyehm klahs
tourist class _____	classe touriste
	klahs tooreest
business class _____	classe affaires
	klahs ahfehr
I'd like to book a seat/couchette/cabin	Je voudrais réserver une place assise/couchette/cabine
	jhuh voodrais rayzehrvay ewn plahs ahseez/koosheht/kahbeen
I'd like to book a berth in the sleeping car	Je voudrais réserver une place dans le wagon-lit
	jhuh voodreh rayzehrvay ewn plahs dohn luh vahgawnlee

60

top/middle/bottom _____	au-dessus/au milieu/au-dessous
	oaduhsew/ oa meelyuh/ oa duhsoo
smoking/no smoking _____	fumeurs/non fumeurs
	fewmuhr/ nawn fewmuhr
by the window _____	à côté de la fenêtre
	ah koatay duh lah fenehtr
single/double _____	une personne/deux personnes
	ewn pehrson/duh pehrson
at the front/back_____	à l'avant/à l'arrière
	ah lahvohn/ah lahryehr
There are...of us_____	Nous sommes...personnes
	noo som...pehrson
a car _____	une voiture
	ewn vwahtewr
a caravan _____	une caravane
	ewn kahrahvahnn
...bicycles_____	...bicyclettes
	...beeseekleht
Do you also have...? _____	Avez-vous aussi...?
	ahvay voo zoasee...?
– season tickets? _____	Avez-vous aussi une carte d'abonnement?
	ahvay voo zoasee ewn kahrt dahbonmohn?
– weekly tickets? _____	Avez-vous aussi une carte hebdomadaire?
	ahvay voo zoasee ewn kahrt ehbdomahdehr?
– monthly season _____ tickets?	Avez-vous aussi une carte mensuelle?
	ahvay voo zoasee ewn kahrt mohnsewehl?

6.4 Information

Where's? _____	Où se trouve...?
	oo suh troov...?
Where's the information ___ desk?	Où se trouve le bureau de renseignements?
	oo suh troov luh bewroa duh rohnsehnyuhmohn?
Where can I find a_____ timetable?	Où se trouvent les horaires des départs/des arrivées?
	oo se troov lay zorehr day daypahr/day zahreevay?
Where's the...desk? _____	Où se trouve la réception de...?
	oo se troov lah raysehpsyawn duh...?
Do you have a city map____ with the bus/the underground routes on it?	Avez-vous un plan du réseau des bus/du métro?
	ahvay voo zuhn plohn dew rayzoa day bews/dew maytroa?
Do you have a _____ timetable?	Avez-vous un horaire des arrivées et des départs?
	ahvay voo zuhn norehr day zahreevay ay day daypahr?
I'd like to confirm/_____ cancel/change my booking for...	Je veux confirmer/annuler/changer ma réservation pour...
	jhuh vuh kawnfeermay/ahnewlay/shohnjhay mah rayzehrvahsyawn poor...
Will I get my money_____ back?	Mon argent me sera rendu?
	mawn nahrjhohn muh suhrah rohndew?

Public transport

6

I want to go to... _____ How do I get there? (What's the quickest way there?)	Je dois aller à...Comment puis-je y aller (le plus vite possible)? *jhuh dwah zahlay ah...komohn pwee jhee ahlay (luh plew veet poseebl?)*
How much is a _____ single/return to...?	Combien coûte un aller simple/un aller-retour pour...? *kawnbyahn koot uhn nahlay sahnpl/uhn nahlay retoor poor...?*
Do I have to pay a_____ supplement?	Dois-je payer un supplément? *dwah jheuh payay uhn sewplaymohn?*
Can I interrupt my_____ journey with this ticket?	Puis-je interrompre mon voyage avec ce billet? *pwee jhahntayrawnpr mawn vwahyahjh ahvehk suh beeyeh?*
How much luggage _____ am I allowed?	J'ai droit à combien de bagages? *jhay drwah ah kawnbyahn duh bahgahjh?*
Does this...travel direct? ___	Ce...est direct? *suh...eh deerehkt?*
Do I have to change? _____ Where?	Dois-je changer? Où? *dwah jhuh shohnjhay? oo?*
Will this plane make any___ stopovers?	L'avion fait escale? *lahvyawn feh tehskahl?*
Does the boat call in at ____ any ports on the way?	Est-ce que le bateau fait escale dans un port pendant son trajet? *ehs kuh luh bahtoa feh tehskahl dohn zuhn por pohndohn sawn trahjheh?*
Does the train/ _____ bus stop at...?	Est-ce que le train/le bus s'arrête à...? *ehs kuh luh trahn/luh bews sahreht ah...?*
Where should I get off? ____	Où dois-je descendre? *oo dwah jhuh duhsohndr?*
Is there a connection _____ to...?	Y a-t-il une correspondance pour...? *ee yah teel ewn korehspawndohns poor...?*
How long do I have to _____ wait?	Combien de temps dois-je attendre? *kawnbyahn duh tohn dwah jhahtohndr?*
When does...leave?_____	Quand part...? *kohn pahr...?*
What time does the _____ first/next/last...leave?	A quelle heure part le premier/prochain/dernier...? *ah kehl uhr pahr luh pruhmyay/proshahn/dehrnyay...?*
How long does...take? _____	Combien de temps met le...? *kawnbyahn duh tohn meh luh...?*
What time does...arrive _____ in...?	A quelle heure arrive...à...? *ah kehl uhr ahreev...ah...?*
Where does the...to... _____ leave from?	D'où part le...pour...? *doo pahr luh...poor...?*
Is this...to...? _____	Est-ce le...pour...? *ehs luh...poor...?*

.5 Aeroplanes

● **At arrival** at a French airport (*aéroport*), you will find the following signs:

arrivée	départ
arrivals	**departures**

.6 Trains

● **The rail network** is extensive. *La Société Nationale des Chemins de Fer Français (SNCF)* is responsible for the national rail traffic. Besides the normal train, there is also *le Train à Grande Vitesse (TGV)* for which you will have to pay a supplement. Reservations before departure are cheaper. The *TGV* operates between the larger cities: Paris, Lyon, Marseille and Nice. A train ticket has to be stamped (*composté*) before departure.

.7 Taxis

● **In nearly all** large cities, there are plenty of taxis. French taxis have no fixed colour. Virtually all taxis have a meter. In the smaller towns, it is usual to agree a fixed price in advance. A supplement is usual for luggage, a journey at night, on a Sunday or Bank holiday, or to an airport. It is advisable in large cities such as Paris and Lyon to check that the meter has been returned to zero at the start of the journey.

libre	occupé	station de taxis
for hire	**booked**	**taxi rank**

Taxi! _____	Taxi!
	tahksee!
Could you get me a taxi, ___ please?	Pouvez-vous m'appeler un taxi?
	poovay voo mahpuhlay uhn tahksee?
Where can I find a taxi_____ around here?	Où puis-je prendre un taxi par ici?
	oo pwee jhuh prohndr uhn tahksee pahr eesee?
Could you take me to..., ___ please?	Conduisez-moi à...s'il vous plaît.
	kawndweezay mwah ah...seel voo pleh
– this address _____	Conduisez-moi à cette adresse.
	kawndweezay mwah ah seht ahdrehs
– the...hotel _____	Conduisez-moi à l'hôtel...
	kawndweezay mwah ah loatehl...
– the town/city centre_____	Conduisez-moi dans le centre.
	kawndweezay mwah dohn luh sohntr
– the station _____	Conduisez-moi à la gare.
	kawndweezay mwah ah lah gahr
– the airport _____	Conduisez-moi à l'aéroport.
	kawndweezay mwah ah layroapor.
How much is the _____ trip to...?	Combien coûte un trajet jusqu'à...?
	kawnbyahn koot uhn trahjheh jhewskah...?

Public transport

How far is it to...?	C'est combien de kilomètres jusqu'à...?
	seh kawnbyahn duh keeloamehtr jhewskah...?
Could you turn on the meter, please?	Voulez-vous mettre le compteur en marche s'il vous plaît?
	voolay voo mehtr luh kawntuhr ohn mahrsh seel voo pleh?
I'm in a hurry	Je suis pressé.
	jhuh swee prehssay
Could you speed up/slow down a little?	Vous pouvez rouler plus vite/plus lentement?
	voo poovay roolay plew veet/plew lohntmohn?
Could you take a different route?	Vous pouvez prendre une autre route?
	voo poovay prohndr ewn oatr root?
I'd like to get out here, please	Je voudrais descendre ici
	jhuh voodreh duhsohndr eesee
You have to go...here	Là vous allez...
	lah voo zahlay...
You have to go straight on here	Là vous allez tout droit
	lah voo zahlay too drwah
You have to turn left here	Là vous allez à gauche
	lah voo zahlay zah goash
You have to turn right here	Là vous allez à droite
	lah voo zahlay zah drwaht
This is it	C'est ici
	seht eesee
Could you wait a minute for me, please?	Vous pouvez m'attendre un instant?
	voo poovay mahtohndr uhn nahnstohn?

Overnight accommodation

7.1 General 66

7.2 Camping 67
Camping equipment 68–69

**7.3 Hotel/B&B/apartment/
holiday house** 70

7.4 Complaints 72

7.5 Departure 73

Overnight accommodation

7 .1 General

● **There is great variety** of overnight accommodation in France.
Hôtels: stars indicate the degree of comfort; from five stars, the most luxurious, to one star, very simple. Beside the star one often finds the letters *NN-Nouvelles Normes* (new classifications). This means that the star-classification is up-to-date. Most hotels offer *pension complète* (full board) or *demi-pension* (half board).
Auberges et Relais de campagne: luxurious; splendid view and lots of rest are guaranteed.
Châteaux, Hôtels de France and *Vieilles Demeures:* a very expensive tourist residence, always within a castle, country manor or an historic building.
Logis de France: an organisation with many hotels with one or two stars, mostly outside the town centre. The hotel can be recognised by the yellow signboards with a green fireplace and the words: *logis de France.*
Motels: especially along the motorway, comparable to UK motels.
Auberges de jeunesse (youth hostel): the number of nights is restricted to between three and seven.
Camping: free camping is allowed, except for forest areas with the sign *attention au feu* (fire hazard). Not all camping sites are guarded.
Refuges et gîtes d'étape (mountain huts): in the Alps and Pyrenees. These huts are owned by the *Club Alpin Français* and are inexpensive.

Combien de temps voulez-vous_____ rester?	How long will you be staying?
Voulez-vous remplir ce questionnaire ___ s'il vous plaît?	Fill out this form, please
Puis-je avoir votre passeport? _____	Could I see your passport?
Vous devez payer un acompte _____	I'll need a deposit
Vous devez payer à l'avance _____	You'll have to pay in advance

My name's...I've made_____ a reservation over the phone/by mail	Mon nom est...J'ai réservé une place par téléphone/par lettre *mawn nawn eh...jhay rayzehrvay ewn plahs pahr taylayfon/pahr lehtr*
How much is it per_____ night/week/ month?	Quel est le prix pour une nuit/une semaine/un mois? *kehl eh luh pree poor ewn nwee/ewn suhmehn/uhn mwah?*
We'll be staying at _____ least...nights/weeks	Nous restons au moins...nuits/semaines. *noo rehstawn zoa mwhan...nwee/suhmehn*
We don't know yet _____	Nous ne le savons pas encore exactement. *noo nuh luh sahvawn pah zohnkor ehgzahktmohn*
Do you allow pets _____ (cats/dogs)?	Est-ce que les animaux domestiques(chiens/chats) sont admis? *ehs kuh lay zahneemoa domehsteek(shyahn/shah) sawn tahdmee?*

66

What time does the _____ gate/door open/close?	A quelle heure on ouvre/ferme le portail/la porte? *ah keh uhr awn noovr/fehrm luh portahy/lah port?*
Could you get me _____ a taxi, please?	Vous voulez m'appeler un taxi? *voo voolay mahplay uhn tahksee?*
Is there any mail _____ for me?	Y a-t-il du courrier pour moi? *ee yah teel dew kooryay poor mwah?*

7 .2 Camping

See the diagram on page 69

Vous pouvez vous-même choisir _____ votre emplacement.	You can pick your own site
Votre emplacement vous sera attribué. _	You'll be allocated a site
Voici votre numéro d'emplacement. _____	This is your site number
Vous devez coller ceci sur votre _____ voiture.	Stick this on your car, please
Ne perdez surtout pas cette carte. _____	Please don't lose this card

Where's the manager? _____	Où est le gardien? *oo eh luh gahrdyahn?*
Are we allowed to _____ camp here?	Pouvons-nous camper ici? *poovawn noo kohnpay eesee?*
There are...of us and _____ ...tents	Nous sommes...personnes et nous avons...tentes. *noo som...pehrson ay nooz ahvawn...tohnt*
Can we pick our _____ own place?	Pouvons-nous choisir nous-mêmes un emplacement? *poovawn noo shwahzeer noo mehm uhn nohnplahsmohn?*
Do you have a quiet _____ spot for us?	Avez-vous un endroit calme pour nous? *ahvay voo zuhn nohndrwah kahlm poor noo?*
Do you have any other _____ pitches available?	Vous n'avez pas d'autre emplacement libre? *voo nahvay pah doatr ohnplahsmohn leebr?*
It's too windy/sunny/ _____ shady here.	Ici il y a trop de vent/soleil/ombre. *eesee eel ee yah troa duh vohn/sohlehy/awnbr*
It's too crowded here _____	Il y a trop de monde ici. *eel ee yah troa duh mawnd eesee*
The ground's too _____ hard/uneven	Le sol est trop dur/irrégulier. *luh sohl eh troa dewr/eeraygewlyay*
Do you have a level _____ spot for the camper/ caravan/folding caravan?	Avez-vous un endroit plat pour le camping-car/la caravane/la caravane pliante? *ahvay voo zuhn nohndrwah plah poor luh kohnpeeng kahr/lah kahrahvahnn/lah kahrahvahnn plyohnt?*
Could we have _____ adjoining pitches?	Pouvons-nous être l'un à côté de l'autre? *poovawn noo zehtr luhn nah koatay duh loatr?*

Overnight accommodation

Camping equipment
(the diagram shows the numbered parts)

luggage space	l'espace (f.) bagages	*lehspahs bahgajh*
can opener	l'ouvre-boîte (m.)	*loovr bwaht*
butane gas bottle	la bouteille de butane	*lah bootehy duh bewtahnn*
1 pannier	la sacoche de vélo	*lah sahkosh duh vayloa*
2 gas cooker	le réchaud à gaz	*luh rayshoa ah gahz*
3 groundsheet	le tapis de sol	*luh tahpee duh sol*
mallet	le marteau	*luh mahrtoa*
hammock	le hamac	*luh ahmahk*
4 jerry can	le bidon d'essence	*luh beedawn dehssohns*
campfire	le feu de camp	*luh fuh duh kohn*
5 folding chair	la chaise pliante	*lah shehz plyohnt*
6 insulated picnic box	la glacière	*lah glahsyehr*
ice pack	le bac à glaçons	*luh bah kah glasawn*
compass	la boussole	*lah boosol*
wick	la mèche	*lah mehsh*
corkscrew	le tire-bouchon	*luh teer booshawn*
7 airbed	le matelas pneumatique	*luh mahtuhlah pnuhmahteek*
8 airbed plug	le bouchon du matelas pneumatique	*luh booshawn dew mahtuhlah pnemahteek*
pump	la pompe à air	*lah pawnp ah ehr*
9 awning	l'auvent (m.)	*loavohn*
10 karimat	la natte	*lah naht*
11 pan	la casserole	*lah kahsrol*
12 pan handle	la poignée de casserole	*lah pwahnnyay duh kahsrol*
primus stove	le réchaud à pétrole	*luh rayshoa ah paytrol*
zip	la fermeture éclair	*lah fehrmuhtewr ayklehr*
13 backpack	le sac à dos	*luh sahk ah doa*
14 guy rope	la corde	*lah kord*
sleeping bag	le sac de couchage	*luh sahk duh kooshajh*
15 storm lantern	la lanterne-tempête	*lah lohntehrn-tohnpeht*
camp bed	le lit de camp	*luh lee duh kohn*
table	la table	*lah tahbl*
16 tent	la tente	*lah tohnt*
17 tent peg	le piquet	*luh peekeh*
18 tent pole	le mât	*luh mah*
vacuum flask	la bouteille thermos	*lah bootehy tehrmos*
19 water bottle	la gourde	*lah goord*
clothes peg	la pince à linge	*lah pahns ah lahnjh*
windbreak	le pare-vent	*luh pahrvohn*
20 torch	la torche électrique	*lah torsh aylehktreek*
pocket knife	le canif	*luh kahneef*

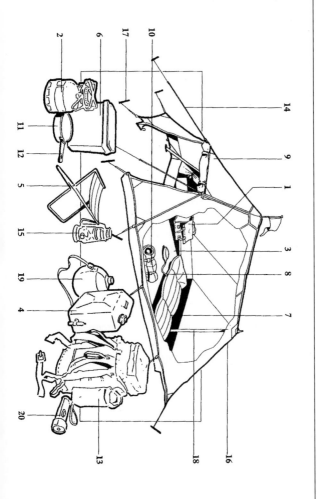

Can we park the car _____ next to the tent?	La voiture, peut-elle être garée à côté de la tente? *lah vwahtewr, puh tehl ehtr gahray ah koatay duh lah tohnt?*
How much is it per _____ person/tent/caravan/car?	Quel est le prix par personne/tente/caravane/voiture? *kehl eh luh pree pahr pehrson/tohnt/kahrahvahnn/vwahtewr?*
Are there any...? _____	Y a-t-il...? *ee yah teel...?*
– any hot showers? _____	Y a-t-il des douches avec eau chaude? *ee yah teel day doosh ahvehk oa shoad?*
– washing machines? _____	Y a-t-il des machines à laver? *ee yah teel day mahsheen ah lahvay?*
Is there a...on the site? _____	Y a-t-il un...sur le terrain? *ee ayh teel uhn...sewr luh tehrahn?*
Is there a children's _____ play area on the site?	Y a-t-il un terrain de jeux pour les enfants? *ee yah teel uhn tehrahn duh jhuh poor lay zohnfohn?*
Are there covered _____ cooking facilities on the site?	Y a-t-il un endroit couvert pour cuisiner? *ee yah teel uhn nohndrwa koovehr poor kweezeenay?*
Can I rent a safe here? _____	Puis-je louer un coffre-fort ici? *pwee jhuh looay uhn kofr for eesee?*
Are we allowed to _____ barbecue here?	Pouvons-nous faire un barbecue? *poovawn noo fehr uhn bahrbuhkew?*
Are there any power _____ points?	Y a-t-il des prises électriques? *ee yah teel day preez aylehktreek?*
Is there drinking water? _____	Y a-t-il de l'eau potable? *ee yah teel duh loa potabl?*
When's the rubbish _____ collected?	Quand vide-t-on les poubelles? *kohn veed-uh-tawn lay poobehl?*
Do you sell gas bottles _____ (butane gas/propane gas)?	Vendez-vous des bouteilles de gaz (butane/propane)? *vohnday voo day bootehuhy duh gahz (bewtahnn/propahnn)?*

7 .3 Hotel/B&B/apartment/holiday house

Do you have a _____ single/double room available?	Avez-vous une chambre libre pour une personne/deux personnes? *ahvay voo zewn shohnbr leebr poor ewn pehrson/duh pehrson?*
per person/per room _____	par personne/par chambre *pahr pehrson/pahr shohnbr*
Does that include _____ breakfast/lunch/dinner?	Est-ce que le petit déjeuner/le déjeuner/le dîner est compris? *ehs kuh luh puhtee dayjhuhnay/luh dayjhuhnay/luh deenay eh kawnpree?*
Could we have two _____ adjoining rooms?	Pouvons-nous avoir deux chambres contiguës? *poovawn noo zahvwahr duh shohnbr kawnteegew?*
with/without _____ toilet/bath/shower	avec/sans toilettes/salle de bains/douche *ahvehk/sohn twahleht/sahl duh bahn/doosh*

(not) facing the street _____	(pas) du côté rue
	(pah) dew koatay rew
with/without a view _____	avec/sans vue sur la mer
of the sea	*ahvehk/sohn vew sewr lah mehr*
Is there...in the hotel? _____	Y a-t-il...dans l'hôtel?
	ee yah teel...dohn loatehl?
Is there a lift in the _____	Y a-t-il un ascenseur dans l'hôtel?
hotel?	*ee yah teel uhn nahsohnsuhr dohn loatehl?*
Do you have room _____	Y a-t-il un service de chambre dans
service?	l'hôtel?
	ee yah teel uhn sehrvees duh shohnbr dohn loatehl?

Les toilettes et la douche sont au _____ même étage/dans votre chambre	You can find the toilet and shower on the same floor/en suite
De ce côté, s'il vous plaît _____	This way, please
Votre chambre est au...étage, c'est le _____ numéro...	Your room is on the... floor, number...

Could I see the room? _____	Puis-je voir la chambre?
	pwee jhuh vwhar lah shohnbr?
I'll take this room _____	Je prends cette chambre.
	jhuh prohn seht shohnbr
We don't like this one _____	Celle-ci ne nous plaît pas.
	sehl see nuh noo pleh pah
Do you have a larger/ _____	Avez-vous une chambre plus
less expensive room?	grande/moins chère?
	avay voo zewn shohnbr plew grohnd/mwahn shehr?
Could you put in a cot? _____	Pouvez-vous y ajouter un lit d'enfant?
	poovay voo zee ahjhootay uhn lee dohnfohn?
What time's breakfast? _____	A quelle heure est le petit déjeuner?
	ah kehl uhr eh luh puhtee dayjhuhnay?
Where's the dining _____	Où est la salle à manger?
room?	*oo eh lah sahl ah mohnjhay?*
Can I have breakfast _____	Puis-je prendre le petit déjeuner dans la
in my room?	chambre?
	pwee jhuh prohndr luh puhtee dayjhuhnay dohn lah shohnbr?
Where's the emergency _____	Où est la sortie de secours/l'escalier de
exit/fire escape?	secours?
	oo eh lah sortee duh suhkoor/lehskahlyay duh suhkoor?
Where can I park my _____	Où puis-je garer ma voiture (en sécurité)?
car (safely)?	*oo pwee jhuh gahray mah vwahtewr (ohn saykewreetay)?*
The key to room..., _____	La clef de la chambre..., s'il vous plaît.
please	*lah klay duh lah shohnbr...,seel voo pleh*
Could you put this in _____	Puis-je mettre ceci dans votre coffre-fort?
the safe, please?	*pwee jhuh mehtr suhsee dohn votr kofr for?*

7 Overnight accommodation

Could you wake me _____ at...tomorrow?	Demain voulez-vous me réveiller à...heures? *duhmahn voolay voo muh rayvehyay ah...uhr?*
Could you find a _____ babysitter for me?	Pouvez-vous m'aider à trouver une baby-sitter? *poovay voo mayday ah troovay ewn behbee seetehr?*
Could I have an extra _____ blanket?	Puis-je avoir une couverture supplémentaire? *pwee jhahvwahr ewn koovehrtewr sewplaymohntehr?*
What days do the _____ cleaners come in?	Quels jours fait-on le ménage? *kehl jhoor feh tawn luh maynahjh?*
When are the sheets/ _____ towels/tea towels changed?	Quand change-t-on les draps/les serviettes-éponge/les torchons? *kohn shohnjh tawn lay drah/lay sehrvyeht aypawnjh/lay tohrshawn?*

7.4 Complaints

We can't sleep for _____ the noise	Nous ne pouvons pas dormir à cause du bruit *noo nuh poovawn pah dormeer ah koaz dew brwee*
Could you turn the _____ radio down, please?	Est-ce que vous pouvez baisser un peu la radio? *ehs kuh voo poovay behssay uhn puh lah rahdyoa?*
We're out of toilet paper ___	Il n'y a plus de papier hygiénique *eel nee yah plew duh pahpyay eejhyayneek*
There aren't any.../there's ___ not enough...	Il n'y a pas de/pas assez de... *eel nee yah pah duh/pah zahssay duh...*
The bed linen's dirty _____	La literie est sale *lah leetree eh sahl*
The room hasn't been _____ cleaned	La chambre n'a pas été nettoyée *lah shohnbr nah pah zayatay nehtwahyay*
The kitchen is not clean ___	La cuisine n'est pas propre *lah kweezeen neh pah propr*
The kitchen utensils are ___ dirty	Les ustensiles de cuisine sont sales *lay zewstohnseel duh kweezeen sawn sahl*
The heater's not _____ working	Le chauffage ne marche pas *luh shoafajh nuh marsh pah*
There's no (hot) _____ water/electricity	Il n'y a pas d'eau(chaude)/d'électricité *eel nee yah pah doa(shoad)/daylehktreeseetay*
...is broken _____	...est cassé *...eh kahssay*
Could you have that _____ seen to?	Vous pouvez le faire réparer? *voo poovay luh fehr raypahray?*
Could I have another _____ room/site?	Puis-je avoir une autre chambre/un autre emplacement pour la tente? *pwee jhuh ahvwahr ewn oatr shohnbr/uhn noatr ohnplasmohn poor lah tohnt?*
The bed creaks terribly ___	Le lit grince énormément *luh lee grahns aynormaymohn*
The bed sags _____	Le lit s'affaisse *luh lee sahfehs*

Overnight accommodation

7

There are bugs/insects in our room	Nous sommes incommodés par des bestioles/insectes
	noo som zahnkomoday pahr day behstyol/day zahnsehkt
This place is full of mosquitos	C'est plein de moustiques ici
	seh plahn duh moosteek eesee
– cockroaches	C'est plein de cafards
	seh plahn duh kahfahr

.5 Departure

See also 8.2 Settling the bill

I'm leaving tomorrow. Could I settle my bill, please?	Je pars demain. Puis-je payer maintenant?
	jhuh pahr duhmahn. pwee jhuh payay mahntuhnohn?
What time should we vacate?	A quelle heure devons-nous quitter la chambre?
	ah kehl uhr duhvawn noo keetay lah shohnbr?
Could I have my passport back, please?	Pouvez-vous me rendre mon passeport?
	poovay voo muh rohndr mawn pahspor?
We're in a terrible hurry	Nous sommes très pressés
	noo som treh prehssay
Could you forward my mail to this address?	Pouvez-vous faire suivre mon courrier à cette adresse?
	poovay voo fehr sweevr mawn kooryay ah seht ahdrehs?
Could we leave our luggage here until we leave?	Nos valises peuvent rester ici jusqu'à notre départ?
	noa vahleez puhv rehstay eesee jhewskah notr daypahr?
Thanks for your hospitality	Merci pour votre hospitalité
	mehrsee poor votr ospeetahleetay

7

Overnight accommodation

Money matters

8.1 Banks   75

8.2 Settling the bill   76

Money matters

● **In general, banks are open** to the public between 9am and 12 noon and between 2 and 4pm; they are closed on Saturdays. In large city centres they are often open at lunchtime. In tourist areas, the bank can be closed on Monday morning and open on Saturday morning. To exchange currency a proof of identity is usually required. The sign *Change* indicates that money can be exchanged. Hotels and railway stations may also offer exchange facilities but at less favourable rates.

8 .1 **B**anks

Where can I find a_____ bank/an exchange office around here?	Où puis-je trouver une banque/un bureau de change par ici? *oo pwee jhuh troovay ewn bohnk/uhn bewroa duh shohnjh pahr eesee?*
Where can I cash this_____ traveller's cheque/giro cheque?	Où puis-je encaisser ce chèque de voyage/chèque postal? *oo pwee jhuh ohnkehssay suh shehk duh vwahyajh/shehk postahl?*
Can I cash this...here? _____	Puis-je encaisser ce...ici? *pweejh ohnkehssay suh...eesee?*
Can I withdraw money_____ on my credit card here?	Puis-je retirer de l'argent avec une carte de crédit? *pwe jhuh ruhteeray duh lahrjhohn ahvehk ewn kahrt duh kraydee?*
What's the minimum/_____ maximum amount?	Quel est le montant minimum/maximum? *kehl eh luh mohntohn meeneemuhm/mahxseemuhm?*
Can I take out less_____ than that?	Puis-je retirer moins? *pwe jhuh ruhteeray mwahn?*
I've had some money_____ transferred here. Has it arrived yet?	J'ai fait virer de l'argent par mandat télégraphique. Est-ce déjà arrivé? *jhay feh veeray duh lahrjhohn pahr mohndah taylaygrahfeek. ehs dayjhah ahreevay?*
These are the details _____ of my bank in the UK	Voici les coordonnées de ma banque au Royaume-Uni *vwahsee lay koa-ordonay duh mah bohnk oa rwahyoam ewnee*
This is my bank/giro_____ account number	Voici mon numéro de compte bancaire/numéro de chèque postal *vwahsee mawn newmayroa duh kawnt bohnkehr/newmayroa duh shehk postahl*
I'd like to change _____ some money	J'aimerais changer de l'argent *jhehmuhreh shohnjhay duh lahrjhohn*
– pounds into... _____	des livres sterling contre... *day leevr stehrleeng kawntr...*
– dollars into... _____	des dollars contre... *day dolahr kawntr...*
What's the exchange _____ rate?	Le change est à combien? *luh shohnjh eh tah kawnbyahn?*
Could you give me _____ some small change with it?	Pouvez-vous me donner de la monnaie? *poovay voo muh donay duh lah moneh?*
This is not right _____	Ce n'est pas exact *suh neh pah zehgzah.*

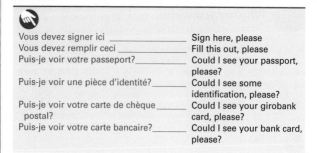

Vous devez signer ici _____	Sign here, please
Vous devez remplir ceci _____	Fill this out, please
Puis-je voir votre passeport?_____	Could I see your passport, please?
Puis-je voir une pièce d'identité? _____	Could I see some identification, please?
Puis-je voir votre carte de chèque _____ postal?	Could I see your girobank card, please?
Puis-je voir votre carte bancaire?_____	Could I see your bank card, please?

8 .2 **S**ettling the bill

Could you put it on_____ my bill?	Pouvez-vous le mettre sur mon compte?
	poovay voo luh mehtr sewr mawn kawnt?
Does this amount _____ include service?	Est-ce que le service est compris(dans la somme)?
	ehs kuh luh sehrvees eh kawnpree(dohn lah som)?
Can I pay by...?_____	Puis-je payer avec...?
	pwee jhuh payay ahvehk...?
Can I pay by credit card?___	Puis-je payer avec une carte de crédit?
	pwee jhuh payay ahvehk ewn kahrt duh kraydee?
Can I pay by traveller's _____ cheque?	Puis-je payer avec un chèque de voyage?
	pwee jhuh payay ahvehk uhn shehk duh vwahyajh?
Can I pay with foreign _____ currency?	Puis-je vous payer en devises étrangères?
	pwee jhuh voo payay ohn duhveez aytrohnjhehr?
You've given me too _____ much/you haven't given me enough change	Vous m'avez trop/pas assez rendu
	voo mahvay troa/pah zahssay rohndew
Could you check this _____ again, please?	Voulez-vous refaire le calcul?
	voolay voo ruhfehr luh kahlkewl?
Could I have a receipt, _____ please?	Pouvez-vous me donner un reçu/le ticket de caisse?
	poovay voo muh donay uhn ruhsew/luh teekeh duh kehs?
I don't have enough _____ money on me	Je n'ai pas assez d'argent sur moi
	jhuh nay pah zahssay dahrjhohn sewr mwah
This is for you _____	Voilà, c'est pour vous
	vwahlah seh poor voo
Keep the change _____	Gardez la monnaie
	gahrday lah moneh

Nous n'acceptons pas les cartes de _____ crédit/les chèques de voyage/les devises étrangères	We don't accept credit cards/traveller's cheques/foreign currency

Post and telephone

9.1 Post   78

9.2 Telephone   79

Post and telephone

9 .1 Post

For giros, see 8 Money matters

● **Post offices** are open from Monday to Friday between 8am and
7pm. In smaller towns the post office closes at lunch. On Saturday they
are open between 8am and 12 noon.
Stamps *(timbres)* are also available in a *tabac* (café that sells cigarettes
and matches).
The yellow letter box *(boîte aux lettres)* in the street and in the post
office has two rates: *tarif normal* (normal rate) and *tarif réduit* (reduced
rate).
It is advisable to opt for the *tarif normal*.

colis	télégrammes	timbres
parcels	telegrams	stamps
mandats		
money orders		

Where's...?	Où est...?
	oo eh...?
Where's the post office?	Où est la poste?
	oo eh lah post?
Where's the main post office?	Où est la poste centrale?
	oo eh lah post sohntrahl?
Where's the postbox?	Où est la boîte aux lettres?
	oo eh lah bwaht oa lehtr?
Which counter should I go to...?	Quel est le guichet pour...?
	kehl eh luh gueesheh poor...?
– to send a fax	Quel est le guichet pour les fax?
	kehl eh luh gueesheh poor lay fahx?
– to change money	Quel est le guichet pour changer de l'argent?
	kehl eh luh gueesheh poor shohnjhay duh lahrjhohn?
-to change giro cheques	Quel est le guichet pour les chèques postaux?
	kehl eh luh gueesheh poor lay shehk postoa?
-for a telegraph money order?	Quel est le guichet pour faire un virement postal télégraphique?
	kehl eh luh gueesheh poor fehr uhn veermohn postahl taylaygrahfeek?
Poste restante	Poste restante
	post rehstohnt
Is there any mail for me? My name's...	Y a-t-il du courrier pour moi? Mon nom est...
	ee yah teel dew kooryay poor mwah? mawn nawn eh...

Stamps

What's the postage _____ for a...to...?	Combien faut-il sur une…pour...? *kawnbyahn foa teel sewr ewn…poor...?*
Are there enough _____ stamps on it?	Y a-t-il suffisamment de timbres dessus? *ee yah teel sewfeezahmohn duh tahnbr duhsew?*
I'd like... ...franc stamps_____	Je voudrais…timbres à... *jhuh voodreh…tahnbr ah...*
I'd like to send this... _____	Je veux envoyer ce/cette… *jhuh vuh zohnvwahyay suh/seht...*
– express _____	Je veux envoyer ce/cette...en express. *jhuh vuh zohnvwahyay suh/seht…ohn nehxprehs*
– by air mail _____	Je veux envoyer ce/cette...par avion. *jhuh vuh zohnvwahyay suh/seht…pahr ahvyawn*
– by registered mail _____	Je veux envoyer ce/cette...en recommandé. *jhuh vuh zohnvwahyay suh/seht…ohn ruhkomohnday*

Telegram / fax

I'd like to send a _____ telegram to...	J'aimerais envoyer un télégramme à... *jhehmuhreh zohnvwahyay uhn taylaygrahm ah...*
How much is that _____ per word?	C'est combien par mot? *seh kawnbyahn pahr moa?*
This is the text I want_____ to send	Voici le texte que je veux envoyer. *vwahsee luh tehxt kuh jhuh vuh zohnvwahyay*
Shall I fill out the form_____ myself?	Puis-je remplir le questionnaire moi-même? *pwee jhuh rohnpleer luh kehstyonehr mwah mehm?*
Can I make photocopies/___ send a fax here?	Puis-je faire des photocopies/envoyer un fax ici? *pwee jhuh fehr day foatoakopee/ ohnvwahyay uhn fahx eesee?*

.2 Telephone

See also 1.8 Telephone alphabet

● **All phone booths** offer a direct international service to the UK or the US (00 + country code 44[UK] or 1[US]+ trunk code minus zero + number). In a few cases these are still payable with coins of 1, 5 and 10 francs, but most phone booths will only accept phone cards. These cards (*télécartes*), with 40 or 120 units (*unités*) can be bought at the post office or in a *tabac*. Phone booths do not take incoming calls. Charges can no longer be reversed in France. A *carte globéo* (special card) can be obtained from any office of the telephone company, on presentation of a credit card and identification. Charges are then deducted from the bank account.

When phoning someone in France, you will not be greeted with the subscriber's name, but with *allô* or *allô oui*?

Is there a phone box _____ around here?	Y a-t-il une cabine téléphonique dans le coin?
	ee ah teel ewn kahbeen taylayfoneek dohn luh kwahn?
Could I use your _____ phone, please?	Puis-je utiliser votre téléphone?
	pwee jhuh ewteeleezay votr taylayfon?
Do you have a _____ (city/region)...phone directory?	Avez-vous un annuaire de la ville de.../de la région de...?
	ahvay voo zuhn ahnnewehr duh lah veel duh.../duh lah rayjhyawn duh...?
Where can I get a _____ phone card?	Où puis-je acheter une télécarte?
	oo pwee jhahshtay ewn taylaykahrt?
Could you give me...? _____	Pouvez-vous me donner...?
	poovay voo muh donay...?
– the number for _____ international directory enquiries	Pouvez-vous me donner le numéro des renseignements pour l'étranger?
	poovay voo muh donay luh newmayroa day rohnsehnyuhmohn poor laytrohnjhay?
– the number of room... ___	Pouvez-vous me donner le numéro de la chambre...?
	poovay voo muh donay luh newmayroa duh lah shohnbr...?
– the international _____ access code	Pouvez-vous me donner le numéro international?
	poovay voo muh donay luh newmayroa ahntehrnahsyonahl?
– the country code for... ___	Pouvez-vous me donner l'indicatif du pays pour...?
	poovay voo muh donay lahndeekahteef dew payee poor...?
– the trunk code for... _____	Pouvez-vous me donner l'indicatif de...?
	poovay voo muh donay lahndeekahteef duh...?
– the number of... _____	Pouvez-vous me donner le numéro d'abonné de...?
	poovay voo muh donay luh newmayroa dahbonay duh...?
Could you check if this ____ number's correct?	Pouvez-vous vérifier si ce numéro est correct?
	poovay voo vayreefyay see suh newmayroa eh korehkt?
Can I dial international_____ direct?	Puis-je téléphoner en automatique à l'étranger?
	pwee jhuh taylayfonay ohn noatoamahteek ah laytrohnjhay?
Do I have to go through ___ the switchboard?	Dois-je appeler en passant par le standard?
	dwah jhahpuhlay ohn pahsohn pahr luh stohndahr?
Do I have to dial '0' first? __	Dois-je d'abord faire le zéro?
	dwah jhuh dahbor fehr luh zayroa?
Do I have to book _____ my calls?	Dois-je demander ma communication?
	dwah jhuh duhmohnday mah komewneekahsyawn?
Could you dial this _____ number for me, please?	Voulez-vous m'appeler ce numéro?
	voolay voo mahpuhlay suh newmayroa?

Could you put me _____ through to.../extension..., please?	Voulez-vous me passer.../le poste...? *voolay voo muh pahsay.../luh post...?*
What's the charge per _____ minute?	Quel est le prix à la minute? *kehl eh luh pree ah lah meenewt?*
Have there been any _____ calls for me?	Quelqu'un m'a-t-il appelé? *kehlkuhn mah teel ahpuhlay?*

The conversation

Hello, this is... _____	Allô, ici... *ahloa, eesee...*
Who is this, please? _____	Qui est à l'appareil? *kee eh tah lahpahrehy?*
Is this...? _____	Je parle à...? *jhuh pahrl ah...?*
I'm sorry, I've dialled _____ the wrong number	Pardon, je me suis trompé(e) de numéro *pahrdawn, jhuh muh swee trawnpay duh newmayroa.*
I can't hear you _____	Je ne vous entends pas *jhuh nuh voo zohntohn pah*
I'd like to speak to... _____	Je voudrais parler à... *jhuh voodreh pahrlay ah...*
Is there anybody _____ who speaks English?	Y a-t-il quelqu'un qui parle l'anglais? *ee yah teel kehlkuhn kee pahrl lohngleh?*
Extension... please _____	Pouvez-vous me passer le poste...? *poovay voo muh pahsay luh post...?*
Could you ask him/her _____ to call me back?	Voulez-vous demander qu'il/qu'elle me rappelle? *voolay voo duhmohnday keel/kehl muh rahpehl?*
My name's... _____ My number's...	Mon nom est...Mon numéro est... *mawn nawn eh...mawn newmayroa eh...*
Could you tell him/her _____ I called?	Voulez-vous dire que j'ai appelé? *voolay voo deer kuh jhay ahpuhlay?*
I'll call back tomorrow _____	Je rappellerai demain *jhuh rahpehluhray duhmahn*

On vous demande au téléphone _____	There's a phone call for you
Vous devez d'abord faire le zéro _____	You have to dial '0' first.
Vous avez un instant? _____	One moment, please
Je n'obtiens pas de réponse _____	There's no answer
La ligne est occupée _____	The line's engaged
Vous voulez attendre? _____	Do you want to hold?
Je vous passe la communication _____	Putting you through
Vous vous êtes trompé de numéro _____	You've got a wrong number
Il/elle n'est pas ici en ce moment _____	He's/she's not here right now
Vous pouvez le/la rappeler à... _____	He'll/she'll be back...
C'est le répondeur automatique de... _____	This is the answering machine of...

Shopping

10.1 Shopping conversations 83

10.2 Food 85

10.3 Clothing and shoes 86

10.4 Photographs and video 87

10.5 At the hairdresser's 89

🔟 **S**hopping

● **Opening times:** Tuesday to Saturday 8/9am-1pm and 2.30-7pm. On Mondays shops are closed in the morning or for the entire day. On Sunday mornings grocers and bakers are usually open, and markets are open until 1pm. Supermarkets and department stores in nearly all cities are open until 8pm once a week. Chemists display the list of *pharmacies de garde* (those open on Sundays and after hours), but you may be charged double in some cities. You may be asked to pay in advance for shoe repairs and dry cleaning.

antiquités	grand magasin	magasin diététique
antiques	**department store**	**health food shop**
appareils électriques	laverie automatique	marché
electrical appliances	**launderette**	**market**
bijoutier	librairie	marché aux puces
jeweller	**bookshop**	**fleamarket**
blanchisserie	magasin	mercerie
laundry	**shop**	**draper**
boucherie	magasin	pâtisserie
butcher	d'ameublement	**cake shop**
boulangerie	**furniture shop**	pharmacie
bakery	magasin d'appareils	**chemist**
centre commercial	photographiques	poissonnerie
shopping centre	**camera shop**	**fishmonger**
charcuterie	magasin de	produits ménagers/
delicatessen	bicyclettes	droguerie
coiffeur	**bicycle shop**	**household goods**
(femmes/hommes)	magasin de	quincaillerie
hairdresser	bricolage	**hardware shop**
(women/men)	**DIY-store**	réparateur de
cordonnier	magasin de jouets	bicyclettes
cobbler	**toy shop**	**bicycle repairs**
crémerie	magasin de disques	salon de beauté
dairy	**record shop**	**beauty parlour**
épicerie	magasin de	salon de dégustation
grocery store	souvenirs	de glaces
fleuriste	**souvenir shop**	**ice-cream parlour**
florist	magasin de sport	supermarché
fruits et légumes	**sports shop**	**supermarket**
greengrocer	magasin de vins et	tabac
galerie marchande	spiritueux	**tobacconist**
shopping arcade	**off-licence**	teinturerie
		dry-cleaner

🔟 .1 **S**hopping conversations

Where can I get...? _____	Dans quel magasin puis-je acheter...?
	dohn kehl mahgahzahn pwee jhahshtay...?
When does this shop _____ open?	A quelle heure ouvre ce magasin?
	ah kehl uhr oovr suh mahgahzahn?
Could you tell me _____ where the...department is?	Pouvez-vous m'indiquer le rayon de...?
	poovay voo mahndeekay luh rayawn duh...?

Could you help me, _____ please? I'm looking for...
Pouvez-vous m'aider? Je cherche...
poovay voo mayday? jhuh shehrsh...

Do you sell English/ _____ American newspapers?
Vendez-vous des journaux anglais/américains?
vohnday voo day jhoornoa ohngleh/ahmayreekahn?

On s'occupe de vous? _____ **Are you being served?**

No, I'd like... _____
Non. J'aimerais...
nawn. jhehmuhreh...

I'm just looking, _____ if that's all right
Je jette un coup d'oeil, si c'est permis
jhuh jheht uhn koo duhy, see seh pehrmee

Vous désirez autre chose? _____ **Anything else?**

Yes, I'd also like... _____
Oui, donnez-moi aussi...
wee, donay mwah oasee...

No, thank you. That's all ___
Non, je vous remercie. Ce sera tout
nawn, jhuh voo ruhmehrsee. suh suhrah too

Could you show me...? ____
Pouvez-vous me montrer...?
poovay voo muh mawntray...?

I'd prefer... _____
Je préfère...
jhuh prayfehr...

This is not what I'm _____ looking for
Ce n'est pas ce que je cherche
suh neh pah suh kuh jhuh shehrsh

Thank you. I'll keep_____ looking
Merci. Je chercherai ailleurs
mehrsee. jhuh shehrshuhray ahyuhr

Do you have _____ something...?
Vous n'avez pas quelque chose de...?
voo nahvay pah kehlkuh shoaz duh...?

– less expensive?_____
Vous n'avez pas quelque chose de moins cher?
voo nahvay pah kehlkuh shoaz duh mwahn shehr?

– something smaller?_____
Vous n'avez pas quelque chose de plus petit?
voo nahvay pah kehlkuh shoaz duh plew puhtee?

– something larger? _____
Vous n'avez pas quelque chose de plus grand?
voo nahvay pah kehlkuh shoaz duh plew grohn?

I'll take this one _____
Je prends celui-ci
jhuh prohn suhlwee see

Does it come with _____ instructions?
Y a-t-il un mode d'emploi avec?
ee yah teel uhn mod dohnplwah ahvehk?

It's too expensive _____
Je le trouve trop cher
jhuh luh troov troa shehr

I'll give you... _____
Je vous offre...
jhuh voo zofr...

Could you keep this for ____ me? I'll come back for it later	Voulez-vous me le mettre de côté? Je reviendrai le chercher tout à l'heure *voolay voo muh luh mehtr duh koatay? jhuh ruhvyahndray luh shehrshay too tah luhr*
Have you got a bag _____ for me, please?	Vous avez un sac? *voo zahvay uhn sahk?*
Could you giftwrap_____ it, please?	Vous pouvez l'emballer dans un papier cadeau? *voo poovay lohnbahlay dohn zuhn pahpyay kahdoa?*

Je suis désolé, nous n'en avons pas ____	I'm sorry, we don't have that
Je suis désolé, le stock est épuisé_____	I'm sorry, we're sold out
Je suis désolé, ce ne sera pas livré_____ avant...	I'm sorry, that won't be in until...
Vous pouvez payer à la caisse _____	You can pay at the cash desk
Nous n'acceptons pas les cartes de ____ crédit	We don't accept credit cards
Nous n'acceptons pas les chèques _____ de voyage	We don't accept traveller's cheques
Nous n'acceptons pas les devises_____ étrangères	We don't accept foreign currency

🔟 .2 Food

I'd like a hundred_____ grams of..., please	Je voudrais cent grammes de... *jhuh voodreh sohn grahm duh...*
– five hundred grams/ _____ half a kilo of...	Je voudrais une livre de... *jhuh voodreh zewn leevr duh...*
– a kilo of... _____	Je voudrais un kilo de... *jhuh voodreh zuhn keeloa duh...*
Could you...it for me, _____ please?	Vous voulez me le...? *voo voolay muh luh...?*
Could you slice it/ _____ dice it for me, please?	Vous voulez me le couper en tranches/morceaux? *voo voolay muh luh koopay ohn trohnsh/mohrsoa?*
Could you grate it _____ for me, please?	Vous voulez me le râper? *voo voolay muh luh rahpay?*
Can I order it?_____	Puis-je le commander? *pwee jhuh luh komohnday?*
I'll pick it up tomorrow/ ____ at...	Je viendrai le chercher demain/à...heures *jhuh vyahndray luh shehrshay duhmahn/ah...uhr*
Can you eat/drink this? ____	Est-ce mangeable/buvable? *ehs mohnjhahbl/bewvahbl?*
What's in it? _____	Qu'y a-t-il dedans? *kee yah teel duhdohn?*

I saw something in the ____ window. Shall I point it out?	J'ai vu quelque chose dans la vitrine. Je vous le montre?
	jhay vew kehlkuh shoaz dohn lah veetreen. jhuh voo lah mawntr?
I'd like something to_____ go with this	J'aimerais quelque chose pour aller avec ceci
	jhehmuhreh kehlkuh shoaz poor ahlay suhsee
Do you have shoes _____ to match this?	Avez-vous des chaussures de la même couleur que ça?
	ahvay voo day shoasewr duh lah mehm kooluhr kuh sah?
I'm a size...in the UK_____	Je fais du...au Royaume-Uni
	jhuh feh dew...oa rwahyoam ewnee
Can I try this on? _____	Puis-je l'essayer?
	pwee jhuh lehsayay?
Where's the fitting room? __	Où est la cabine d'essayage?
	oo eh lah kahbeen dehsayahjh?
It doesn't fit_____	Cela ne me va pas
	suhlah nuh muh vah pah
This is the right size _____	C'est la bonne taille
	seh lah bon tahy
It doesn't suit me_____	Cela ne me convient pas
	suhlah nuh muh kawnvyahn pah
Do you have this in...? _____	L'avez-vous aussi en...?
	lahvay voo zoasee ohn...?
The heel's too high/low ____	Je trouve le talon trop haut/bas
	jhuh troov luh tahlawn troa oa/bah
Is this/are these _____ genuine leather?	Est-ce/sont-elles en cuir?
	eh suh/sawn tehl ohn kweer?
I'm looking for a..._____ for a...-year-old baby/child	Je cherche un...pour un bébé/enfant de...ans
	jhuh shehrsh uhn...poor uhn baybay/ohnfohn duh...ohn
I'd like a... ... _____	J'aurais aimé un...de...
	jhoareh zaymay uhn... duh...
– silk _____	J'aurais aimé un...de soie
	jhoareh zaymay uhn...duh swah
– cotton _____	J'aurais aimé un...de coton
	jhoareh zaymay uhn...duh koatawn
– woollen_____	J'aurais aimé un...de laine
	jhoareh zaymay uhn...duh lehn
– linen_____	J'aurais aimé un...de lin
	jhoareh zaymay uhn...duh lahn
What temperature_____ can I wash it at?	A quelle température puis-je le laver?
	ah kehl tohnpayrahtewr pwee jhuh luh lahvay?
Will it shrink in the _____ wash?	Cela rétrécit au lavage?
	suhlah raytraysee oa lahvahjh?

Shopping

10

86

Ne pas repasser	Étendre humide	Laver à la main
Do not iron	**Drip dry**	**Hand wash**
Ne pas essorer	Nettoyage à sec	Laver à la machine
Do not spin dry	**Dry clean**	**Machine wash**

At the cobbler

Could you mend _____ these shoes?
Pouvez-vous réparer ces chaussures?
poovay voo raypahray say shoasewr?

Could you put new _____ soles/heels on these?
Pouvez-vous y mettre de nouvelles semelles/nouveaux talons?
poovay voo zee mehtr duh noovehl suhmehl/noovoa tahlawn?

When will they be _____ ready?
Quand seront-elles prêtes?
kohn suhrawn tehl preht?

I'd like..., please _____
Je voudrais...
jhuh voodreh...

– a tin of shoe polish _____
Je voudrais une boîte de cirage
jhuh voodreh zewn bwaht duh seerahjh

– a pair of shoelaces_____
Je voudrais une paire de lacets
jhuh voodreh zewn pehr duh lahseh

🔟 .4 Photographs and video

I'd like a film for this_____ camera, please
Je voudrais un rouleau de pellicules pour cet appareil
jhuh voodreh zuhn rooloa duh payleekewl poor seht ahpahrehy

– a 126 _____ cartridge
Je voudrais une cartouche de cent vingt-six
jhuh voodreh zewn kahrtoosh duh sohn vahn sees

– a slide film _____
Je voudrais un rouleau de pellicules pour diapositives
jhuh voodreh zuhn rooloa duh payleekewl poor deeahpoaseeteev

– a film _____
Je voudrais un rouleau de pellicules
jhuh voodreh zuhn rooloa duh payleekewl

– a videotape _____
Je voudrais une vidéocassette
jhuh voodreh zewn veedayoakahseht

colour/black and white_____
couleur/noir et blanc
kooluhr/nwahr ay blohn

super eight _____
super huit mm
sewpehr wee meeleemehtr

12/24/36 exposures _____
douze/vingt-quatre/trente-six poses
dooz/vahn kahtr/trohnt see poaz

ASA/DIN number_____
nombre d'ASA/DIN
nohnbr dahzah/deen

daylight film _____
film pour la lumière du jour
feelm poor lah lewmyehr dew joor

film for artificial light _____
film pour la lumière artificielle
feelm poor lah lewmyehr ahrteefeesyehl

Shopping

🔟

Problems

Could you load the _____ film for me, please?	Voulez-vous mettre le film dans l'appareil? *voolay voo mehtr luh feelm dohn lahpahrehy?*
Could you take the film _____ out for me, please?	Voulez-vous enlever le film de l'appareil-photo? *voolay voo zohnluhvay luh feelm duh lahpahrehy foatoa?*
Should I replace_____ the batteries?	Dois-je changer les piles? *dwah jhuh shohnjhay lay peel?*
Could you have a look _____ at my camera, please? It's not working	Voulez-vous jeter un coup d'oeil à mon appareil-photo? Il ne marche plus *voolay voo jhuhtay uhn koo duhy ah mawn nahpahrehy foatoa? eel nuh mahrsh plew*
The...is broken _____	Le...est cassé *luh...eh kahssay*
The film's jammed _____	La pellicule est bloquée *lah payleekewl eh blokay*
The film's broken_____	La pellicule est cassée *lah payleekewl eh kahssay*
The flash isn't working ____	Le flash ne marche pas *luh flahsh nuh mahrsh pah*

Processing and prints

I'd like to have this film _____ developed/printed, please	Je voudrais faire développer/tirer ce film *jhuh voodreh fehr dayvuhlopay/teeray suh feelm*
I'd like...prints from_____ each negative	Je voudrais...tirages de chaque négatif *jhuh voodreh...teerahjh duh shahk naygahteef*
glossy/mat_____	brillant/mat *breeyohn/maht*
6x9_____	six sur neuf *sees sewr nuhf*
I'd like to re-order _____ these photos	Je veux faire refaire cette photo *jhuh vuh fehr ruhfehr seht foatoa*
I'd like to have this _____ photo enlarged	Je veux faire agrandir cette photo *jhuh vuh fehr ahgrohndeer seht foatoa*
How much is_____ processing?	Combien coûte le développement? *kawnbyahn koot luh dayvuhlopmohn?*
– printing _____	Combien coûte le tirage? *kawnbyahn koot luh teerahjh?*
– to re-order _____	Combien coûte la commande supplémentaire? *kawnbyahn koot lah komohnd sewplaymohntehr?*
– the enlargement_____	Combien coûte l'agrandissement? *kawnbyahn koot lahgrohndeesmohn?*
When will they_____ be ready?	Quand seront-elles prêtes? *kohn suhrawn tehl preht?*

Do I have to make an _____ appointment?	Dois-je prendre un rendez-vous? *dwah jhuh prohndr uhn rohnday voo?*
Can I come in straight _____ away?	Pouvez-vous vous occuper de moi immédiatement? *poovay voo voo zokewpay duh mwah eemaydyahtmohn?*
How long will I have_____ to wait?	Combien de temps dois-je attendre? *kawnbyahn duh tohn dwah jhahtohndr?*
I'd like a shampoo/ _____ haircut	Je veux me faire laver/couper les cheveux *jhuh vuh muh fehr lahvay/koopay lay shuhvuh*
I'd like a shampoo for _____ oily/dry hair, please	Je voudrais un shampooing pour cheveux gras/secs *jhuh voodreh zuhn shohnpwahn poor shuhvuh grah/sehk*
an anti-dandruff_____ shampoo	Je voudrais un shampooing anti-pelliculaire *jhuh voodreh zuhn shohnpwahn ohnteepayleekewlehr*
– a shampoo for_____ permed/coloured hair	Je voudrais un shampooing pour cheveux permanentés/colorés *jhuh voodreh zuhn shohnpwahn poor shuhvuh pehrmahnohntay/kohlohray*
– a colour rinse shampoo __	Je voudrais un shampooing colorant *jhuh voodreh zuhn shohnpwahn kolorohn*
– a shampoo with _____ conditioner	Je voudrais un shampoing avec un soin traitant *jhuh voodreh zuhn shohnpwahn ahvehk uhn swahn trehtohn*
– highlights _____	Je voudrais me faire faire des mèches *jhuh voodreh muh fehr fehr day mehsh*
Do you have a colour_____ chart, please?	Avez-vous une carte de coloration s'il vous plaît? *ahvay voo zewn kahrt duh kolorahsyawn seel voo pleh?*
I want to keep it the _____ same colour	Je veux garder la même couleur *jhuh vuh gahrday lah mehm kooluhr*
I'd like it darker/lighter _____	Je les veux plus sombres/clairs *jhuh lay vuh plew sawmbr/klehr*
I'd like/I don't want _____ hairspray	Je veux de la/ne veux pas de laque *jhuh vuh duh la/nuh vuh pah duh lahk*
– gel_____	Je veux du/ne veux pas de gel *jhuh vuh dew/ nuh vuh pah duh jhehl*
– lotion _____	Je veux de la/ne veux pas de lotion *jhuh vuh duh lah/nuh vuh pah duh loasyawn*
I'd like a short fringe _____	Je veux ma frange courte *jhuh vuh mah frohnjh koort*
Not too short at the _____ back	Je ne veux pas la nuque trop courte *jhuh nuh vuh pah lah newk troa koort*
Not too long here _____	Ici je ne les veux pas trop longs *eesee jhuh nuh lay vuh pah troa lawn*
I'd like/I don't want _____ (many) curls	Je (ne) veux (pas) être (trop) frisée *jhuh (nuh) vuh (pah) ehtr (troa) freezay*

It needs a little/ a lot taken off	Il faut en enlever une petite/grande quantité *eel foa ohn nohnluhvay ewn puhteet/grohnd kohnteetay*
I want a completely _____ different style	Je veux une toute autre coupe *jhuh vuh zewn toot oatr koop*
I'd like it like..._____	Je veux mes cheveux comme... *jhuh vuh may shuhvuh kom...*
– the same as that lady's ___	Je veux la même coiffure que cette femme *jhuh vuh lah mehm kwahfewr kuh seht fahm*
– the same as in this photo	Je veux la même coiffure que sur cette photo *jhuh vuh lah mehm kwahfewr kuh sewr seht foatoa*
Could you put the _____ drier up/down a bit?	Pouvez-vous mettre le casque plus haut/plus bas? *poovay voo mehtr luh kahsk plew oa/plew bah?*
I'd like a facial_____	J'aimerais un masque de beauté *jhehmuhreh zuhn mahsk duh boatay*
– a manicure _____	J'aimerais qu'on me fasse les ongles *jhehmuhreh kawn muh fahs lay zawngl*
– a massage _____	J'aimerais un massage *jhehmuhreh zuhn mahsahjh*

Quelle coupe de cheveux_____ désirez-vous?	How do you want it cut?
Quelle coiffure désirez-vous? _____	What style did you have in mind?
Quelle couleur désirez-vous? _____	What colour do you want?
Est-ce la bonne température? _____	Is the temperature all right for you?
Voulez-vous lire quelque chose? _____	Would you like something to read?
Voulez-vous boire quelque chose? _____	Would you like a drink?
C'est ce que vous vouliez?_____	Is this what you had in mind?

Could you trim_____ my fringe?	Pouvez-vous égaliser ma frange? *poovay voo zaygahleezay mah frohnjh?*
– my beard? _____	Pouvez-vous égaliser ma barbe? *poovay voo zaygahleezay mah bahrb?*
– my moustache? _____	Pouvez-vous égaliser ma moustache? *poovay voo zaygahleezay mah moostahsh?*
I'd like a shave, please_____	Pouvez-vous me raser s'il vous plaît? *poovay voo muh rahzay seel voo pleh?*
I'd like a wet shave, _____ please	Je veux être rasé au rasoir à main *jhuh vuh zehtr rahzay oa rahzwahr ah mahn*

At the Tourist Information Centre

11.1 Places of interest   92

11.2 Going out   94

11.3 Booking tickets   95

11 .1 Places of interest

Where's the Tourist Information, please?	Où est l'office de tourisme?
	oo eh lofees duh tooreesm?
Do you have a city map?	Avez-vous un plan de la ville?
	ahvay voo zuhn plohn duh lah veel?
Where is the museum?	Où est le musée?
	oo eh luh mewzay?
Where can I find a church?	Où puis-je trouver une église?
	oo pwee jhuh troovay ewn aygleez?
Could you give me some information about...?	Pouvez-vous me renseigner sur...?
	poovay voo muh rohnsehnyay sewr...?
How much is that?	Combien ça coûte?
	kawnbyahn sah koot?
What are the main places of interest?	Quelles sont les curiosités les plus importantes?
	kehl sawn lay kewryoseetay lay plewz ahnportohnt?
Could you point them out on the map?	Pouvez-vous les indiquer sur la carte?
	poovay voo lay zahndeekay sewr lah kahrt?
What do you recommend?	Que nous conseillez-vous?
	kuh noo kawnsehyay voo?
We'll be here for a few hours	Nous restons ici quelques heures.
	noo rehstawn zeesee kehlkuh zuhr.
– a day	Nous restons ici une journée.
	noo rehstawn zeesee ewn jhoornay.
– a week	Nous restons ici une semaine.
	noo rehstawn zeesee ewn suhmehn.
We're interested in...	Nous sommes intéressés par...
	noo som zahntayrehsay pahr...
Is there a scenic walk around the city?	Pouvons-nous faire une promenade en ville?
	poovawn noo fehr ewn promuhnahd ohn veel?
How long does it take?	Combien de temps dure-t-elle?
	kawnbyahn duh tohn dewr tehl?
Where does it start/end?	Où est le point de départ/d'arrivée?
	oo eh luh pwahn duh daypahr/dahreevay?
Are there any boat cruises here?	Y a-t-il des bateaux-mouches?
	ee yah teel day bahtoa moosh?
Where can we board?	Où pouvons-nous embarquer?
	oo poovawn noo zohnbahrkay?
Are there any bus tours?	Y a-t-il des promenades en bus?
	ee yah teel day promuhnahd ohn bews?
Where do we get on?	Où devons-nous monter?
	oo devawn noo mawntay?
Is there a guide who speaks English?	Y a-t-il un guide qui parle l'anglais?
	ee yah teel uhn gueed kee pahrl lohngleh?
What trips can we take around the area?	Quelles promenades peut-on faire dans la région?
	kehl promuhnahd puh tawn fehr dohn lah rayjhyawn?

Are there any _____ excursions?	Y a-t-il des excursions?
	ee yah teel day zehxkewrsyawn?
Where do they go to? ___	Où vont-elles?
	oo vawn tehl?
We'd like to go to..._____	Nous voulons aller à...
	noo voolawn zahlay ah...
How long is the trip? _____	Combien de temps dure l'excursion?
	kawnbyahn duh tohn dewr lehxkewrsyawn?
How long do we _____ stay in...?	Combien de temps restons-nous à...?
	kawnbyahn duh tohn rehstawn noo zah...?
Are there any guided _____ tours?	Y a-t-il des visites guidées?
	ee yah teel day veezeet gueeday?
How much free time_____ will we have there?	Combien de temps avons-nous de libre?
	kawnbyahn duh tohn ahvawn noo duh leebr?
We want to go hiking_____	Nous voulons faire une randonnée
	noo voolawn fehr ewn rohndonay
Can we hire a guide? _____	Pouvons-nous prendre un guide?
	poovawn noo prohndr uhn gueed?
Can I book mountain _____ huts?	Puis-je réserver un refuge?
	pwee jhuh rayzehrvay uhn ruhfewjhuh?
What time does... _____ open/close?	A quelle heure ouvre/ferme...?
	ah kehl uhr oovr/fehrm...?
What days is...open/_____ closed?	Quels sont les jours d'ouverture/de fermeture de...?
	kehl sawn lay jhoor doovehrtewr/duh fehrmuhtewr duh...?
What's the admission_____ price?	Quel est le prix d'entrée?
	kehl eh luh pree dohntray?
Is there a group _____ discount?	Y a-t-il une réduction pour les groupes?
	ee yah teel ewn raydewksyawn poor lay groop?
Is there a child _____ discount?	Y a-t-il une réduction pour les enfants?
	ee yah teel ewn raydewksyawn poor lay zohnfohn?
Is there a discount_____ for pensioners?	Y a-t-il une réduction pour les personnes de plus de soixante-cinq ans?
	ee yah teel ewn raydewksyawn poor lay pehrson duh plew duh swahssohnt sahnk ohn?
Can I take (flash) _____ photos/can I film here?	M'est-il permis de prendre des photos(avec flash)/filmer ici?
	meh teel pehrmee duh prohndr day foatoa(ahvehk flahsh)/feelmay eesee?
Do you have any _____ postcards of...?	Vendez-vous des cartes postales de...?
	vohnday voo day kahrt postahl duh...?
Do you have an _____ English...?	Avez-vous un...en anglais?
	ahvay voo zuhn...ohn nohngleh?
– an English catalogue?___	Avez-vous un catalogue en anglais?
	ahvay voo zuhn kahtahlog ohn nohngleh?
– an English programme?__	Avez-vous un programme en anglais?
	ahvay voo zuhn prograhm ohn nohngleh?
– an English brochure? ___	Avez-vous une brochure en anglais?
	ahvay voo zewn broshewr ohn nohngleh?

At the Tourist Information Centre

11

11 .2 Going out

● **In French theatres** you are usually shown to your seat by an usherette from whom you can buy a programme. It is customary to tip. At the cinema most films are dubbed (*version française*). In large cities subtitled versions are often screened, advertised as *version originale* or *V.O.* If the publicity does not mention *V.O.*, the film will be dubbed. *L'Officiel des spectacles* (an entertainment guide) can be obtained from newspaper kiosks.

Do you have this _____ week's/month's entertainment guide?	Avez-vous le journal des spectacles de cette semaine/de ce mois? *ahvay voo luh jhoornal day spehktahkl duh seht suhmehn/duh suh mwah?*
What's on tonight? _____	Que peut-on faire ce soir? *kuh puh tawn fehr suh swahr?*
We want to go to... _____	Nous voulons aller au... *noo voolawn zahlay oa...*
Which films are _____ showing?	Quels films passe-t-on? *kehl feelm pah stawn?*
What sort of film is that? ___	Qu'est-ce que c'est comme film? *kehs kuh seh kom feelm?*
suitable for all ages _____	pour tous les âges *poor too lay zahjh*
not suitable for children under 12/16 years	pour les plus de douze ans/seize ans *poor lay plew duh dooz ohn/sehz ohn*
original version _____	version originale *vehrsyawn oreejheenahl*
subtitled _____	sous-titré *soo teetray*
dubbed _____	doublé *dooblay*
Is it a continuous _____ showing?	Est-ce un spectacle permanent? *ehs uhn spehktahkl pehrmahnohn?*
What's on at...? _____	Qu'y a-t-il au...? *kee yah teel oa...?*
– the theatre? _____	Qu'y a-t-il au théâtre? *kee yah teel oa tayahtr?*
– the concert hall? _____	Qu'y a-t-il à la salle des concerts? *kee yah teel ah lah sahl day kawnsehr?*
– the opera? _____	Qu'y a-t-il à l'opéra? *kee yah teel ah loapayrah?*
Where can I find a good ___ disco around here?	Où se trouve une bonne disco par ici? *oo suh troov ewn bon deeskoa pahr eesee?*
Is it members only? _____	Exige-t-on une carte de membre? *ehgzeejh-tawn ewn kahrt duh mohnbr?*
Where can I find a good nightclub around here?	Où se trouve une bonne boîte de nuit par ici? *oo suh troov ewn bon bwaht duh nwee pahr eesee?*
Is it evening wear only? ___	La tenue de soirée, est-elle obligatoire? *lah tuhnew duh swahray, eh tehl obleegahtwahr?*
Should I/we dress up? _____	La tenue de soirée, est-elle souhaitée? *lah tuhnew duh swahray ehtehl sooehtay?*

What time does the _____ show start?	A quelle heure commence la représentation? *ah kehl uhr komohns lah ruhprayzohntahsyawn?*
When's the next soccer ____ match?	Quand est le prochain match de football? *kohn teh luh proshahn mahtch duh footbohl?*
Who's playing?_____	Qui joue contre qui? *kee jhoo kawntr kee?*
I'd like an escort for _____ tonight. Could you arrange that for me?	Je veux une hôtesse pour ce soir. Pouvez-vous arranger ça? *jhuh vuh zewn oatehs poor suh swahr.* *poovay voo zahrohnjhay sah?*

11 .3 Booking tickets

Could you book some _____ tickets for us?	Pouvez-vous nous faire une réservation? *poovay voo noo fehr ewn rayzehrvahsyawn?*
We'd like to book... _____ seats/a table...	Nous voulons...places/une table... *noo voolawn...plahs/ewn tahbl...*
– in the stalls_____	Nous voulons...places à l'orchestre. *noo voolawn...plahs ah lorkehstr*
– on the balcony _____	Nous voulons...places au balcon. *noo voolawn...plahs oa bahlkawn*
– box seats _____	Nous voulons...places dans les loges. *noo voolawn...plahs dohn lay lojh*
– a table at the front _____	Nous voulons...une table à l'avant. *noo voolawn...ewn tahbl ah lahvohn*
– in the middle _____	Nous voulons...places au milieu. *noo voolawn...plahs oa meelyuh*
– at the back _____	Nous voulons...places à l'arrière. *noo voolawn...plahs ah lahryehr*
Could I book...seats for ____ the...o'clock performance?	Puis-je réserver...places pour la représentation de...heures? *pwee jhuh rayzehrvay...plahs poor lah ruhprayzohntahsyawn duh...uhr?*
Are there any seats left ____ for tonight?	Reste-t-il encore des places pour ce soir? *rehst-uh-teel ohnkor day plahs poor suh swahr?*
How much is a ticket? _____	Combien coûte un billet? *kawnbyahn koot uhn beeyeh?*
When can I pick the _____ tickets up?	Quand puis-je venir chercher les billets? *kohn pwee jhuh vuhneer shehrshay lay beeyeh?*
I've got a reservation _____	J'ai réservé *jhay rayzehrvay*
My name's... _____	Mon nom est... *mawn nawn eh...*

Vous voulez réserver pour quelle représentation?	Which performance do you want to book for?
Où voulez-vous vous asseoir?	Where would you like to sit?
Tout est vendu	Everything's sold out
Il ne reste que des places debout	It's standing room only
Il ne reste que des places au balcon	We've only got balcony seats left
Il ne reste que des places au poulailler	We've only got seats left in the gallery
Il ne reste que des places d'orchestre	We've only got stalls seats left
Il ne reste que des places à l'avant	We've only got seats left at the front
Il ne reste que des places à l'arrière	We've only got seats left at the back
Combien de places voulez-vous?	How many seats would you like?
Vous devez venir chercher les billets avant...heures	You'll have to pick up the tickets before...o'clock
Puis-je voir vos billets?	Tickets, please
Voici votre place	This is your seat
Vous n'êtes pas aux bonnes places	You're in the wrong seats

Sports

12.1 Sporting questions   98

12.2 By the waterfront   98

12.3 In the snow   99

12.1 Sporting questions

Where can we... around here?	Où pouvons-nous...?
	oo poovawn noo...?
Is there a... around here?	Y a-t-il un...dans les environs?
	ee yah teel uhn...dohn lay zohnveerawn?
Can I hire a...here?	Puis-je louer un...ici?
	pwee jhuh looay uhn...eesee?
Can I take...lessons?	Puis-je prendre des cours de...?
	pwee jhuh prohndr day koor duh...?
How much is that per hour/per day/a turn?	Quel est le prix à l'heure/à la journée/à chaque fois?
	kehl eh luh pree ah luhr/ah lah jhoornay/ah shahk fwah?
Do I need a permit for that?	A-t-on besoin d'un permis?
	ah tawn buhzwahn duhn pehrmee?
Where can I get the permit?	Où puis-je obtenir le permis?
	oo pwee jhuh obtuhneer luh pehrmee?

12.2 By the waterfront

Is it a long way to the sea still?	La mer, est-elle encore loin?
	lah mehr eh tehl ohnkor lwahn?
Is there a...around here?	Y a-t-il un...dans les environs?
	ee yah teel uhn...dohn lay zohnveerawn?
– a public swimming pool	Y a-t-il une piscine dans les environs?
	ee yah teel ewn peeseen dohn lay zohnveerawn?
– a sandy beach	Y a-t-il une plage de sable dans les environs?
	ee yah teel ewn plahjh duh sahbl dohn lay zohnveerawn?
– a nudist beach	Y a-t-il une plage pour nudistes dans les environs?
	ee yah teel ewn plahjh poor newdeest dohn lay zohnveerawn?
– mooring	Y a-t-il un embarcadère pour les bateaux dans les environs?
	ee yah teel uhn nohnbahrkahdehr poor lay bahtoa dohn lay zohnveerawn?
Are there any rocks here?	Y a-t-il aussi des rochers ici?
	ee yah teel oasee day roshay eesee?
When's high/low tide?	Quand est la marée haute/basse?
	kohn teh lah mahray oat/bahs?
What's the water temperature?	Quelle est la température de l'eau?
	kehl eh lah tohnpayratewr duh loa?
Is it (very) deep here?	Est-ce (très) profond ici?
	ehs (treh) proafawn eesee?
Can you stand here?	A-t-on pied ici?
	ah tawn pyay eesee?
Is it safe to swim here?	Peut-on nager en sécurité ici?
	puh tawn nahjhay ohn saykewreetay eesee?
Are there any currents?	Y a-t-il des courants?
	ee yah teel day koorohn?

Are there any rapids/_____ waterfalls in this river?	Est-ce que cette rivière a des courants rapides/des chutes d'eau?
	ehs kuh seht reevyehr ah day koorohn rahpeed/day shewt doa?
What does that flag/_____ buoy mean?	Que signifie ce drapeau/cette bouée là-bas?
	kuh seenyeefee suh drahpoa/seht booway lah bah?
Is there a life guard_____ on duty here?	Y a-t-il un maître nageur qui surveille?
	ee yah teel uhn mehtr nahjhuhr kee sewrvehy?
Are dogs allowed here?____	Les chiens sont admis ici?
	lay shyahn sawn tahdmee eesee?
Is camping on the _____ beach allowed?	Peut-on camper sur la plage?
	puh tawn kohnpay sewr lah plahjh?
Are we allowed to_____ build a fire here?	Peut-on faire un feu ici?
	puh tawn fehr uhn fuh eesee?

Danger	Pêche interdite	Baignade interdite
Danger	**No fishing**	**No swimming**
Pêche	Surf interdit	Seulement avec
Fishing water	**No surfing**	permis
		Permits only

⑫ .3 In the snow

Can I take ski lessons _____ here?	Puis-je prendre des leçons de ski?
	pwee jhuh prohndr day luhsawn duh skee?
for beginners/advanced____	pour débutants/initiés
	poor daybewtohn/eeneesyay
How large are the _____ groups?	Quelle est la taille des groupes?
	kehl eh lah tahy day groop?
What language are _____ the classes in?	En quelle langue donne-t-on les leçons de ski?
	ohn kehl lohng don tawn lay luhsawn duh skee?
I'd like a lift pass,_____ please	Je voudrais un abonnement pour les remontées mécaniques.
	jhuh voodreh zuhn nahbonmohn poor lay ruhmawntay maykahneek
Must I give you a_____ passport photo?	Dois-je donner une photo d'identité?
	dwah jhuh donay ewn foatoa deedohnteetay?
Where can I have a _____ passport photo taken?	Où puis-je faire faire une photo d'identité?
	oo pwee jhuh fehr fehr ewn foatoa deedohnteetay?
Where are the_____ beginners' slopes?	Où sont les pistes de ski pour débutants?
	oo sawn lay peest duh skee poor daybewtohn?
Are there any runs for ____ cross-country skiing?	Y a-t-il des pistes de ski de fond dans les environs?
	ee yah teel day peest duh skee duh fawn dohn lay zohnveerawn?

Sports

⑫

99

Have the cross-country _____ Les pistes de ski de fond, sont-elles
runs been marked? indiquées?
*lay peest duh skee duh fawn, sawn tehl
ahndeekay?*

Are the...in operation? _____ Est-ce que les...marchent?
ehs kuh lay...mahrsh?

– the ski lifts _____ Est-ce que les remontées mécaniques
marchent?
*ehs kuh lay ruhmawntay maykahneek
mahrsh?*

– the chair lifts _____ Est-ce que les télésièges marchent?
ehs kuh lay taylaysyehjh mahrsh?

Are the slopes usable?_____ Est-ce que les pistes sont ouvertes?
ehs kuh lay peest sawn toovehrt?

Are the cross-country_____ Est-ce que les pistes de ski de fond sont
runs usable? ouvertes?
*ehs kuh lay peest duh skee duh fawn sawn
toovehrt?*

Sickness

13.1 Call (fetch) the doctor   102

13.2 Patient's ailments   102

13.3 The consultation   103

13.4 Medication and
prescriptions   105

13.5 At the dentist's   106

13 Sickness

13.1 Call (fetch) the doctor

Could you call/fetch a _____ doctor quickly, please?	Voulez-vous vite appeler/aller chercher un médecin s'il vous plaît? *voolay voo veet ahpuhlay/ahlay shehrshay uhn maydsahn seel voo pleh?*
When does the doctor _____ have surgery?	Quand est-ce que le médecin reçoit? *kohn tehs kuh luh maydsahn ruhswah?*
When can the doctor _____ come?	Quand est-ce que le médecin peut venir? *kohn tehs kuh luh maydsahn puh vuhneer?*
I'd like to make an _____ appointment to see the doctor	Pouvez-vous me prendre un rendez-vous chez le médecin? *poovay voo muh prohndr uhn rohnday voo shay luh maydsahn?*
I've got an appointment ___ to see the doctor at...	J'ai un rendez-vous chez le médecin à...heures *jhay uhn rohnday voo shay luh maydsahn a...uhr*
Which doctor/chemist _____ has night/weekend duty?	Quel médecin/Quelle pharmacie est de garde cette nuit/ce week-end? *kehl maydsahn/kehl fahrmahsee eh duh gahrd seht nwee/suh week-ehnd?*

13.2 Patient's ailments

I don't feel well _____	Je ne me sens pas bien *jhuh nuh muh sohn pah byahn*
I'm dizzy _____	J'ai des vertiges *jhay day vehrteejh*
– ill _____	Je suis malade *jhuh swee mahlahd*
– sick _____	J'ai mal au coeur *jhay mahl oa kuhr*
I've got a cold _____	Je suis enrhumé(e) *jhuh swee zohnrewmay*
It hurts here _____	J'ai mal ici *jhay mahl eesee*
I've been throwing up _____	J'ai vomi *jhay vomee*
I've got... _____	Je souffre de... *jhuh soofr duh...*
I'm running a _____ temperature	J'ai de la fièvre *jhayduh lah fyehvr*
I've been stung by _____ a wasp.	J'ai été piqué(e) par une guêpe *jhay aytay peekay pahr ewn gehp*
I've been stung by an _____ insect	J'ai été piqué(e) par un insecte *jhay aytay peekay pahr uhn nahnsehkt*
I've been bitten by _____ a dog	J'ai été mordu(e) par un chien *jhay aytay mordew pahr uhn shyahn*
I've been stung by _____ a jellyfish	J'ai été piqué(e) par une méduse *jhay aytay peekay pahr ewn maydewz*
I've been bitten by _____ a snake	J'ai été mordu(e) par un serpent *jhay aytay mordew pahr uhn sehrpohn*

I've been bitten by	J'ai été mordu(e) par un animal
an animal	*jhay aytay mordew pahr uhn nahneemahl*
I've cut myself	Je me suis coupé(e)
	jhuh muh swee koopay
I've burned myself	Je me suis brûlé(e)
	jhuh muh swee brewlay
I've grazed myself	Je me suis égratigné(e)
	jhuh muh swee zaygrahteenyay
I've had a fall	Je suis tombé(e)
	jhuh swee tawnbay
I've sprained my ankle	Je me suis foulé(e) la cheville
	jhuh muh swee foolay lah shuhveey
I've come for the	Je viens pour la pilule du lendemain
morning-after pill	*jhuh vyahn poor lah peelewl dew lohndmahn*

13 .3 The consultation

👋

Quels sont vos symptômes?	What seems to be the problem?
Depuis combien de temps avez-vous ces symptômes?	How long have you had these symptoms?
Avez-vous eu ces symptômes auparavant?	Have you had this trouble before?
Avez-vous de la fièvre?	How high is your temperature?
Déshabillez-vous s'il vous plaît?	Get undressed, please
Pouvez-vous vous mettre torse nu?	Strip to the waist, please
Vous pouvez vous déshabiller là-bas.	You can undress there
Pouvez-vous remonter la manche de votre bras gauche/droit?	Roll up your left/right sleeve, please
Allongez-vous ici	Lie down here, please
Ceci vous fait mal?	Does this hurt?
Aspirez et expirez profondément	Breathe deeply
Ouvrez la bouche	Open your mouth

Patient's medical history

I'm a diabetic	Je suis diabétique
	jhuh swee dyahbayteek
I have a heart condition	Je suis cardiaque
	jhuh swee kahrdyahk
I have asthma	J'ai de l'asthme
	jhay duh lahsm
I'm allergic to...	Je suis allergique à...
	jhuh swee zahlehrjheek ah...
I'm...months pregnant	Je suis enceinte de...mois
	jhuh swee zohnsahnt duh...mwah
I'm on a diet	Je suis au régime
	jhuh swee zoa rayjheem
I'm on medication/the pill	Je prends des médicaments/la pilule
	jhuh prohn day maydeekahmohn/lah peelewl

Sickness

13

I've had a heart attack once before	J'ai déjà eu une crise cardiaque *jhay dayjhah ew ewn kreez kahrdyahk*
I've had a(n)...operation	J'ai été opéré(e) de... *jhay aytay oapayray duh...*
I've been ill recently	Je viens d'être malade *jhuh vyahn dehtr mahlahd*
I've got an ulcer	J'ai un ulcère à l'estomac *jhay uhn newlsehr ah lehstomah*
I've got my period	J'ai mes règles *jhay may rehgl*

Avez-vous des allergies?	Do you have any allergies?
Prenez-vous des médicaments?	Are you on any medication?
Suivez-vous un régime?	Are you on a diet?
Etes-vous enceinte?	Are you pregnant?
Etes-vous vacciné(e) contre le tétanos?	Have you had a tetanus injection?

The diagnosis

Is it contagious?	Est-ce contagieux? *ehs kawntahjhyuh?*
How long do I have to stay...?	Combien de temps dois-je rester...? *kawnbyahn duh tohn dwah jhuh rehstay...?*
– in bed	Combien de temps dois-je rester au lit? *kawnbyahn duh tohn dwah jhuh rehstay oa lee?*
– in hospital	Combien de temps dois-je rester à l'hôpital? *kawnbyahn duh tohn dwah jhuh rehstay ah loapeetahl?*

Ce n'est rien de grave	It's nothing serious
Vous vous êtes cassé le/la...	Your...is broken
Vous vous êtes foulé le/la...	You've sprained your...
Vous vous êtes déchiré le/la...	You've got a torn...
Vous avez une inflammation	You've got an inflammation
Vous avez une crise d'appendicite	You've got appendicitis
Vous avez une bronchite	You've got bronchitis
Vous avez une maladie vénérienne	You've got a venereal disease
Vous avez une grippe	You've got the flu
Vous avez eu une crise cardiaque	You've had a heart attack
Vous avez une infection (virale/bactérielle)	You've got an infection (viral/bacterial)
Vous avez une pneumonie	You've got pneumonia

3 Sickness

Vous avez un ulcère à l'estomac _____	You've got an ulcer
Vous vous êtes froissé un muscle _____	You've pulled a muscle
Vous avez une infection vaginale _____	You've got a vaginal infection
Vous avez une intoxication alimentaire _____	You've got food poisoning
Vous avez une insolation _____	You've got sunstroke
Vous êtes allergique à... _____	You're allergic to...
Vous êtes enceinte _____	You're pregnant
Je veux faire analyser votre sang/urine/vos selles _____	I'd like to have your blood/urine/stools tested
Il faut faire des points de suture _____	It needs stitching
Je vous envoie à un spécialiste/l'hôpital _____	I'm referring you to a specialist/sending you to hospital.
Il faut faire des radios _____	You'll need to have some x-rays taken
Voulez-vous reprendre place un petit instant dans la salle d'attente? _____	Could you wait in the waiting room, please?
Il faut vous opérer _____	You'll need an operation

Do I have to go on a special diet? _____	Dois-je suivre un régime? *dwah jhuh sweevr uhn rayjheem?*
Am I allowed to travel? _____	Puis-je voyager? *pwee jhuh vwahyahjhay?*
Can I make a new appointment? _____	Puis-je prendre un autre rendez-vous? *pwee jhuh prohndr uhn noatr rohnday voo?*
When do I have to come back? _____	Quand dois-je revenir? *kohn dwah jhuh ruhvuhneer?*
I'll come back tomorrow _____	Je reviendrai demain *jhuh ruhvyahndray duhmahn*

Vous devez revenir demain /dans...jours _____	Come back tomorrow/in...days' time

13 .4 Medication and prescriptions

How do I take this medicine? _____	Comment dois-je prendre ces médicaments? *komohn dwah jhuh prohndr say maydeekahmohn?*
How many capsules/ drops/injections/spoonfuls/ tablets each time? _____	Combien de capsules/gouttes/piqûres/cuillères/comprimés à chaque fois? *kawnbyahn duh kahpsewl/goot/peekewr/kweeyehr/kawnpreemay ah shahk fwah?*
How many times a day? _____	Combien de fois par jour? *kawnbyahn duh fwah pahr jhoor?*
I've forgotten my medication. At home I take... _____	J'ai oublié mes médicaments. A la maison je prends... *jhay oobleeyay may maydeekahmohn. ah lah mehzawn jhuh prohn...*
Could you make out a prescription for me? _____	Pouvez-vous me faire une ordonnance? *poovay voo muh fehr ewn ordonohns?*

Sickness

13

105

Je vous prescris un antibiotique/un _____ sirop/un tranquillisant/un calmant		I'm prescribing antibiotics/a mixture/a tranquillizer/pain killer
Vous devez rester au calme_____		Have lots of rest
Vous ne devez pas sortir _____		Stay indoors
Vous devez rester au lit_____		Stay in bed

avaler entièrement **swallow whole**	cuillerées (...à soupe/...à café) **spoonfuls (tablespoons/ teaspoons)**	pendant...jours **for...days**
avant chaque repas **before meals**		piqûres **injections**
capsules **capsules**	dissoudre dans l'eau **dissolve in water**	pommade **ointment**
la prise de ce médicament peut rendre dangereuse la conduite automobile **this medication impairs your driving**	enduire **rub on**	prendre **take**
	finir le traitement **finish the course**	toutes les...heures **every...hours**
	...fois par jour **...times a day**	uniquement pour usage externe **not for internal use**
comprimés **tablets**	gouttes **drops**	

13 .5 At the dentist's

Do you know a good _____ dentist?	Connaissez-vous un bon dentiste? *konehsay voo zuhn bawn dohnteest?*
Could you make a _____ dentist's appointment for me? It's urgent	Pouvez-vous me prendre un rendez-vous chez le dentiste? C'est urgent *poovay voo muh prohndr uhn rohnday voo shay luh dohnteest? seh tewrjhohn*
Can I come in today, _____ please?	Puis-je venir aujourd'hui s'il vous plaît? *pwee jhuh vuhneer oajhoordwee seel voo pleh?*
I have (terrible) _____ toothache	J'ai une rage de dents/un mal de dents(épouvantable) *jhay ewn rahjh duh dohn/uhn mahl duh dohn (aypoovohntahbl)*
Could you prescribe/ _____ give me a painkiller?	Pouvez-vous me prescrire/donner un calmant? *poovay voo muh prehskreer/donay uhn kahlmohn?*
A piece of my tooth _____ has broken off	Ma dent s'est cassée *mah dohn seh kahssay*
My filling's come out _____	Mon plombage est parti *mawn plawnbahjh eh pahrtee*
I've got a broken crown_____	Ma couronne est cassée *mah kooron eh kahssay*
I'd like/I don't want a _____ local anaesthetic	Je (ne) veux (pas) une anesthésie locale *jhuh (nuh) vuh (paz) ewn ahnehstayzee lokahl*

Can you do a makeshift repair job?	Pouvez-vous me soigner de façon provisoire?
	poovay voo muh swahnyay duh fahsawn proveezwahr?
I don't want this tooth pulled	Je ne veux pas que cette dent soit arrachée
	jhuh nuh vuh pah kuh seht dohn swaht ahrahshay
My dentures are broken. Can you fix them?	Mon dentier est cassé. Pouvez-vous le réparer?
	mawn dohntyay eh kahssay. poovay voo luh raypahray?

Quelle dent/molaire vous fait mal?	Which tooth hurts?
Vous avez un abcès	You've got an abscess
Je dois faire une dévitalisation	I'll have to do a root canal
Je vais vous faire une anesthésie locale	I'm giving you a local anaesthetic
Je dois plomber/extraire/polir cette dent	I'll have to fill/pull/file down this tooth
Je dois utiliser la roulette	I'll have to drill
Ouvrez bien la bouche	Open wide, please
Fermez la bouche	Close your mouth, please
Rincez	Rinse, please
Sentez-vous encore la douleur?	Does it hurt still?

14

In trouble

14.1 Asking for help 109

14.2 Loss 110

14.3 Accidents 110

14.4 Theft 111

14.5 Missing person 111

14.6 The police 112

14 .1 Asking for help

Help!	Au secours!
	oa suhkoor!
Fire!	Au feu!
	oa fuh!
Police!	Police!
	pohlees!
Quick!	Vite!
	veet!
Danger!	Danger!
	dohnjhay
Watch out!	Attention!
	ahtohnsyawn!
Stop!	Stop!
	stop!
Be careful!	Prudence!
	prewdohns!
Don't!	Arrêtez!
	ahrehtay!
Let go!	Lâchez!
	lahshay!
Stop that thief!	Au voleur!
	oa voluhr!
Could you help me, please?	Voulez-vous m'aider?
	voolay voo mayday?
Where's the police station/emergency exit/fire escape?	Où est le poste de police/la sortie de secours/l'escalier de secours?
	oo eh luh post duh polees/lah sortee duh suhkoor/lehskahlyay duh suhkoor?
Where's the nearest fire extinguisher?	Où y a-t-il un extincteur?
	oo ee yah teel uhn nehxtahnktuhr?
Call the fire brigade!	Prévenez les sapeurs-pompiers!
	prayvuhnay lay sahpuhr pawnpyay!
Call the police!	Appelez la police!
	ahpuhlay lah polees!
Call an ambulance!	Appelez une ambulance!
	ahpuhlay ewn ohnbewlohns!
Where's the nearest phone?	Où est le téléphone le plus proche?
	oo eh luh taylayfon luh plew prosh?
Could I use your phone?	Puis-je utiliser votre téléphone?
	pwee jhuh ewteeleezay votr taylayfon?
What's the emergency number?	Quel est le numéro d'urgence?
	kehl eh luh newmayroa dewrjhohns?
What's the number for the police?	Quel est le numéro de téléphone de la police?
	kehl eh luh newmayroa duh taylayfon duh lah polees?

14.2 Loss

I've lost my purse/_____ J'ai perdu mon porte-monnaie/
  wallet   portefeuille
                                jhay pehrdew mawn port moneh/portfuhy

I lost my...yesterday _____ Hier j'ai oublié mon/ma...
                                yehr jhay oobleeay mawn/mah...

I left my...here _____ J'ai laissé mon/ma...ici
                                jhay layssay mawn/mah...eesee

Did you find my...? _____ Avez-vous trouvé mon/ma...?
                                ahvay voo troovay mawn/mah...?

It was right here_____ Il était là
                                eel ayteh lah

It's quite valuable _____ C'est un objet de valeur
                                seh tuhn nobjheh duh vahluhr

Where's the lost_____ Où est le bureau des objets trouvés?
  property office?   *oo eh luh bewroa day zobjheh troovay?*

14.3 Accidents

There's been an accident __ Il y a eu un accident
                                eel ee yah ew uhn nahkseedohn

Someone's fallen into _____ Quelqu'un est tombé dans l'eau
  the water   *kehlkuhn eh tawnbay dohn loa*

There's a fire_____ Il y a un incendie.
                                eel ee yah uhn nahnsohndee

Is anyone hurt? _____ Y a-t-il quelqu'un de blessé?
                                ee yah teel kehlkuhn duh blehssay?

Some people have _____ Il (n)y a des(pas de) blessés
  been/no one's been   *eel (n)ee yah day(pah duh) blehssay*
  injured

There's someone in _____ Il y a encore quelqu'un dans la voiture/le
  the car/train still   train
                                eel ee ah ohnkor kehlkuhn dohn lah
                                vwahtewr/luh trahn

It's not too bad. Don't____ Ce n'est pas si grave. Ne vous inquiétez
  worry   pas
                                suh neh pah see grahv. nuh voo zahnkyaytay
                                pah

Leave everything the _____ Ne touchez à rien s'il vous plaît
  way it is, please   *nuh tooshay ah ryahn seel voo pleh*

I want to talk to the_____ Je veux d'abord parler à la police
  police first   *jhuh vuh dahbor pahrlay ah lah polees*

I want to take a _____ Je veux d'abord prendre une photo
  photo first   *jhuh vuh dahbor prohndr ewn foatoa*

Here's my name_____ Voici mon nom et mon adresse
  and address   *vwahsee mawn nawn ay mawn nahdrehs*

Could I have your _____ Puis-je connaître votre nom et votre
  name and address?   adresse?
                                pwee jhuh konehtr votr nawn ay votr
                                ahdrehs?

In trouble

4

Could I see some_____ dentification/your insurance papers?	Puis-je voir vos papiers d'identité/papiers d'assurance?
	pwee jhuh vwahr voa pahpyay deedohnteetay/pahpyay dahsewrohns?
Will you act as a _____ witness?	Voulez-vous être témoin?
	voolay voo zehtr taymwahn?
I need the details for _____ the insurance	Je dois avoir les données pour l'assurance.
	jhuh dwah zahvwahr lay donay poor lahsewrohns
Are you insured?_____	Etes-vous assuré?
	eht voo zahsewray?
Third party or_____ comprehensive?	Responsabilité civile ou tous risques?
	rehspawnsahbeeleetay seeveel oo too reesk?
Could you sign here, _____ please?	Voulez-vous signer ici?
	voolay voo seenyay eesee?

🔞 .4 Theft

I've been robbed _____	On m'a volé.
	awn mah volay
My...has been stolen _____	Mon/ma...a été volé(e).
	mawn/mah...ah aytay volay
My car's been_____ broken into	On a cambriolé ma voiture.
	awn nah kohnbreeolay mah vwahtewr

🔞 .5 Missing person

I've lost my child/_____ grandmother	J'ai perdu mon enfant/ma grand-mère
	jhay pehrdew mawn nohnfohn/mah grohnmehr
Could you help me _____ find him/her?	Voulez-vous m'aider à le/la chercher?
	voolay voo mayday ah luh/lah shehrshay?
Have you seen a _____ small child?	Avez-vous vu un petit enfant?
	ahvay voo vew uhn puhtee tohnfohn?
He's/she's...years old _____	Il/elle a...ans.
	eel/ehl ah...ohn
He's/she's got _____ short/long/blond/red/ brown/black/grey/curly/ straight/frizzy hair	Il/elle a les cheveux courts/longs/blonds/ roux/bruns/noirs/gris/bouclés/raides/frisés
	eel/ehl ah lay shuhvuh koor/lawn/blawn/roo/bruhn/nwahr/gree rehd/freezay
with a ponytail _____	avec une queue de cheval
	ahvehk ewn kuh duh shuhvahl
with plaits _____	avec des nattes
	ahvehk day naht
in a bun _____	avec un chignon
	ahvehk uhn sheenyawn
He's/she's got _____ blue/brown/green eyes	Il/elle a les yeux bleus/bruns/verts
	eel/ehl ah lay zyuh bluh/bruhn/vehr
He's wearing swimming ___ trunks/mountaineering boots	Il porte un maillot de bain/des chaussures de montagne.
	eel port uhn mahyoa duh bahn/day shoasewr duh mawntahnyuh

In trouble

14

111

with/without glasses/ a bag	avec/sans lunettes/un sac
	ahvehk/sohn lewneht/uhn sahk
tall/short	grand(e)/petit(e)
	grohn(d)/puhtee(t)
This is a photo of him/her	Voici une photo de lui/d'elle.
	vwahsee ewn foatoa duh lwee/dehl
He/she must be lost	Il/elle s'est certainement égaré(e).
	eel/ehl seh sehrtehnmohn aygahray

14 .6 The police

An arrest

Vos papiers de voiture s'il vous plaît.	Your registration papers, please
Vous rouliez trop vite	You were speeding
Vous êtes en stationnement interdit	You're not allowed to park here
Vous n'avez pas mis d'argent dans le parcmètre	You haven't put money in the meter
Vos phares ne marchent pas	Your lights aren't working
Vous avez une contravention de...francs	That's a...franc fine
Vous voulez payer immédiatement?	Do you want to pay on the spot?
Vous devez payer immédiatement	You'll have to pay on the spot

I don't speak French	Je ne parle pas français.
	jhuh nuh pahrl pah frohnseh
I didn't see the sign	Je n'ai pas vu ce panneau.
	jhuh nay pah vew suh pahnoa
I don't understand what it says	Je ne comprends pas ce qu'il y est écrit.
	jhuh nuh kawnprohn pah suh keel ee yeh taykree
I was only doing... kilometres an hour	Je ne roulais qu'à...kilomètres à l'heure.
	jhuh nuh rooleh kah...keeloamehtr ah luhr
I'll have my car checked	Je vais faire réviser ma voiture.
	jhuh veh fehr rayveezay mah vwahtewr
I was blinded by oncoming lights	J'ai été aveuglé(e) par une voiture en sens inverse.
	jhay aytay ahvuhglay pahr ewn vwahtewr ohn sohns ahnvehrs

In trouble

4

112

At the police station

I want to report a _____ Je viens faire la déclaration d'une
collision/missing collision/d'une disparition/d'un viol
person/rape *jhuh vyahn fehr lah dayklahrasyawn dewn koleezyawn/dewn deespahreesyawn/duhn vyol*

Could you make out _____ Voulez-vous faire un rapport?
a report, please? *voolay voo fehr uhn rahpor?*

Could I have a copy _____ Puis-je avoir une copie pour l'assurance?
for the insurance? *pwee jhahvwahr ewn kopee poor lahsewrohns?*

I've lost everything _____ J'ai tout perdu
jhay too pehrdew

I'd like an interpreter _____ J'aimerais un interprète
jhehmuhreh zuhn nahntehrpreht

I'm innocent _____ Je suis innocent(e)
jhuh swee zeenosohn(t)

I don't know anything _____ Je ne sais rien
about it *jhuh nuh seh ryahn*

I want to speak to _____ Je veux parler à quelqu'un du consulat
someone from the British britannique
consulate *jhuh vuh pahrlay ah kehlkuhn dew kawnsewlah breetahneek*

I need to see someone _____ Je dois parler à quelqu'un de l'ambassade
from the British embassy britannique
jhuh dwah pahrlay ah kehlkuhn duh lohnbahsahd breetahneek

I want a lawyer who_____ Je veux un avocat qui parle anglais
speaks English *jhuh vuh uhn nahvokah kee pahrl ohngleh*

In trouble

14

113

15

Word list

Word list English - French

● **This word list** is meant to supplement the previous chapters.
Nouns are always accompanied by the French definite article in order
to indicate whether it is a masculine (le) or feminine (la) word. In the
case of an abbreviated article (l'), the gender is indicated by (m.) or (f.).
In a number of cases, words not contained in this list can be found
elsewhere in this book, namely alongside the diagrams of the car, the
bicycle and the tent. Many food terms can be found in the French-
English list in 4.7.

A

about	environ	*ohnveerawn*
above	au-dessus	*oadsew*
abroad	l'étranger (m.)	*laytrohnjhay*
accident	l'accident (m.)	*lahkseedohn*
adder	la vipère	*lah veepehr*
addition	l'addition (f.)	*lahdeesyawn*
address	l'adresse (f.)	*lahdrehs*
admission	l'entrée (f.)	*lohntray*
admission price	le prix d'entrée	*luh pree dohntray*
advice	le conseil	*luh kawnsehy*
after	après	*ahpreh*
afternoon	l'après-midi (m., f.)	*lahpreh meedee*
aftershave	la lotion après-rasage	*lah loasyawn ahpreh rahzahjh*
again	à nouveau	*ah noovoa*
against	contre	*kawntr*
age	l'âge (m.)	*lahjh*
Aids	le sida	*luh seedah*
air conditioning	l'air conditionné (m.)	*lehr kawndeesyonay*
air mattress	le matelas pneumatique	*luh mahtlah pnuhmahteek*
air sickness bag	le petit sac à vomissements	*luh puhtee sahk ah vomeesmohn*
aircraft	l'avion (m.)	*lahvyawn*
airport	l'aéroport (m.)	*lahayroapor*
alarm	l'alarme (f.)	*lahlahrm*
alarm clock	le réveil	*luh rayvehy*
alcohol	l'alcool (m.)	*lahlkol*
A-level equivalent	le bac	*luh bahk*
a little	un peu	*uhn puh*
allergic	allergique	*ahlehrjheek*
alone	seul	*suhl*
always	toujours	*toojhoor*
ambulance	l'ambulance (f.)	*lohnbewlohns*
amount	le montant	*luh mawntohn*
amusement park	le parc d'attractions	*luh pahrk dahtrahksyawn*
anaesthetize	anesthésier	*ahnehstayzyay*
anchovy	l'anchois (m.)	*lohnshwah*
and	et	*ay*
angry	en colère	*ohn kolehr*
animal	l'animal (m.)	*lahneemahl*
answer	la réponse	*lah raypawns*
ant	la fourmi	*lah foormee*

antibiotics	l'antibiotique (m.)	*lohnteebyoteek*
antifreeze	l'antigel (m.)	*lohnteejhehl*
antique	ancien	*ohnsyahn*
antiques	antiquités (f.)	*ohnteekeetay*
anus	l'anus (m.)	*lahnews*
apartment	l'appartement (m.)	*lahpahrtuhmohn*
aperitif	l'apéritif (m.)	*lahpayreeteef*
apologies	les excuses	*lay zehxkewz*
apple	la pomme	*lah pom*
apple juice	le jus de pommes	*luh jhew duh pom*
apple pie	la tarte aux pommes	*lah tahrt oa pom*
apple sauce	la compote de pommes	*lah kawnpot duh pom*
appointment	le rendez-vous	*luh rohndayvoo*
apricot	l'abricot (m.)	*lahbreekoa*
April	avril	*ahvreel*
archbishop	l'archevêque (m.)	*lahrshuhvehk*
architecture	l'architecture (f.)	*lahrsheetehktewr*
area	les environs	*lay zohnveerawn*
arm	le bras	*luh brah*
arrive	arriver	*ahreevay*
arrow	la flèche	*lah flehsh*
art	l'art (m.)	*lahr*
artery	l'artère (f.)	*lahrtehr*
artichoke	l'artichaut (m.)	*lahrteeshoa*
article	l'article (m.)	*lahrteekl*
artificial respiration	la respiration artificielle	*lah rehspeerahsyawn ahrteefeesyehl*
arts and crafts	l'artisanat d'art	*lahrteezahnah dahr*
ashtray	le cendrier	*luh sohndreeay*
ask	demander	*duhmohnday*
ask	prier	*preeay*
asparagus	les asperges	*lay zahspehrjh*
aspirin	l'aspirine (f.)	*lahspeereen*
assault	l'agression (f.)	*lahgrehsyawn*
at home	à la maison	*ah lah mehzawn*
at night	la nuit	*lah nwee*
at the back	à l'arrière	*ah lahryehr*
at the front	à l'avant	*ah lahvohn*
at the latest	au plus tard	*oa plew tahr*
aubergine	l'aubergine (f.)	*loabehrjheen*
August	août	*oot*
automatic	automatique	*loatoamahteek*
automatically	automatiquement	*oatoamahteekmohn*
autumn	l'automne (m.)	*loatonn*
avalanche	l'avalanche (f.)	*lahvahlohnsh*
awake	réveillé	*rayvay-yay*
awning	le parasol	*luh pahrahsol*

B

baby	le bébé	*luh baybay*
baby food	la nourriture pour bébé	*lah nooreetewr poor baybay*
babysitter	le/la baby-sitter	*luh/lah behbee seetehr*
back	le dos	*luh doa*
backpack	le sac à dos	*luh sahk ah doa*

bacon	le lard	*luh lahr*
bad	mauvais	*moaveh*
bag	le sac	*luh sahk*
baker (cakes)	le pâtissier	*luh pahteesyay*
baker	le boulanger	*luh boolohnjhay*
balcony (theatre)	le balcon	*luh bahlkawn*
balcony (to building)	le balcon	*luh bahlkawn*
ball	la balle	*lah bahl*
ballet	le ballet; la danse	*luh bahleh; la dohns*
ballpoint pen	le stylo à bille	*luh steeloa ah beey*
banana	la banane	*lah bahnahn*
bandage	le pansement	*luh pohnsmohn*
bank (river)	la rive	*lah reev*
bank	la banque	*lah bohnk*
bank card	la carte bancaire	*lah kahrt bohnkehr*
bar (café)	le bar	*luh bahr*
bar (drinks' cabinet)	le bar	*luh bahr*
barbecue	le barbecue	*luh bahrbuhkew*
bath	le bain	*luh bahn*
bath attendant	le maître nageur	*luh mehtr nahjhuhr*
bath foam	la mousse de bain	*lah moos duh bahn*
bath towel	la serviette de bain	*lah sehrvyeht duh bahn*
bathing cap	le bonnet de bain	*luh boneh duh bahn*
bathing cubicle	la cabine de bain	*lah kahbeen duh bahn*
bathing suit	le maillot de bain	*luh mahyoa duh bahn*
bathroom	la salle de bain	*lah sahl duh bahn*
battery (car)	l'accumulateur (m.)	*lahkewmewlahtuhr*
battery	la pile	*lah peel*
beach	la plage	*lah plahjh*
beans	les haricots	*lay ahreekoa*
beautiful	beau/belle	*boa/behl*
beautiful	magnifique	*mahnyeefeek*
beauty parlour	le salon de beauté	*luh sahlawn duh boatay*
bed	le lit	*luh lee*
bee	l'abeille (f.)	*lahbehy*
beef	la viande de boeuf	*lah vyohnd duh buhf*
beer	la bière	*lah byehr*
beetroot	la betterave	*lah behtrahv*
begin	commencer	*komohnsay*
beginner	le débutant	*luh daybewtohn*
behind	derrière	*dehryehr*
Belgian (f)	la belge	*lah behljh*
Belgian (m)	le belge	*luh behljh*
Belgium	la Belgique	*lah behljheek*
belt	la ceinture	*lah sahntewr*
berth	la couchette	*lah koosheht*
better	mieux	*myuh*
bicarbonate of soda	le bicarbonate de soude	*luh beekahrbonaht duh sood*
bicycle	la bicyclette/le vélo	*lah beeseekleht/luh vayloa*
bicycle pump	la pompe à bicyclette	*lah pawnp ah beeseekleht*
bicycle repairman	le réparateur de vélos	*luh raypahrahtuhr duh vayloa*
bikini	le bikini	*luh beekeenee*
bill	l'addition	*lahdeesyawn*

birthday	l'anniversaire (m.)	lahneevehrsehr
biscuit	le biscuit	luh beeskwee
bite	mordre	mordr
bitter	amer	ahmehr
black	noir	nwahr
bland	fade	fahd
blanket	la couverture	lah koovehrtewr
bleach	blondir	blawndeer
blister	la cloque	lah klok
blond	blond	blawn
blood	le sang	luh sohn
blood pressure	la tension	lah tohnsyawn
blouse	le chemisier	luh shuhmeezyay
blow dry	sécher	sayshay
blue	bleu	bluh
blunt	épointé/émoussé	aypwahntay/aymoosay
boat	le bateau	luh bahtoa
body	le corps	luh kor
body milk	le lait corporel	luh leh korporehl
boil	bouillir	boo-yeer
boiled	cuit	kwee
boiled ham	jambon cuit	jhohnbawn kwee
bone	l'os (m.)	los
bonnet	le capot	luh kahpoa
book (verb)	réserver	raysehrvay
book	le livre	luh leevr
booked	réservé	rayzehrvay
booking office	le bureau de réservation	luh bewroa duh rayzehrvahsyawn
bookshop	la librairie	lah leebrehree
border	la frontière	lah frawntyehr
bored (to be)	s'ennuyer	sonweeyay
boring	ennuyeux	onweeyuh
born	né	nay
botanical gardens	le jardin botanique	luh jhahrdahn botahneek
both	tous/toutes les deux	too/toot lay duh
bottle-warmer	le chauffe-biberon	luh shoaf beebrawn
bottle (baby's)	le biberon	luh beebrawn
bottle	la bouteille	lah bootehy
box	la boîte	lah bwaht
box (theatre)	la loge	lah lojh
boy	le garçon	luh gahrsawn
bra	le soutien-gorge	luh sootyahn gorjh
bracelet	le bracelet	luh brahsleh
braised	braisé	brehzay
brake	le frein	luh frahn
brake fluid	le liquide de freins	luh leekeed duh frahn
brake oil	l'huile à frein (f.)	lweel ah frahn
bread	le pain	luh pahn
break	casser	kahssay
breakfast	le petit déjeuner	luh puhtee dayjhuhnay
breast	la poitrine	lah pwahtreen
bridge	le pont	luh pawn
briefs	la culotte	lah kewlot
brochure	la brochure	lah broshewr
broken	cassé	kahssay

broth	le consommé	*luh kawnsomay*
brother	le frère	*luh frehr*
brown	brun	*bruhn*
brush	la brosse	*lah bros*
Brussels sprouts	les choux de Bruxelles	*lay shoo duh brewxehl*
bucket	le seau	*luh soa*
bugs	les insectes nuisibles	*lay zahnsehkt nweezeebl*
building	le bâtiment	*luh bahteemohn*
buoy	la bouée	*lah booway*
burglary	le cambriolage	*luh kohnbryolajh*
burn (verb)	brûler	*brewlay*
burn	la brûlure	*lah brewlewr*
burnt	brûlé	*brewlay*
bus	l'autobus (m.)	*loatoabews*
bus station	la station d'autobus	*lah stahsyawn doatoabews*
bus stop	l'arrêt d'autobus (m.)	*lahreh doatoabews*
business class	la classe affaire (f.)	*lah klahs ahfehr*
business trip	le voyage d'affaires	*luh vwahyahjh dahfehr*
busy	animé	*ahneemay*
butane gas	le gaz butane	*luh gahz bewtahnn*
butcher	le boucher	*luh booshay*
butter	le beurre	*luh buhr*
button	le bouton	*luh bootawn*
buy	acheter	*ahshtay*
by airmail	la poste aérienne/ par avion	*lah post ahayryehn/ pahr ahvyawn*

C

cabbage	le chou	*luh shoo*
cabin	la cabine	*lah kahbeen*
cake	le gâteau	*luh gahtoa*
call	appeler	*ahpuhlay*
called (to be)	s'appeler	*sahpuhlay*
camera	l'appareil-photo (m.)	*lahpahrehy foatoa*
camp	faire du camping	*fehr dew kohnpeeng*
camp shop	le magasin du camping	*luh mahgahzahn dew kohnpeeng*
camp site	le camping	*luh kohnpeeng*
camper	le camping-car	*luh kohnpeeng kahr*
campfire	le feu de camp	*luh fuh duh kohn*
camping guide	le guide de camping	*luh gueed duh kohnpeeng*
camping permit	le permis de camping	*luh pehrmee duh kohnpeeng*
canal boat	la péniche	*lah payneesh*
cancel	annuler	*ahnewlay*
candle	la bougie	*lah boojhee*
canoe (verb)	faire du canoë	*fehr dew kahnoaeh*
canoe	le canoë	*luh kahnoaeh*
car (train)	le wagon	*luh vahgawn*
car	la voiture	*lah vwahtewr*
car deck	le pont à voitures	*luh pawn ah vwahtewr*
car documents	les papiers de voiture	*lay pahpyay duh vwahtewr*

car trouble	la panne	*lah pahnn*
carafe	la carafe	*lah kahrahf*
caravan	la caravane	*lah kahrahvahnn*
cardigan	le cardigan/le gilet	*luh kahrdeegahn/ luh jheeleh*
careful	prudent	*prewdohn*
carrot	la carotte	*lah kahrot*
cartridge	la cartouche	*lah kahrtoosh*
cartridge	la cassette	*lah kahseht*
cascade	la cascade	*lah kahskahd*
cash desk	la caisse	*lah kehss*
casino	le casino	*luh kahzeenoa*
cassette	la cassette	*lah kahseht*
castle	le château	*luh shahtoa*
cat	le chat	*luh shah*
catalogue	le catalogue	*luh kahtahlog*
cathedral	la cathédrale	*lah kahtaydrahl*
cauliflower	le chou-fleur	*luh shoo fluhr*
cave	la grotte	*lah grot*
CD	le compact disc	*luh kawnpahkt deesk*
celebrate	célébrer	*saylaybray*
cellotape	le scotch	*luh skoch*
cemetery	le cimetière	*luh seemtyehr*
centimetre	le centimètre	*luh sohnteemehtr*
central heating	le chauffage central	*luh shoafahjh sohntrahl*
centre (in the)	au milieu	*oa meelyuh*
centre	le centre	*luh sohntr*
cereal	la céréale	*lah sayrayahl*
chair	la chaise	*lah shehz*
chambermaid	la femme de chambre	*lah fahm duh shohnbr*
chamois	la peau de chamois	*lah poa duh shahmwah*
champagne	le champagne	*luh shohnpany*
change (verb)	modifier	*modeefyay*
	changer	*shohnjhay*
change	la monnaie	*lah moneh*
change the baby's nappy	changer la couche du bébé	*shohnjhay lah koosh dew baybay*
change the oil	changer l'huile	*shohnjhay lweel*
chapel	la chapelle	*lah shahpehl*
charcoal tablets	les pastilles de charbon	*lay pahsteey duh shahrbawn*
charter flight	le vol charter	*luh vol shahrtehr*
chat up	draguer	*drahgay*
check (verb)	contrôler	*kawntroalay*
check in	enregistrer	*ohnruhjheestray*
cheers	à votre santé	*ah votr sohntay*
cheese	le fromage	*luh fromahjh*
chef	le chef	*luh shehf*
chemist	la pharmacie	*lah fahrmahsee*
cheque	le chèque	*luh shehk*
cherries	les cerises	*lay suhreez*
chess (play)	jouer aux échecs	*jhooay oa zayshehk*
chewing gum	le chewing-gum	*luh shweenguhm*
chicken	le poulet	*luh pooleh*
chicory	les endives	*lay zohndeev*
child	l'enfant (m./f.)	*lohnfohn*
child seat	le siège-enfant	*luh seeyehjh ohnfohn*

chilled	rafraîchi	*rahfrehshee*
chin	le menton	*luh montawn*
chips	les pommes-frites	*lay pom freet*
chocolate	le chocolat	*luh shoakoalah*
choose	choisir	*shwahzeer*
chop	la côtelette	*lah koatuhleht*
christian name	le prénom	*luh praynawn*
church	l'église (f.)	*laygleez*
church service	le service religieux	*luh sehrvees ruhleejhyuh*
cigar	le cigare	*luh seegahr*
cigar shop	le tabac	*luh tahbah*
cigarette	la cigarette	*lah seegahreht*
cigarette paper	le papier à cigarettes	*luh pahpyay ah seegahreht*
cine camera	la caméra	*lah kahmayrah*
circle	le cercle	*luh sehrkl*
circus	le cirque	*luh seerk*
city	la ville	*lah veel*
map	le plan	*luh plohn*
classical concert	le concert classique	*luh kawnsehr klahsseek*
clean (verb)	nettoyer	*nehtwahyay*
clean	propre	*propr*
clear	clair	*klehr*
clearance	les soldes	*lay sold*
closed	fermé	*fehrmay*
closed off	bloqué	*blokay*
clothes	les habits	*lay zahbee*
clothes hanger	le cintre	*luh sahntr*
clothes peg	la pince à linge	*lah pahns ah lahnjh*
clothing	vêtements	*vehtmohn*
coach	l'autobus (m.)	*loatoabews*
coat	le manteau	*luh mohntoa*
cockroach	le cafard	*luh kahfahr*
cocoa	le cacao	*luh kahkahoa*
cod	le cabillaud	*luh kahbeeyoa*
coffee	le café	*luh kahfay*
coffee filter	le filtre de cafetière	*luh feeltr duh kahftyehr*
cognac	le cognac	*luh konyahk*
cold	froid	*frwah*
cold	le rhume	*luh rewm*
cold cuts	la charcuterie	*lah shahrkewtree*
collarbone	la clavicule	*lah klahveekewl*
colleague	le collègue	*luh kolehg*
collision	la collision	*lah koleezyawn*
cologne	l'eau de toilette (f.)	*loa duh twahleht*
colour	la couleur	*lah kooluhr*
colour pencils	les crayons de couleur	*lay krayawn duh kooluhr*
colour TV	la télévision en couleurs	*lah taylayveezyawn ohn kooluhr*
colouring book	l'album de coloriage (m.)	*lahlbuhm duh koloryajh*
comb	le peigne	*luh pehnyuh*
come	venir	*vuhneer*
come back	revenir	*ruhvuhneer*

compartment	le compartiment	*luh kawnpahrteemohn*
complaint	la plainte	*lah plahnt*
complaints book	le cahier de réclamations	*luh kahyay duh rayklahmahsyawn*
completely	entièrement	*ohntyehrmohn*
compliment	le compliment	*luh kawnpleemohn*
compulsory	obligatoire	*obleegahtwahr*
concert	le concert	*luh kawnsehr*
concert hall	la salle de concert	*lah sahl duh kawnsehr*
concussion	la commotion cérébrale	*lah koamoasyawn sayraybrahl*
condensed milk	le lait condensé	*luh leh kawndohnsay*
condom	le préservatif	*luh prayzehrvahteef*
congratulate	féliciter	*fayleeseetay*
connection	la liaison	*lah lyehzawn*
constipation	la constipation	*lah kawnsteepahsyawn*
consulate	le consulat	*luh kownsewlah*
consultation	la consultation	*lah kawnsewltahsyawn*
contact lens	la lentille de contact	*lah lohnteey duh kawntahkt*
contact lens solution	le liquide pour lentille de contact	*luh leekeed poor lohnteey duh kawntahkt*
contagious	contagieux	*kawntahjhyuh*
contraceptive	le contraceptif	*luh kawntrahsehpteef*
contraceptive pill	la pilule anticonceptionnelle	*lah peelewl ohnteekawnseh-psyonehl*
convent	le couvent	*luh koovohn*
cook (verb)	cuisiner	*kweezeenay*
cook	le cuisinier	*luh kweezeenyay*
copper	le cuivre	*luh kweevr*
copy	la copie	*lah kopee*
corkscrew	le tire-bouchon	*luh teerbooshawn*
cornflour	la maïzena	*lah maheezaynah*
corner	le coin	*luh kwahn*
correct	correct	*korehkt*
correspond	correspondre	*korehspawndr*
corridor	le couloir	*luh koolwahr*
costume	le costume	*luh kostewm*
cot	le lit d'enfant	*luh lee dohnfohn*
cotton	le coton	*luh koatawn*
cotton wool	le coton	*luh koatawn*
cough	la toux	*lah too*
cough mixture	le sirop pectoral	*luh seeroa pehktoaral*
counter	la réception	*lah raysehpsyawn*
country	le pays	*luh pehy*
country	la campagne	*lah kohnpahnyuh*
country code	l'indicatif du pays (m.)	*lahndeekahteef dew pehy*
courgette	la courgette	*lah koorjheht*
cousin (f)	la cousine	*lah koozeen*
cousin (m)	le cousin	*luh koozahn*
crab	le crabe	*luh krahb*
cream	la crème	*lah krehm*

credit card	la carte de crédit	*lah kahrt duh kraydee*
crisps	les chips	*lay sheeps*
croissant	le croissant	*luh krwahssohn*
cross-country run	la piste de ski de fond	*lah peest duh skee duh fawn*
cross-country skiing	faire du ski de fond	*fehr dew skee duh fawn*
cross-country skis	les skis de fond	*lay skee duh fawn*
cross the road	traverser	*trahvehrsay*
crossing	la traversée	*lah trahvehrsay*
crossing	le croisement	*luh krwahzmohn*
cry	pleurer	*pluhray*
cubic metre	le mètre cube	*luh mehtr kewb*
cucumber	le concombre	*luh kawnkawnbr*
cuddly toy	l'animal en peluche (m.)	*lahneemahl ohn plewsh*
cuff links	les boutons de manchette	*lay bootawn duh mohnsheht*
cup	la tasse	*lah tahs*
curly	frisé	*freezay*
current	la circulation	*lah seerkewlahsyawn*
cushion	le coussin	*luh koossahn*
customary	habituel	*ahbeetewehl*
customs	la douane	*lah dwahnn*
customs	le contrôle douanier	*luh kawntrol dwahnnyay*
cut (verb)	couper	*koopay*
cutlery	couverts	*koovehr*
cycling	faire de la bicyclette/ du vélo	*fehr duh lah beeseekleht/dew vayloa*

D

dairy produce	les produits laitiers	*lay prodwee laytyay*
damaged	abîmé	*ahbeemay*
dance	danser	*dohnsay*
dandruff	les pellicules	*lay payleekewl*
danger	le danger	*luh dohnjhay*
dangerous	dangereux	*dohnjhuhruh*
dark	sombre	*sawnbr*
date	le rendez-vous	*luh rohndayvoo*
daughter	la fille	*lah feey*
day	le jour	*luh jhoor*
day after tomorrow	après-demain	*ahpreh duhmahn*
day before yesterday	avant-hier	*ahvohn tyehr*
death	la mort	*lah mor*
decaffeinated	le décaféiné	*luh daykahfayeenay*
December	décembre	*daysohnbr*
deck chair	la chaise longue	*lah shehz lawng*
declare(customs)	déclarer	*dayklahray*
deep	profond	*profawn*
deep sea diving	la plongée sous-marine	*lah plawnjhay soo mahreen*
deepfreeze	le congélateur	*luh kawnjhaylahtuhr*
degrees	les degrés	*lay duhgray*
delay	le retard	*luh ruhtahr*
delicious	délicieux	*dayleesyuh*

Word list

123

dentist	le dentiste	*luh dohnteest*
dentures	le dentier	*luh dohntyay*
deodorant	le déodorant	*luh dayodorohn*
department	le rayon	*luh rayawn*
department store	le grand magasin	*luh grohn mahgahzahn*
departure	le départ	*luh daypahr*
departure time	l'heure de départ (f.)	*ler duh daypahr*
depilatory cream	la crème épilatoire	*lah krehm aypeelahtwahr*
deposit	arrhes, acompte	*ahr, ahkawnt*
dessert	le dessert	*luh dehssehr*
destination	la destination	*lah dehsteenahsyawn*
develop	développer	*dayvlopay*
diabetes	le diabète	*luh deeahbeht*
diabetic	le diabétique	*luh dyahbayteek*
dial	composer	*kawnpoazay*
diamond	le diamant	*luh deeahmohn*
diarrhoea	la diarrhée	*lah deeahray*
dictionary	le dictionnaire	*luh deeksyonehr*
diesel	le diesel	*luh dyayzehl*
diesel oil	le gas-oil	*luh gahzwahl*
diet	le régime	*luh rayjheem*
difficulty	la difficulté	*lah deefeekewltay*
dining room	la salle à manger	*lah sahl ah mohnjhay*
dining/buffet car	le wagon-restaurant	*luh vahgawn rehstoaron*
dinner (to have)	dîner	*deenay*
dinner	le dîner	*luh deenay*
dinner jacket	le smoking	*luh smokeeng*
direction	la direction	*lah deerehksyawn*
directly	directement	*deerehktuhmohn*
dirty	sale	*sahl*
disabled	l'invalide (m./f.)	*lahnvahleed*
disco	la discothèque	*lah deeskotehk*
discount	la réduction	*lah raydewksyawn*
disgusting	dégoûtant	*daygootohn*
dish	le plat	*luh plah*
dish of the day	le plat du jour	*luh plah dew jhoor*
disinfectant	le désinfectant	*luh dayzahnfehktohn*
distance	la distance	*lah deestohns*
distilled water	l'eau distillée (f.)	*loa deesteelay*
disturb	déranger	*dayrohnjhay*
disturbance	troubles, tapage	*troobl, tapahjh*
dive	plonger	*plawnjhay*
diving	la plongée	*lah plawnjhay*
diving board	le plongeoir	*luh plawnjhwahr*
diving gear	l'équipement de plongeur (m.)	*laykeepmohn duh plawnjhuhr*
DIY-shop	le magasin de bricolage	*luh mahgahzahn duh breekolajh*
dizzy	pris de vertige	*pree duh vehrteejh*
do (verb)	faire	*fehr*
doctor	le médecin	*luh maydsahn*
dog	le chien	*luh shyahn*
doll	la poupée	*lah poopay*

Word list

15

124

domestic	l'intérieur (m.)	*lahntayryuhr*
	du pays	*dew pehy*
door	la porte	*lah port*
down	en bas	*ohn bah*
draught	le courant d'air	*luh koorohn dehr*
dream	rêver	*rehvay*
dress	la robe	*lah rob*
dressing gown	le peignoir	*luh paynywahr*
drink (verb)	boire	*bwahr*
drink	le verre	*luh vehr*
drinking chocolate	le chocolat au lait	*luh shoakoalah oa leh*
drinking water	l'eau potable (f.)	*loa potabl*
drive	conduire	*kawndweer*
driver	le chauffeur	*luh shoafuhr*
driving licence	le permis de	*luh pehrmee duh*
	conduire	*kawndweer*
drought	la sécheresse	*lah sayshrehs*
dry (verb)	sécher	*sayshay*
dry	sec	*sehk*
dry clean	nettoyer à sec	*nehtwahay ah sehk*
dry cleaner's	la teinturerie	*lah tahntewruhree*
dry shampoo	le shampooing sec	*luh shohnpwahn sehk*
dummy	la tétine	*lah tayteen*
during	pendant	*pohndohn*
during the day	de jour	*duh jhoor*

E

each time	chaque fois	*shahk fwah*
ear	l'oreille (f.)	*lorehy*
ear, nose and throat (ENT) specialist	l'oto-rhino (m.)	*loatoa reenoa*
earache	le mal d'oreille	*luh mahl dorehy*
eardrops	les gouttes pour	*lay goot poor*
	les oreilles	*lay zorehy*
early	tôt	*toa*
earrings	les boucles d'oreilles	*lay bookl dorehy*
earth	la terre	*lah tehr*
earthenware	la poterie	*lah potree*
east	l'est (m.)	*lehst*
easy	facile	*fahseel*
eat	manger	*mohnjhay*
eczema	l'eczéma (m.)	*lehgzaymah*
eel	l'anguille (f.)	*lohngeey*
egg	l'oeuf (m.)	*luhf*
elastic band	l'élastique (m.)	*laylahsteek*
electric	électrique	*aylehktreek*
electric current	le courant	*luh koorohn*
electricity	l'électricité (f.)	*laylehktreeseetay*
embassy	l'ambassade (f.)	*lohnbahsahd*
emergency brake	le frein de secours	*luh frahn duh suhkoor*
emergency exit	la sortie de secours	*lah sortee duh suhkoor*
emergency number	le numéro	*luh newmayroa*
	d'urgence (m.)	*dewrzhohns*
emergency phone	le téléphone	*luh taylayfon*
	d'urgence (m.)	*dewrjhohns*
emergency triangle	le triangle de	*luh treeohngl duh*
	signalisation	*seenyahleezahsyawn*

Word list

15

emery board	la lime à ongles	lah leem ah awngl
empty	vide	veed
engaged	occupé	okewpay
England	Angleterre	ohngluhtehr
English	anglais	ohngleh
entertainment guide	le journal des spectacles	luh jhoornal day spehktahkl
envelope	l'enveloppe (f.)	lohnvlop
escort	l'hôtesse	loatehs
evening	le soir	luh swahr
evening wear	la tenue de soirée	lah tuhnew duh swahray
event	l'évènement (m.)	layvehnmohn
everything	tout	too
everywhere	partout	pahrtoo
examine	examiner	ehgzahmeenay
excavation	les fouilles	lay fooeey
excellent	excellent	ehxaylohn
exchange	échanger	ayshohnjhay
exchange office	le bureau de change	luh bewroa duh shohnjh
exchange rate	le cours du change	luh koor dew shohnjh
excursion	l'excursion (f.)	lehxkewrsyawn
exhibition	l'exposition (f.)	lehxpoazeesyawn
exit	la sortie	lah sortee
expenses	les frais	lay freh
expensive	cher	shehr
explain	expliquer	ehxpleekay
express	l'express (m.)	lehxprehs
external	extérieur	ehxtayryuhr
eye	l'oeil (m.)	luhy
eye drops	les gouttes pour les yeux	lay goot poor lay zyuh
eye shadow	le fard à paupières	luh fahr ah poapyehr
eye specialist	l'ophtalmologue (m.)	loftahmolog
eyeliner	l'eye-liner (m.)	lahy leehnehr

F

face	le visage	luh veezajh
factory	l'usine (f.)	lewzeen
fair	la foire	lah fwahr
fall	tomber	tawnbay
family	la famille	lah fahmeey
famous	célèbre	saylehbr
far away	éloigné	aylwahnyay
farm	la ferme	lah fehrm
farmer	le fermier	luh fehrmyay
fashion	la mode	lah mod
fast	rapidement	rahpeedmohn
father	le père	luh pehr
fault	la faute	lah foat
fax	faxer	fahxay
fear	la peur	lah puhr
February	février	fayvryay
feel	sentir	sohnteer
feel like	avoir envie (de)	ahvvwahr ohnvee (duh)
fence	la clôture	lah kloatewr

fever	la fièvre	*lah feeyehvr*
fill (tooth)	plomber	*plawnbay*
fill out	remplir	*rohnpleer*
filling	le plombage	*luh plawnbahjh*
film	la pellicule	*lah payleekewl*
filter	le filtre	*luh feeltr*
filthy	crasseux	*krahssuh*
find	trouver	*troovay*
fine	la caution	*lah koasyawn*
fine (parking)	la contravention	*lah kawntrahvohn-syawn*
finger	le doigt	*luh dwah*
fire	le feu	*luh fuh*
fire brigade	les sapeurs-pompiers	*lay sahpuhr pawnpyay*
fire escape	l'escalier de secours (m.)	*lehskahlyay duh suhkoor*
fire extinguisher	l'extincteur (m.)	*lehxtahntuhr*
first	le premier	*luh pruhmyay*
first aid	les premiers soins	*lay pruhmyay swahn*
first class	la première classe	*lah pruhmyehr klahs*
fish (verb)	pêcher	*payshay*
fish	le poisson	*luh pwahssawn*
fishing rod	la canne à pêche	*lah kahnn ah pehsh*
fitness centre	le centre de mise en forme	*luh sohntr duh meez ohn form*
fitness training	l'entraînement de mise en forme (m.)	*lohntrehnmohn duh meez ohn form*
fitting room	la cabine d'essayage	*lah kahbeen dehsayahjh*
fix	réparer	*raypahray*
flag	le drapeau	*luh drahpoa*
flash bulb	l'ampoule de flash (f.)	*lohnpool duh flahsh*
flash cube	le cube-flash	*luh kewb flahsh*
flash gun	le flash	*luh flahsh*
flat	l'appartement (m.)	*lahpahrtuhmohn*
flea market	le marché aux puces	*luh mahrshay oa pews*
flight	le vol	*luh vol*
flight number	le numéro de vol	*luh newmayroa duh vol*
flood	l'inondation (f.)	*leenawndahsyawn*
floor	l'étage (m.)	*laytahjh*
flour	la farine	*lah fahreen*
flu	la grippe	*lah greep*
fly-over	l'autopont (m.)	*loatoapawn*
fly (insect)	la mouche	*lah moosh*
fly (verb)	voler	*volay*
fog	le brouillard	*luh brooy-yahr*
foggy (to be)	faire du brouillard	*fehr dew brooy-yahr*
folding caravan	la caravane pliante	*lah kahrahvahnn pleeohnt*
folkloristic	folklorique	*folkloreek*
follow	suivre	*sweevr*
food	la nourriture	*lah nooreetewr*
food poisoning	l'intoxication alimentaire (f.)	*lahntoxeekahsyawn ahleemohntehr*
foodstuffs	les produits alimentaires	*lay prohdwee zahleemohntehr*
foot	le pied	*luh pyay*

for hire	à louer	*ah looay*
forbidden	interdit	*ahntehrdee*
forehead	le front	*luh frawn*
foreign	étranger	*aytrohnjhay*
forget	oublier	*oobleeay*
fork	la fourchette	*lah foorsheht*
form	le questionnaire	*luh kehstyonehr*
fort	le fort	*luh for*
fountain	la fontaine	*lah fawntehn*
four star petrol	le super	*luh sewpehr*
frame	la monture	*lah mawntewr*
franc	le franc	*luh frohn*
free	libre	*leebr*
free of charge	gratuit	*grahtwee*
free time	les loisirs	*lay lwahzeer*
freeze	geler	*jhuhlay*
French	français	*frohnseh*
French (language)	le français	*luh frohnseh*
French bread	la baguette	*lah bahgeht*
fresh	frais	*freh*
Friday	vendredi	*vohndruhdee*
fried	frit	*free*
fried egg	l'oeuf sur le plat (m.)	*luhf sewr luh plah*
friend	l'ami(e) (m./f.)	*lahmee*
friendly	amical	*ahmeekahl*
fringe	la frange	*lah frohnjh*
fruit	le fruit	*luh frwee*
fruit juice	le jus de fruits	*luh jhew duh frwee*
frying pan	la poêle à frire	*lah pwahl ah freer*
full	plein	*plahn*
fun	le plaisir	*luh playzeer*
funny	drôle	*droal*

G

gallery	la galerie	*lah gahlree*
game	le jeu	*luh jhuh*
garage	le garage	*luh gahrahjh*
garbage bag	le sac poubelle	*luh sahk poobehl*
garden	le jardin	*luh jhahrdahn*
gastroenteritis	la gastro-entérite	*gahstroa ohntayreet*
gauze	la compresse de gaze	*lah kawnprehs duh gahz*
gel	le gel	*luh jhehl*
German	allemand	*ahlmohn*
get married	(se) marier	*(suh) mahryay*
get off	descendre	*daysohndr*
gift	le cadeau	*luh kahdoa*
gilt	doré	*doray*
ginger	le gingembre	*luh jhahnjhohnbr*
girl	la fille	*lah feey*
girlfriend	l'amie	*lahmee*
giro card	la carte de chèque postal	*lah kahrt duh shehk postahl*
giro cheque	le chèque postal	*luh shehk postahl*
glacier	le glacier	*luh glahsyay*
glass (wine -)	le verre	*luh vehr*
glasses (sun -)	les lunettes	*lay lewneht*

glide	faire du vol à voile	*fehr dew vol ah vwahl*
glove	le gant	*luh gohn*
glue	la colle	*lah kol*
go	aller	*ahlay*
go back	reculer, retourner	*ruhkewlay, ruhtoornay*
go out	sortir	*sorteer*
goat's cheese	le fromage de chèvre	*luh fromajh duh shehvr*
gold	l'or (m.)	*lor*
golf course	le terrain de golf	*luh tehrahn duh golf*
good afternoon	bonjour	*bawnjhoor*
good evening	bonsoir	*bawnswahr*
good morning	bonjour	*bawnjhoor*
good night	bonne nuit	*bon nwee*
goodbye	au revoir	*oa ruhvwahr*
gram	le gramme	*luh grahm*
grandchild	le petit enfant	*luh puhtee tohnfohn*
grandfather	le grand-père	*luh grohn pehr*
grandmother	la grand-mère	*lah grohn mehr*
grape juice	le jus de raisin	*luh jhew duh rayzahn*
grapefruit	le pamplemousse	*luh pohnpluhmoos*
grapes	les raisins	*lay rayzahn*
grass	l'herbe (f.)	*lehrb*
grave	la tombe	*lah townb*
greasy	gras	*grah*
green	vert	*vehr*
green card	la carte verte	*lah kahrt vehrt*
greet	saluer	*sahleway*
grey	gris	*gree*
grill	griller	*greeyay*
grilled	grillé	*greeyay*
grocer	l'épicier (m)	*laypeesyay*
ground	le sol	*luh sol*
group	le groupe	*luh groop*
guest house	la pension	*lah pohnsyawn*
guide (book)	le guide	*luh gueed*
guide (person)	le/la guide	*luh/lah gueed*
guided tour	la visite guidée	*lah veezeet gueeday*
gynaecologist	le gynécologue	*luh jheenaykolog*

H

hair	les cheveux	*lay shuhvuh*
hairbrush	la brosse à cheveux	*lah bros ah shuhvuh*
hairdresser	le coiffeur	*luh kwahfuhr*
hairslides	les barrettes	*lay bahreht*
hairspray	la laque	*lah lahk*
half (adj.)	demi	*duhmee*
half	la moitié	*lah mwahtyay*
half full	à moitié plein	*ah mwahtyay plahn*
hammer	le marteau	*luh mahrtoa*
hand	la main	*lah mahn*
hand brake	le frein à main	*luh frahn ah mahn*
handbag	le sac à main	*luh sahk ah mahn*
handkerchief	le mouchoir	*luh mooshwahr*
handmade	fait-main	*feh mahn*
happy	heureux	*uhruh*
harbour	le port	*luh por*
hard	dur	*dewr*

Word list

15

hat	le chapeau	*luh shahpoa*
hay fever	le rhume des foins	*luh rewm day fwahn*
hazelnut	la noisette	*lah nwahzeht*
head	la tête	*lah teht*
headache	le mal de tête	*luh mahl duh teht*
headscarf	le foulard	*luh foolahr*
health	la santé	*lah sohntay*
health food shop	le magasin diététique	*luh mahgahzahn dyaytayteek*
hear	entendre	*ohntohndr*
hearing aid	la correction auditive	*lah korehksyawn oadeeteev*
heart	le coeur	*luh kuhr*
heater	le chauffage	*luh shoafahjh*
heavy	lourd	*loor*
heel	le talon	*luh tahlawn*
hello	bonjour, salut	*bawnjhoor, sahlew*
helmet	le casque	*luh kahsk*
help (verb)	aider	*ayday*
help	l'aide (f.)	*lehd*
herbal tea	l'infusion (f.)	*lahnfewzyawn*
here	ici	*eesee*
herring	le hareng	*luh ahrohn*
high	haut	*oa*
high tide	le flux	*luh flew*
highchair	la chaise d'enfant	*lah shehz dohnfohn*
hiking	la marche à pied	*lah mahrsh ah pyay*
hiking trip	la randonnée	*lah rohndonay*
hip	la hanche	*lah ohnsh*
hire	louer	*looay*
hitchhike	faire de l'auto-stop	*fehr duh loatoastop*
hobby	le passe-temps	*luh pahstohn*
hold-up	l'attaque (f.)	*lahtahk*
holiday house	la maison de vacances	*lah mehzawn duh vahkohns*
holidays	les vacances	*lay vahkohns*
homesickness	le mal du pays	*luh mahl dew pehy*
honest	honnête	*oneht*
honey	le miel	*luh myehl*
horizontal	horizontal	*oareezawntahl*
horrible	horrible	*oareebl*
horse	le cheval	*luh shuhvahl*
hospital	l'hôpital (m.)	*loapeetahl*
hospitality	l'hospitalité(f.)	*lospeetahleetay*
hot	chaud	*shoa*
hot-water bottle	la bouillotte	*lah booy-yot*
hot (spicy)	pimenté	*peemohntay*
hotel	l'hôtel (m.)	*loatehl*
hour	l'heure (f.)	*luhr*
house	la maison	*lah mehzawn*
household appliances	les appareils	*lay zahpahrehy*
houses of parliament	le parlement	*luh pahrluhmohn*
housewife	la femme au foyer	*lah fahm oa fwahyay*
how far?	c'est loin?	*seh lwahn?*
how long?	combien de temps?	*kawnbyahn duh tohn?*
how much?	combien?	*kawnbyahn?*

how?	comment?	*komohn?*
hungry (to be)	avoir faim	*ahvwahr fahn*
hurricane	l'ouragan (m.)	*loorahgohn*
hurry	la hâte	*lah aht*
husband	le mari	*luh mahree*
hut	la cabane	*lah kahbahnn*
hyperventilation	l'hyperventilation (f.)	*leepehrvohnteelah-syawn*

I

ice cream	la glace	*lah glahs*
ice cubes	les glaçons	*lay glahsawn*
ice skate	patiner	*pahteenay*
idea	l'idée (f.)	*leeday*
identification	la pièce d'identité	*lah pyehs deedohnteetay*
identify	identifier	*eedohnteefyay*
ignition key	la clef de contact	*lah klay duh kawntahkt*
ill	malade	*mahlahd*
illness	la maladie	*lah mahlahdee*
imagine	imaginer	*eemahjheenay*
immediately	immédiatement	*eemaydyahtmohn*
import duty	les droits de douane	*lay drwah duh dwahnn*
impossible	impossible	*ahnposeebl*
in	dans	*dohn*
in the evening	le soir	*luh swahr*
in the morning	le matin	*luh mahtahn*
included	compris	*kawnpree*
indicate	indiquer	*ahndeekay*
indicator	le clignotant	*luh kleenyotohn*
inexpensive	bon marché	*bawn mahrshay*
infection (viral/ bacterial)	l'infection (virale/ bactérielle) (f.)	*lahnfehksyawn (veerahl, bahktayryehl)*
inflammation	l'inflammation (f.)	*lahnflahmahsyawn*
information	l'information (f.)	*lahnformahsyawn*
information	le renseignement	*luh rohnsehnymohn*
information office	le bureau de renseignements	*luh bewroa duh rohnsehnymohn*
injection	la piqûre	*lah peekewr*
injured	blessé	*blehssay*
inner ear	l'oreille interne (f.)	*lorehy ahntehrn*
inner tube	la chambre à air	*lah shohnbr ah ehr*
innocent	innocent	*eenosohn*
insect	l'insecte (m.)	*lahnsehkt*
insect bite	la piqûre d'insecte	*lah peekewr dahnsehkt*
insect repellant	l'huile contre les moustiques	*lweel kawntr lay moosteek*
inside	à l'intérieur	*ah lahntayryuhr*
instructions	le mode d'emploi	*luh mod dohnplwah*
insurance	l'assurance (f.)	*lahsewrohns*
intermission	la pause	*lah poaz*
international	international	*ahntehrnahsyonahl*
interpreter	l'interprète (m./f.)	*lahntehrpreht*
intersection	le carrefour	*luh kahrfoor*
introduce oneself	se présenter	*suh prayzohntay*
invite	inviter	*ahnveetay*

Word list

invoice	la facture	*lah fahktewr*
iodine	l'iode (m.)	*lyod*
Ireland	l'Irlande (f.)	*leerlohnd*
Irish	irlandais	*leerlohndeh*
iron (verb)	repasser	*ruhpahsay*
iron	le fer à repasser	*luh fehr ah ruhpahsay*
ironing board	la table à repasser	*lah tahbl ah ruhpahsay*
island	l'île (f.)	*leel*
it's a pleasure	je vous en prie	*jhuh voo zohn pree*
Italian	italien	*eetahlyahn*
itch	la démangeaison	*lah daymohnjhehzawn*

J

jack	le cric	*luh kreek*
jacket	la veste	*lah vehst*
jam	la confiture	*lah kawnfeetewr*
January	janvier	*jhohnvyay*
jaw	la mâchoire	*lah mahshwahr*
jellyfish	la méduse	*lah maydewz*
jeweller	le bijoutier	*luh beejhootyay*
jewellery	les bijoux	*lay beejhoo*
jog	faire du jogging	*fehr dew jogeeng*
joke	la blague	*lah blahg*
juice	le jus	*luh jhew*
July	juillet	*jhweeyeh*
jump leads	le câble de démarrage	*luh kahbl duh daymahrahjh*
jumper	le pull-over	*luh pewlovehr*
June	juin	*jhwahn*

K

key	la clef/clé	*lah klay*
kilo	le kilo	*luh keeloa*
kilometre	le kilomètre	*luh keeloamehtr*
king	le roi	*luh rwah*
kiss (verb)	embrasser	*ohnbrahssay*
kiss	le baiser	*luh bayzay*
kitchen	la cuisine	*lah kweezeen*
knee	le genou	*luh jhuhnoo*
knee socks	les mi-bas	*lay mee bah*
knife	le couteau	*luh kootoa*
knit	tricoter	*treekotay*
know	savoir	*sahvwahr*

L

lace	la dentelle	*lah dohntehl*
ladies' toilets	les toilettes pour dames	*lay twahleht poor dahm*
lake	le lac	*luh lahk*
lamp	la lampe	*lah lohnp*
land	atterrir	*ahtayreer*
lane	la voie	*lah vwah*
language	la langue	*lah lohng*
large	grand	*grohn*
last	dernier, passé	*dehrnyay, pahssay*
last night	la nuit passée	*lah nwee pahssay*

late	tard	*tahr*
later	tout à l'heure	*too tah luhr*
laugh	rire	*reer*
launderette	la laverie	*lah lahvree*
	automatique	*oatoamahteek*
law	la loi	*lah lwah*
laxative	le laxatif	*luh lahxahteef*
leaky	crevé	*kruhvay*
leather	le cuir	*luh kweer*
leather goods	les articles	*lay zahrteekl*
	de maroquinerie	*duh mahrokeenree*
leave	partir	*pahrteer*
leek	le poireau	*luh pwahroa*
left	gauche	*goash*
left luggage	la consigne	*lah kawnseeny*
left, on the	à gauche	*ah goash*
leg	la jambe	*lah jhohnb*
lemon	le citron	*luh seetrawn*
lemonade	la limonade	*lah leemonahd*
lend	prêter (à)	*prehtay (ah)*
lens	la lentille	*lah lohnteey*
lentils	les lentilles	*lay lohnteey*
less	moins	*mwahn*
lesson	la leçon	*lah luhsawn*
letter	la lettre	*lah lehtr*
lettuce	la laitue	*lah laytew*
level crossing	le passage à niveau	*luh pahssahjh ah neevoa*
library	la bibliothèque	*lah beebleeotehk*
lie (down)	s'étendre	*saytohndr*
lie (verb)	mentir	*mohnteer*
hitch-hiking	l'auto-stop	*loatoastop*
lift (in building)	l'ascenseur (m.)	*lahsohnsuhr*
lift (chair)	le télésiège	*luh taylaysyehjh*
light (not dark)	clair	*klehr*
light (not heavy)	léger	*layjhay*
light	la lumière	*lah lewmyehr*
lighter	le briquet	*luh breekeh*
lighthouse	le phare	*luh fahr*
lightning	la foudre	*lah foodr*
like	aimer	*aymay*
line	la ligne	*lah leenyuh*
linen	le lin	*luh lahn*
lipstick	le rouge à lèvres	*luh roojh ah lehvr*
liquorice	le réglisse	*luh rayglees*
listen	écouter	*aykootay*
literature	la littérature	*lah leetayrahtewr*
litre	le litre	*luh leetr*
little	peu	*puh*
live	habiter	*ahbeetay*
live	vivre	*veevr*
live together	habiter ensemble	*ahbeetay ohnsohnbl*
lobster	le homard	*luh omahr*
locally	localement	*lokahlmohn*
lock	la serrure	*lah sehrewr*
long	long	*lawn*
look	regarder	*ruhgahrday*

Word list

15

133

look for	chercher	shehrshay
look up	rechercher	ruhshehrshay
lorry	le camion	luh kahmyawn
lose	perdre	pehrdr
loss	la perte	lah pehrt
lost	introuvable, perdu	ahntroovahbl, pehrdew
lost item	l'objet perdu (m.)	lohbjeh pehrdew
lost property office	les objets trouvés	lay zobjheh troovay
lotion	la lotion	lah loasyawn
loud	fort	for
love (to be in)	être amoureux	ehtr ahmooruh
love (verb)	aimer	aymay
love	l'amour (m.)	lahmoor
low	bas	bah
low tide	le reflux	luh ruhflew
luck	la chance	lah shohns
luggage	le bagage	luh bahgahjh
luggage locker	la consigne automatique	lah kawnseenyuh oatoamahteek
lunch	le déjeuner	luh dayjhuhnay
lunchroom	le café	luh kahfay
lungs	les poumons	lay poomawn

M

macaroni	les macaronis	lay mahkahroanee
madam	madame	mahdahm
magazine	la revue	lah ruhvew
mail	le courrier	luh kooryay
main post office	le bureau de poste central	luh bewroa duh post sohntral
main road	la grande route	lah grohnd root
make an appointment	prendre un rendez-vous	prohndr uhn rohndayvoo
make love	faire l'amour	fehr lahmoor
makeshift	provisoirement	proveezwahrmohn
man	l'homme (m.)	lom
manager	le directeur	luh deerehktuhr
mandarin	la mandarine	lah mohndahreen
manicure	la manucure	lah mahnewkewr
map	la carte géographique	lah kahrt jhayoagrahfeek
marble	le marbre	luh mahrbruh
March	mars	mahrs
margarine	la margarine	lah mahrgahreen
marina	le port de plaisance	luh por duh playzohns
market	le marché	luh mahrshay
marriage	le mariage	luh mahryajh
married	marié	mahreeay
mass	la messe	lah mehs
massage	le massage	luh mahsahjh
mat	mat	maht
match	le match	luh mahch
matches	les allumettes	lay zahlewmeht
May	mai	meh
maybe	peut-être	puh tehtr
mayonnaise	la mayonnaise	lah mahyonehz
mayor	le maire	luh mehr

15

meal	le repas	*luh ruhpah*
mean	signifier	*seenyeefyay*
meat	la viande	*lah vyohnd*
medical insurance	l'assurance	*lahsewrohns*
	maladie (f.)	*mahlahdee*
medication	le médicament	*luh maydeekahmohn*
medicine	le médicament	*luh maydeekahmohn*
meet	rencontrer	*rohnkohntray*
melon	le melon	*luh muhlawn*
membership	l'adhésion (f.)	*lahdayzyawn*
menstruate	avoir ses règles	*ahvwahr say rehgl*
menstruation	les règles	*lay rehgl*
menu	la carte	*lah kahrt*
menu of the day	le menu du jour	*luh muhnew dew jhoor*
message	le message	*luh mehsahjh*
metal	le métal	*luh maytahl*
meter	le compteur	*luh kawntuhr*
metre	le mètre	*luh mehtr*
migraine	la migraine	*lah meegrehn*
mild (tobacco)	léger	*layjhay*
milk	le lait	*luh leh*
millimetre	le millimètre	*luh meeleemehtr*
milometer	le compteur	*luh kawntuhr*
	kilométrique	*keeloamaytreek*
mince	la viande hachée	*lah vyohnd ahshay*
mineral water	l'eau minérale (f.)	*loa meenayral*
minute	la minute	*lah meenewt*
mirror	le miroir	*luh meerwahr*
miss	manquer	*mohnkay*
missing (to be)	manquer	*mohnkay*
mistake	l'erreur (f.)	*lehruhr*
misunderstanding	le malentendu	*luh mahlohntohndew*
mocha	le moka	*luh mokah*
modern art	l'art moderne (m.)	*lahr modehrn*
molar	la molaire	*lah molehr*
moment	le moment	*luh momohn*
Monday	lundi	*luhndee*
money	l'argent (m.)	*lahrjhohn*
month	le mois	*luh mwah*
moped	le cyclomoteur	*luh seekloamotuhr*
morning-after pill	la pilule du	*lah peelewl dew*
	lendemain	*lohnduhmahn*
mosque	la mosquée	*lah moskay*
motel	le motel	*luh moatehl*
mother	la mère	*lah mehr*
moto-cross	le moto-cross	*luh moatoakros*
motorbike	la motocyclette	*lah moatoaseekleht*
motorboat	le bateau à moteur	*luh bahtoa ah motuhr*
motorway	l'autoroute (f.)	*loatoaroot*
mountain	la montagne	*lah mawntanyuh*
mountain hut	le refuge	*luh ruhfewjh*
mountaineering	l'alpinisme (m.)	*lahlpeeneesm*
mountaineering shoes	les chaussures	*lay shoasewr duh*
	de montagne	*mawntanyuh*
mouse	la souris	*lah sooree*
mouth	la bouche	*lah boosh*
much/many	beaucoup	*boakoo*

Word list

15

135

multi-storey car park	le parking	*luh pahrkeeng*
muscle	le muscle	*luh mewskl*
muscle spasms	les crampes musculaires	*lay krohnp mewskewlehr*
museum	le musée	*luh mewzay*
mushrooms	les champignons	*lay shohnpeenyawn*
music	la musique	*lah mewzeek*
musical	la comédie musicale	*lah komaydee mewzeekahl*
mussels	les moules	*lay mool*
mustard	la moutarde	*lah mootahrd*

N

nail (on hand)	l'ongle (m.)	*lawngl*
nail	le clou	*luh kloo*
nail polish	le vernis à ongles	*luh vehrnee ah awngl*
nail polish remover	le dissolvant	*luh deesolvohn*
nail scissors	le coupe-ongles	*luh koop awngl*
naked	nu	*new*
nappy	la couche	*lah koosh*
nationality	la nationalité	*lah nahsyonahleetay*
natural	naturel	*nahtewrehl*
nature	la nature	*lah nahtewr*
naturism	le naturisme (m.)	*luh nahtewreesm*
nauseous	(avoir) mal au coeur	*(ahvwahr) mahl oa kuhr*
near	près	*preh*
nearby	tout près	*too preh*
necessary	nécessaire	*naysehsehr*
neck	le collier	*luh kolyay*
necklace	la chaîne	*lah shehn*
nectarine	la nectarine	*lah nehktahreen*
needle	l'aiguille (f.)	*laygweey*
negative	le négatif	*luh naygahteef*
neighbours	les voisins	*lay vwahzahn*
nephew	le neveu	*luh nuhvuh*
Netherlands	les Pays-Bas	*lay pehy bah*
never	jamais	*jhahmeh*
new	nouveau	*noovoa*
news	les informations	*lay zahnformahsyawn*
news stand	le kiosque	*luh kyosk*
newspaper	le journal	*luh jhoornahl*
next	le prochain	*luh proshahn*
next to	à côté de	*ah koatay duh*
nice (friendly)	gentil	*jhohntee*
nice	agréable, bon	*ahgrayahbl, bawn*
niece	la nièce	*lah nyehs*
night	la nuit	*lah nwee*
night duty	le service de nuit	*luh sehrvees duh nwee*
nightclub	la boîte de nuit/ le night-club	*lah bwaht duh nwee/ luh naheet kluhb*
nightlife	la vie nocturne	*lah vee noktewrn*
nipple	la tétine	*lah tayteen*
no-one	personne	*pehrson*
no	non	*nawn*
no overtaking	l'interdiction de dépasser (f.)	*lahntehrdeeksyawn duh daypahsay*
noise	le bruit	*luh brwee*

nonstop	continu	*kawnteenew*
normal	normal, ordinaire	*normahl, ordeenehr*
north	le nord	*luh nor*
nose	le nez	*luh nay*
nose bleed	le saignement de nez	*luh sehnyuhmohn dew nay*
nose drops	les gouttes pour le nez	*lay goot poor luh nay*
notepaper	le papier postal	*luh pahpyay postahl*
nothing	rien	*ryahn*
November	novembre	*novohnbr*
nowhere	nulle part	*newl pahr*
nudist beach	la plage de nudistes	*lah plahjh duh newdeest*
number	le numéro	*luh newmayroa*
number plate	la plaque d'immatriculation	*lah plahk deemahtree-kewlahsyawn*
nurse	l'infirmière (f.)	*lahnfeermyehr*
nutmeg	la noix de muscade	*lah nwah duh mewskahd*
nuts	les noix	*lay nwah*

O

October	octobre	*oktobr*
off licence	le marchand de vin	*luh mahrshohn duh vahn*
offer	offrir	*ofreer*
office	le bureau	*luh bewroa*
oil	l'huile (f.)	*lweel*
oil level	le niveau d'huile	*luh neevoa dweel*
ointment	le baume	*luh boam*
ointment for burns	la pommade contre les brûlures	*lah pomahd kawntr lay brewlewr*
okay	d'accord	*dahkor*
old	vieux	*vyuh*
old town	la vieille ville	*lah vyehy veel*
olive oil	l'huile d'olive	*lweel doleev*
olives	les olives	*lay zoleev*
omelette	l'omelette (f.)	*lomleht*
on	sur	*sewr*
on board	à bord	*ah bor*
on the way	en cours de route	*ohn koor duh root*
oncoming car	le véhicule en sens inverse	*luh vayeekewl ohn sohns ahnvehr*
one-way traffic	la circulation à sens unique	*lah seerkewlahsyawn ah sohns ewneek*
one hundred grams	cent grammes	*sohn grahm*
onion	l'oignon (m.)	*lonyawn*
open (verb)	ouvrir	*oovreer*
open	ouvert	*oovehr*
opera	l'opéra (m.)	*loapayrah*
operate	opérer	*oapayray*
operator (telephone)	la téléphoniste	*lah taylayfoneest*
operetta	l'opérette (f.)	*loapayreht*
opposite	en face	*ohn fahs*
optician	l'opticien (m.)	*lopteesyahn*
or	ou	*oo*

orange	l'orange (f.)	lorohnjh
orange (adj.)	orange	orohnjh
orange juice	le jus d'orange	luh jhew dorohnjh
order (verb)	commander	komohnday
order	la commande	lah kohmohnd
other	l'autre	loatr
other side	l'autre côté	loatr koatay
outside	dehors	duh-or
overtake	doubler	dooblay
oysters	les huîtres	lay zweetr

P

package (post)	le paquet postal	luh pahkeh postahl
packed lunch	le casse-croûte	luh kahs kroot
page	la page	lah pahjh
pain	la douleur	lah dooluhr
painkiller	le calmant	luh kahlmohn
paint	la peinture	lah pahntewr
painting (art)	le tableau	luh tahbloa
palace	le palais	luh pahleh
pan	la casserole	lah kahsrol
pancake	la crêpe	lah krehp
pane	la vitre	lah veetr
pants	la culotte	lah kewlot
panty liner	le protège-slip	luh protehjh sleep
paper	le papier	luh pahpyay
paraffin oil	le pétrole	luh paytrol
parasol	le parasol	luh pahrahsol
parcel	le colis	luh kolee
pardon	pardon	pahrdawn
parents	les parents	lay pahrohn
park	le parc	luh pahrk
park (verb)	garer	gahray
parking space	la place de parking	lah plahs duh pahrkeeng
parsley	le persil	luh pehrsee
part	la pièce	lah pyehs
partition	la séparation	lah saypahrahsyawn
partner	le/la partenaire	luh/lah pahrtuhnehr
party	la fête	lah feht
passable	praticable	prahteekahbl
passenger	le passager	luh pahsahjhay
passport	le passeport	luh pahspor
passport photo	la photo d'identité	lah foatoa deedohnteetay
patient	le patient	luh pahsyohn
pavement	le trottoir	luh trotwahr
pay	payer	payay
peach	la pêche	lah pehsh
peanuts	les cacahuètes	lay kahkahweht
pear	la poire	lah pwahr
peas	les petits pois	lay puhtee pwah
pedal	la pédale	lah paydahl
pedestrian crossing	le passage clouté	luh pahsahjh klootay
pedicure	le/la pédicure	luh/lah paydeekewr
pen	le stylo	luh steeloa
pencil	le crayon	luh krayawn

penis	le pénis	_luh paynees_
pepper (capsicum)	le poivron	_luh pwahvrawn_
pepper	le poivre	_luh pwahvr_
performance	la représentation	_lah_
	de théâtre	_ruhprayzohntahsyawn_
		duh tayahtr
perfume	le parfum	_luh pahrfuhn_
perm (verb)	faire une	_fehr ewn_
	permanente à	_pehrmahnohnt ah_
perm	la permanente	_lah pehrmahnohnt_
permit	le permis	_luh pehrmee_
person	la personne	_lah pehrson_
personal	personnel	_pehrsonehl_
petrol	l'essence (f.)	_lehssohns_
petrol station	la station-service	_lah stahsyawn_
		sehrvees
pets	les animaux	_lay zahneemoa_
	domestiques	_domehsteek_
pharmacy	la pharmacie	_lah fahrmahsee_
phone (by)	par téléphone	_pahr taylayfon_
phone (tele-)	le téléphone	_luh taylayfon_
phone (verb)	téléphoner	_taylayfonay_
phone box	la cabine	_lah kahbeen_
	téléphonique	_taylayfoneek_
phone directory	l'annuaire	_lahnnwehr_
phone number	le numéro	_luh newmayroa_
	de téléphone	_duh taylayfon_
photo	la photo	_la foatoa_
photocopier	le photocopieur	_luh foatoakopyuhr_
photocopy (verb)	photocopier	_foatoakopyay_
photocopy	la photocopie	_lah foatoakopee_
pick up	aller chercher	_ahlay shehrshay_
picnic	le pique-nique	_luh peek neek_
pier	la jetée	_lah jhuhtay_
pigeon	le pigeon	_luh peejhyawn_
pill (contraceptive)	la pilule	_lah peelewl_
pillow	le coussin	_luh koossahn_
pillowcase	la taie d'oreiller	_lah tay dorehyay_
pin	l'épingle (f.)	_laypahngl_
pineapple	l'ananas (m.)	_lahnahnahs_
pipe	la pipe	_lah peep_
pipe tobacco	le tabac à pipe	_luh tahbah ah peep_
pity	dommage	_domahjh_
places of entertainment	les possibilités	_lay poseebeeleetay_
	de sortie	_duh sortee_
places of interest	les curiosités	_lay kewryozeetay_
plan	l'intention (f.)	_lahntohnsyawn_
plant	la plante	_lah plohnt_
plaster	le sparadrap	_luh spahrahdrah_
plastic	plastique	_plahsteek_
plastic bag	le sac en plastique	_luh sahk ohn plahsteek_
plate	l'assiette (f.)	_lahsyeht_
platform	la voie, le quai	_lah vwah, luh kay_
play (theatre)	la pièce de théâtre	_lah pyehs duh tayahtr_
play (verb)	jouer	_jhooay_
play basketball	jouer au basket	_jhooay oa bahskeht_
play billiards	jouer au billiard	_jhooay oa biy-yahr_

play chess	jouer aux échecs	*jhooay oa zayshehk*
play draughts	jouer aux dames	*jhooay oa dahm*
play golf	jouer au golf	*jhooay oa golf*
playing cards	les cartes à jouer	*lay kahrt ah jhooay*
pleasant	agréable	*ahgrayahbl*
please	s'il vous plaît	*seel voo pleh*
pleasure	la satisfaction	*lah sahteesfahksyawn*
plum	la prune	*lah prewn*
pocketknife	le canif	*luh kahneef*
point	indiquer	*ahndeekay*
poison	le poison	*luh pwahzawn*
police	la police	*lah polees*
police station	le poste de police	*luh post duh polees*
policeman	l'agent de police (m.)	*lahjhohn duh polees*
pond	le bassin	*luh bahsahn*
pony	le poney	*luh poaneh*
pop concert	le concert pop	*luh kawnsehr pop*
population	la population	*lah popewlahsyawn*
pork	la viande de porc	*lah vyohnd duh por*
port	le porto	*luh portoa*
porter	le porteur	*luh portuhr*
post code	le code postal	*luh kod postahl*
post office	la poste	*lah post*
postage	le port	*luh por*
postbox	la boîte aux lettres	*lah bwaht oa lehtr*
postcard	la carte postale	*lah kahrt postahl*
postman	le facteur	*luh fahktuhr*
potato	la pomme de terre	*lah pom duh tehr*
poultry	la volaille	*lah vohlahy*
pound	la livre	*lah leevr*
powdered milk	le lait en poudre	*luh leh ohn poodr*
prawns	les crevettes roses	*lay kruhveht roaz*
precious	précieux	*praysyuh*
prefer	préférer	*prayfayray*
preference	la préférence	*lah prayfayrohns*
pregnant	enceinte	*ohnsahnt*
present (adj.)	présent	*prayzohn*
present	le cadeau	*luh kahdoa*
press	appuyer	*ahpweeyay*
pressure	la pression	*lah prehsyawn*
price	le prix	*luh pree*
price list	la liste de prix	*lah leest duh pree*
print (verb)	faire tirer	*fehr teeray*
print	l'épreuve (f.)	*laypruhv*
probably	probablement	*probahbluhmohn*
problem	le problème	*luh problehm*
profession	la profession	*lah profehsyawn*
programme	le programme	*luh prograhm*
pronounce	prononcer	*proanawnsay*
propane gas	le gaz propane	*luh gahz propahn*
pull	arracher	*ahrahshay*
pull a muscle	froisser un muscle	*frwahsay uhn mewskl*
pure	pur	*pewr*
purple	violet	*veeoleh*
purse	le porte-monnaie	*luh port moneh*
push	pousser	*poossay*
pushchair	la poussette	*lah poosseht*

| puzzle | le puzzle | *luh puhzl* |
| pyjamas | le pyjama | *luh peejhahmah* |

Q

quarter	le quart	*luh kahr*
quarter of an hour	le quart d'heure	*luh kahr duhr*
queen	la reine	*lah rehn*
question	la question	*lah kehstyawn*
quick	rapide	*rahpeed*
quiet	tranquille	*trohnkeey*

R

radio	la radio	*lah rahdyoa*
railways	les chemins	*lay shuhmahn*
	de fer (m.)	*duh fehr*
rain (verb)	pleuvoir	*pluhvwahr*
rain	la pluie	*lah plwee*
raincoat	l'imperméable (m.)	*lahnpehrmayahbl*
raisins	les raisins secs	*lay rehzahn sehk*
rape	le viol	*luh vyol*
rapids	le courant rapide	*luh koorohn rahpeed*
raspberries	les framboises	*lay frohnbwahz*
raw	cru	*krew*
raw ham	le jambon cru	*luh jhohnbawn krew*
raw vegetables	les crudités	*lay krewdeetay*
razor blades	les lames de rasoir	*lay lahm duh rahzwahr*
read (verb)	lire	*leer*
ready	prêt	*preh*
really	vraiment	*vrehmohn*
receipt (till)	le ticket de caisse	*luh teekeh duh kehs*
receipt	le reçu, la quittance	*luh ruhsew, lah keetohns*
recipe	la recette	*lah ruhseht*
reclining chair	la chaise longue	*lah shehz lawng*
recommend	recommander	*ruhkomohnday*
recovery service	l'assistance routiere (f.)	*lahseestohns rootyehr*
rectangle	le rectangle	*luh rehktohngl*
red	rouge	*roojh*
red wine	le vin rouge	*luh vahn roojh*
reduction	la réduction	*lah raydewksyawn*
refrigerator	le réfrigérateur	*luh rayfreejhayrahtuhr*
regards	les amitiés	*lay zahmeetyay*
region	la région	*lah rayjhyawn*
registration	la carte grise	*lah kahrt greez*
relatives	la famille	*lah fahmeey*
reliable	sûr	*sewr*
religion	la religion	*lah ruhleejhyawn*
rent out	louer	*looay*
repair (verb)	réparer	*raypahray*
repairs	la réparation	*lah raypahrahsyawn*
repeat	répéter	*raypaytay*
report	le procès-verbal	*luh proseh vehrbahl*
resent	prendre mal	*prohndr mahl*
responsible	responsable	*rehspawnsahbl*
rest	se reposer	*suh ruhpoazay*
restaurant	le restaurant	*luh rehstoarohn*

result	le résultat	*luh rayzewltah*
retired	à la retraite	*ah lah ruhtreht*
retirement	la retraite	*lah ruhtreht*
return (ticket)	l'aller-retour (m.)	*lahlay ruhtoor*
reverse (vehicle)	faire marche arrière	*fehr mahrsh ahryehr*
rheumatism	le rhumatisme	*luh rewmahteesm*
rice	le riz	*luh ree*
ridiculous	ridicule	*reedeekewl*
riding (horseback)	faire du cheval	*fehr dew shuhvahl*
riding school	le manège	*luh mahnehjh*
right	la droite	*lah drwaht*
right of way	la priorité	*lah preeoreetay*
right, on the	à droite	*ah drwaht*
ripe	mûr	*mewr*
risk	le risque	*luh reesk*
river	la rivière	*reevyehr*
road	la route	*lah root*
roasted	rôti	*roatee*
rock	le rocher	*luh roshay*
roll	le petit pain	*luh puhtee pahn*
rolling tobacco	le tabac à rouler	*luh tahbah ah roolay*
roof rack	la galerie	*lah gahlree*
room	la pièce	*lah pyehs*
room number	le numéro de chambre	*luh newmayroa duh shohnbr*
room service	le service de chambre	*luh sehrvees duh shohnbr*
rope	la corde	*lah kord*
rose	la rose	*lah roaz*
rosé	le rosé	*luh roazay*
roundabout	le rond-point	*luh rawn pwahn*
route	l'itinéraire (m.)	*leeteenayrehr*
rowing boat	la barque	*la bahrk*
rubber	le caoutchouc	*luh kah-oochoo*
rubbish	les détritus	*luh daytreetews*
rucksack	le sac à dos	*luh sahk ah doa*
rude	mal élevé	*mahl aylvay*
ruins	les ruines (f.)	*lay rween*
run into	rencontrer	*rohnkawntray*
running shoes	les chaussures de sport	*lay shoasewr duh spor*

s

sad	triste	*treest*
safari	le safari	*luh sahfahree*
safe (adj.)	en sécurité	*ohn saykewreetay*
safe	le coffre-fort	*luh kofr for*
safety pin	l'épingle de nourrice (f.)	*laypahngl duh noorees*
sail	faire de la voile	*fehr duh lah vwahl*
sailing boat	le voilier	*luh vwahlyay*
salad	la salade	*lah sahlahd*
salad oil	l'huile de table (f.)	*lweel duh tahbl*
salami	le salami	*luh sahlahmee*
sale	les soldes	*lay sold*
salt	le sel	*luh sehl*
same	le même	*luh mehm*

sandwich	le sandwich	*luh sohndweech*
sandy beach	la plage de sable	*lah plahjh duh sahbl*
sanitary towel	la serviette hygiénique	*lah sehrvyeht eejhyayneek*
sardines	les sardines	*lay sahrdeen*
satisfied	content (de)	*kawntohn (duh)*
Saturday	samedi	*sahmdee*
sauce	la sauce	*lah soas*
sauna	le sauna	*luh soanah*
sausage	la saucisse	*lah soasees*
savoury	salé	*sahlay*
say	dire	*deer*
scarf	l'écharpe (f.)	*layshahrp*
scenic walk	le circuit pédestre	*luh seerkwee paydehstr*
school	l'école (f.)	*laykol*
scissors	les ciseaux	*lay seezoa*
scooter	le scooter	*luh skootehr*
scorpion	le scorpion	*luh skorpyawn*
Scotland	l'Ecosse (f.)	*laykos*
Scottish	écossais	*aykosseh*
scrambled eggs	l'oeuf brouillé (m.)	*lef brooy-yay*
screw	la vis	*lah vees*
screwdriver	le tournevis	*luh toornuhvees*
sculpture	la sculpture	*lah skewltewr*
sea	la mer	*lah mehr*
seasick (to be)	avoir le mal de mer	*ahvwahr luh mahl duh mehr*
seat	la place	*lah plahs*
second-hand	d'occasion	*dokahzyawn*
second (adj.)	deuxième	*duhzyehm*
second	la seconde	*lah suhgawnd*
sedative	le tranquillisant	*luh trohnkeeleezohn*
self-timer	le déclencheur automatique	*luh dayklohnshuhr oatoamahteek*
semi-skimmed	demi-écrémé	*duhmee aykraymay*
send	expédier	*ehxpaydyay*
sentence	la phrase	*lah frahz*
separated	séparé	*saypahray*
September	septembre	*sehptohnbr*
serious	sérieux	*sayryuh*
service	le service	*luh sehrvees*
serviette	la serviette	*lah sehrvyeht*
set (hair)	faire une mise en plis	*fehr ewn meez ohn plee*
sewing thread	le fil à coudre	*luh feel ah koodr*
shade	l'ombre (f.)	*lawnbr*
shallow	peu profond	*puh profawn*
shampoo	le shampooing	*luh shohnpwahn*
shark	le requin	*luh ruhkahn*
shave (verb)	se raser	*suh rahzay*
shaver	le rasoir électrique	*luh rahzwahr aylehktreek*
shaving brush	le blaireau	*luh blayroa*
shaving cream	la crème à raser	*lah krehm ah rahzay*
shaving soap	le savon à raser	*luh sahvawn ah rahzay*
sheet	le drap	*luh drah*

sherry	le xérès	*luh ksayrehz*
shirt	la chemise	*lah shuhmeez*
shoe	la chaussure	*lah shoasewr*
shoe polish	le cirage	*luh seerajh*
shoe shop	le magasin de chaussures	*luh mahgahzahn duh shoasewr*
shoelace	le lacet	*luh lahseh*
shoemaker	le cordonnier	*luh kordonyay*
shop (verb)	faire les courses	*fehr lay koors*
shop	le magasin	*luh mahgahzahn*
shop assistant	la vendeuse	*lah vohnduhz*
shop window	la vitrine	*lah veetreen*
shopping bag	le cabas	*luh kahbah*
shopping centre	le centre commercial	*luh sohntr komehrsyahl*
short	court	*koor*
short circuit	le court-circuit	*luh koor seerkwee*
shorts	le bermuda	*luh behrmewdah*
shoulder	l'épaule (f.)	*laypoal*
show	le spectacle	*luh spehktahkl*
shower	la douche	*lah doosh*
shutter	l'obturateur (m.)	*lobtewrahtuhr*
sieve	la passoire	*lah pahswahr*
sign (verb)	signer	*seenyay*
sign	le panneau	*luh pahnoa*
signature	la signature	*lah seenyahtewr*
silence	le silence	*luh seelohns*
silver	l'argent (m.)	*lahrjhohn*
silver-plated	argenté	*ahrjhohntay*
simple	simple	*sahnpl*
single (ticket)	l'aller simple (m.)	*lahlay sahnpl*
single (unmarried)	célibataire	*sayleebahtehr*
single	le célibataire	*luh sayleebahtehr*
sir	monsieur	*muhsyuh*
sister	la soeur	*lah suhr*
sit (verb)	s'asseoir	*sahswahr*
size	la pointure, la taille	*lah pwahntewr, lah tahy*
ski (verb)	skier, faire du ski	*skeeay, fehr dew skee*
ski boots	les chaussures de ski	*lay shoasewr duh skee*
ski goggles	les lunettes de ski	*lay lewneht duh skee*
ski instructor	le moniteur de ski	*luh moneetuhr duh skee*
ski lessons/class	le cours de ski, la classe de ski	*luh koor duh skee, lah klahs duh skee*
ski lift	le remonte-pente	*luh ruhmawnt pohnt*
ski pants	le pantalon de ski	*luh pohntahlawn duh skee*
ski pass	le forfait de ski	*luh forfeh duh skee*
ski slope	la piste de ski	*lah peest duh skee*
ski stick	le bâton de ski	*luh bahtawn duh skee*
ski suit	la combinaison de ski	*lah kawnbeenehzawn duh skee*
ski wax	le fart à ski	*luh fahr ah skee*
skimmed	écrémé	*aykraymay*
skin	la peau	*lah poa*
skirt	la jupe	*lah jhewp*
skis	les skis	*lay skee*

144

sledge	la luge	*lah lewjh*
sleep (verb)	dormir	*dormeer*
sleep well	dormez-bien	*dormay byahn*
sleeping car	le wagon-lit	*luh vahgawn lee*
sleeping pills	les somnifères	*lay somneefehr*
slide	la diapositive	*lah deeahpozeeteev*
slim	mince	*mahns*
slip	la combinaison	*lah kawnbeenehzawn*
slip road	la bretelle d'accès	*lah bruhtehl dahkseh*
slow	lentement	*lohntuhmohn*
small	petit	*puhtee*
small change	la monnaie	*lah moneh*
smell (verb)	puer	*peway*
smoke	la fumée	*lah fewmay*
smoke (verb)	fumer	*fewmay*
smoked	fumé	*fewmay*
smoking compartment	le compartiment fumeurs	*luh kawnpahrteemohn fewmuhr*
snake	le serpent	*luh sehrpohn*
snorkel	le tuba	*luh tewbah*
snow (verb)	neiger	*nehjhay*
snow	la neige	*lah nehjh*
snow chains	les chaînes	*lay shehn*
soap	le savon	*luh sahvawn*
soap box	la boîte à savon	*lah bwaht ah sahvawn*
soccer (play)	jouer au football, le football	*jhooay oa footbol, luh footbol*
soccer match	le match de football	*luh mahch duh footbol*
socket	la prise	*lah preez*
socks	les chaussettes	*lay shoasseht*
soft drink	la boisson fraîche	*lah bwahssawn frehsh*
sole (fish)	la sole	*lah sol*
sole (shoe)	la semelle	*lah suhmehl*
solicitor	l'avocat	*lahvoakah*
someone	quelqu'un	*kehlkuhn*
something	quelque chose	*kehlkuhshoaz*
sometimes	parfois	*pahrfwah*
somewhere	quelque part	*kehlkuhpahr*
son	le fils	*luh fees*
soon	bientôt	*byahntoa*
sorbet	le sorbet	*luh sorbeh*
sore (be)	faire mal	*fehr mal*
sore throat	le mal de gorge	*luh mahl duh gorjh*
sorry	pardon	*pahrdawn*
sort	la sorte	*lah sort*
soup	la soupe	*lah soop*
sour	acide	*ahseed*
sour cream	la crème fraîche	*lah krehm frehsh*
source	la source	*lah soors*
south	le sud	*luh sewd*
souvenir	le souvenir	*luh soovneer*
spaghetti	les spaghetti	*lay spahgehtee*
spanner (open-ended)	las clé plate	*lay klay plaht*
spanner	la clef à molette	*lah klay ah moleht*
spare parts	les pièces détachées	*lay pyehs daytashay*

spare tyre	le pneu de rechange	luh pnuh duh ruhshohnjh
spare wheel	la roue de secours	lah roo duh suhkoor
speak (verb)	parler	pahrlay
special	spécial	spaysyahl
specialist	le spécialiste	luh spaysyahleest
specialty	la spécialité	lah spaysyahleetay
speed limit	la vitesse maximum	lah veetehs mahxeemuhm
spell (verb)	épeler	aypuhlay
spices	les épices	lay zaypees
spicy	épicé	aypeesay
splinter	l'écharde (f.)	layshahrd
spoon	la cuillère	lah kweeyehr
spoonful	la cuillerée	lah kweeyuhray
sport	le sport	luh spor
sports centre	la salle de sport	lah sahl duh spohr
spot	l'endroit (m.)	lohndrwah
sprain	fouler	foolay
spring	le printemps	luh prahntohn
square	le carré	luh kahray
square (town)	la place	lah plahs
square metre	le mètre carré	luh mehtr kahray
squash	le squash	luh skwahsh
stadium	le stade	luh stahd
stain	la tache	lah tahsh
stain remover	le détachant	luh daytahshohn
stairs	l'escalier (m.)	lehskahlyay
stalls	la salle	lah sahl
stamp	le timbre	luh tahnbr
start (verb)	démarrer	daymahray
station	la gare	lah gahr
statue	la statue	lah stahtew
stay (lodge)	loger	lohjhay
stay (remain)	rester	rehstay
stay	le séjour	luh sayjhoor
steal	voler	volay
steel	acier	ahsyay
stench	la mauvaise odeur	lah moavehz oduhr
sting	piquer	peekay
stitch (med.)	la suture	lah sewtewr
stitch (verb)	suturer	sewtewray
stock	le consommé	luh kawnsomay
stockings	les bas	lay bah
stomach	l'estomac (m.)	lehstomah
stomach	le ventre	luh vohntr
stomach ache	mal au ventre	mahl oa vohntr
stomach ache	le mal d'estomac	luh mahl dehstomah
stomach cramps	les spasmes abdominaux	lay spahzm zahbdomeenoa
stools	les selles	lay sehl
stop	arrêter	ahrehtay
stop	l'arrêt (m.)	lahreh
stopover	l'escale (f.)	lehskahl
storm	la tempête	lah tohnpeht
straight	raide	rehd
straight ahead	tout droit	too drwah

straw	la paille	*lah pahy*
street	la rue	*lah rew*
street (side)	côté rue	*koatay rew*
strike	la grève	*lah grehv*
study	faire des études	*fehr day zaytewd*
subscriber's number	le numéro d'abonné	*luh newmayroa dahbonay*
subtitled	sous-titré	*soo teetray*
succeed	réussir	*rayewsseer*
sugar	le sucre	*luh sewkr*
sugar lumps	les morceaux de sucre	*lay morsoa duh sewkr*
suit	le costume	*luh kostewm*
suitcase	la valise	*lah vahleez*
summer	l'été (m.)	*laytay*
summertime	l'heure d'été (f.)	*luhr daytay*
sun	le soleil	*luh solehy*
sun hat	le chapeau de soleil	*luh shahpoa duh solehy*
sun hat	le bonnet	*luh boneh*
sunbathe	prendre un bain de soleil	*prohndr uhn bahn duh solehy*
sunburn	le coup de soleil	*luh koo duh solehy*
Sunday	dimanche	*deemohnsh*
sunglasses	les lunettes de soleil	*lay lewneht duh solehy*
sunrise	le lever du soleil	*luh luhvay duh solehy*
sunset	le coucher du soleil	*luh kooshay duh solehy*
suntan lotion	la crème solaire	*lah krehm solehr*
suntan oil	l'huile solaire (f.)	*lweel sohlehr*
supermarket	le supermarché	*luh sewpehrmahrshay*
surcharge	le supplément	*luh sewplaymohn*
surf board	la planche à voile	*lah plohnsh ah vwahl*
surgery	la consultation	*lah kawnsewltahsyawn*
surname	le nom	*luh nawn*
surprise	la surprise	*lah sewrpreez*
swallow	avaler	*ahvahlay*
swamp	le marais	*luh mahreh*
sweat	la transpiration	*lah trohnspeerahsyawn*
sweet	le bonbon	*luh bawnbawn*
sweet (kind)	gentil	*jhohntee*
sweet (adj.)	sucré	*sewkray*
sweetcorn	le maïs	*luh mahees*
sweets	les friandises	*lay freeohndeez*
swim	nager	*nahjhay*
swimming pool	la piscine	*lah peeseen*
swimming trunks	le maillot de bain	*luh mahyoa duh bahn*
swindle	l'escroquerie (f.)	*lehskrokree*
switch	l'interrupteur (m.)	*lahntayrewptuhr*
synagogue	la synagogue	*lah seenahgog*

T

table	la table	*lah tahbl*
table tennis	jouer au ping-pong	*jhooay oa peeng pawng*
tablet	le comprimé	*luh kawnpreemay*
take (use)	utiliser	*ewteeleezay*
take	prendre	*prohndr*
take (time)	durer	*dewray*
take pictures	photographier	*foatoagrahfyay*

taken	occupé	*okewpay*
talcum powder	le talc	*luh tahlk*
talk	parler	*pahrlay*
tall	grand	*grohn*
tampons	les tampons	*lay tohnpawn*
tanned	brun	*bruhn*
tap	le robinet	*luh robeeneh*
tap water	l'eau du robinet (f.)	*loa dew robeeneh*
tartlet	la tartelette	*lah tahrtuhleht*
taste	goûter	*gootay*
tax free shop	le magasin	*luh mahgahzahn*
	hors-taxes	*or tahx*
taxi	le taxi	*luh tahxee*
taxi stand	la station de taxis	*lah stahsyawn duh*
		tahxee
tea	le thé	*luh tay*
teapot	la théière	*lah tay-yehr*
teaspoon	la petite cuillère	*lah puhteet kweeyehr*
telegram	le télégramme	*luh taylaygrahm*
telephoto lens	le téléobjectif	*luh taylayobjhehkteef*
television	la télévision	*lah taylayveezyawn*
telex	le télex	*luh taylehx*
temperature	la température	*lah tohnpayrahtewr*
temporary filling	le plombage	*luh plawnbahjh*
	provisoire	*proveezwahr*
tender	tendre	*tohndr*
tennis (play)	jouer au tennis	*jhooay oa taynees*
tennis ball	la balle de tennis	*lah bahl duh taynees*
tennis court	le court de tennis	*luh koor duh taynees*
tennis racket	la raquette de tennis	*lah rahkeht duh*
		taynees
tent	la tente	*lah tohnt*
tent peg	le piquet	*luh peekay*
terrace	la terrasse	*lah tehrahs*
terrible	épouvantable	*aypoovohntahbl*
thank	remercier	*ruhmehrsyay*
thank you	merci bien	*mehrsee byahn*
thanks	merci	*mehrsee*
thaw	dégeler	*dayjhuhlay*
theatre	le théâtre	*luh tayahtr*
theft	le vol	*luh vol*
there	là	*lah*
thermal bath	le bain thermal	*luh bahn tehrmahl*
thermometer	le thermomètre	*luh tehrmomehtr*
thick	gros	*groa*
thief	le voleur	*luh voluhr*
thigh	la cuisse	*lah kwees*
thin	maigre	*mehgr*
think	penser	*pohnsay*
third	le tiers	*luh tyehr*
thirsty, to be	la soif	*lah swahf*
this afternoon	cet après-midi	*seht ahpreh meedee*
this evening	ce soir	*suh swahr*
this morning	ce matin	*suh mahtahn*
thread	le fil	*luh feel*
throat	la gorge	*lah gorjh*

Word list

throat lozenges	les pastilles pour la gorge	*lay pahsteey poor lah gorjh*
throw up	vomir	*vomeer*
thunderstorm	l'orage (m.)	*lorajh*
Thursday	jeudi	*jhuhdee*
ticket (admission)	le billet	*luh beeyeh*
ticket (travel)	le ticket	*luh teekeh*
tickets	les billets	*lay beeyeh*
tidy	ranger	*rohnjhay*
tie	la cravate	*lah krahvaht*
tights	le collant	*luh kolohn*
time (clock)	l'heure (f.)	*luhr*
time (occasion)	la fois	*lah fwah*
timetable	l'horaire des arrivées et des départs	*lorehr day zahreevay ay day daypahr*
tin	la boîte de conserve	*lah bwaht duh kawnsehrv*
tip	le pourboire	*luh poorbwahr*
tissues	les mouchoirs en papier	*lay mooshwahr ohn pahpyay*
toast	le toast	*luh toast*
tobacco	le tabac	*luh tahbah*
toboggan	la luge	*lah lewjh*
today	aujourd'hui	*oajhoordwee*
toe	l'orteil (m.)	*lortehy*
together	ensemble	*ohnsohnbl*
toilet	les toilettes	*lay twahleht*
toilet paper	le papier hygiénique	*luh pahpyay eejhyayneek*
toiletries	les articles de toilette	*lay zahrteekl duh twahleht*
tomato	la tomate	*lah tomaht*
tomato purée	le concentré de tomates	*luh kawnsohntray duh tomaht*
tomato sauce	le ketchup	*luh kehtchuhp*
tomorrow	demain	*duhmahn*
tongue	la langue	*lah lohng*
tonic water	le tonic	*luh toneek*
tonight	ce soir	*suh swahr*
tonight	cette nuit	*seht nwee*
too much	trop	*troa*
tools	les outils	*lay zootee*
tooth	la dent	*lah dohn*
toothache	le mal de dents	*luh mahl duh dohn*
toothbrush	la brosse à dents	*lah bros ah dohn*
toothpaste	le dentifrice	*luh dohnteefrees*
toothpick	le cure-dent	*luh kewrdohn*
top up	remplir	*rohnpleer*
total	le total	*luh totahl*
tough	dur	*dewr*
tour	le tour	*luh toor*
tour guide	le guide	*luh geed*
tourist card	la carte touristique	*lah kahrt tooreesteek*
tourist class	la classe touriste	*lah klahs tooreest*
Tourist Information office	l'office de tourisme	*lofees duh tooreesm*
tow	remorquer	*ruhmorkay*

Word list

15

tow cable	le câble	*luh kahbl*
towel	la serviette de toilette	*lah sehrvyeht duh twahleht*
tower	la tour	*lah toor*
town	la ville	*lah veel*
town hall	la mairie	*lah mayree*
toy	le jouet	*luh jhooeh*
traffic	la circulation	*lah seerkewlahsyawn*
traffic light	le feu de signalisation	*luh fuh duh seenyahleezahsyawn*
train	le train	*luh trahn*
train ticket	le billet de train	*luh beeyeh duh trahn*
train timetable	l'indicateur des chemins de fer	*lahndeekahtuhr day shuhmahn duh fehr*
translate	traduire	*trahdweer*
travel	voyager	*vwahyahjhay*
travel agent	l'agence de voyages (f.)	*lahjhohns duh vwahyahjh*
travel guide	le guide touristique	*luh geed tooreesteek*
traveller	le voyageur	*luh vwahyahjhuhr*
traveller's cheque	le chèque de voyage	*luh shehk duh vwahyahjh*
treacle	la mélasse	*lah maylahs*
treatment	le traitement	*luh trehtmohn*
triangle	le triangle	*luh treeohngl*
trim	tailler	*tahy-yay*
trip	l'excursion (f.)	*lehxkewrsyawn*
trip	le voyage	*luh vwahyahjh*
trout	la truite	*lah trweet*
trunk call	interurbain	*ahntehrewrbahn*
trunk code	l'indicatif (m.)	*lahndeekahteef*
trustworthy	de confiance	*duh kawnfyohns*
try on	essayer	*ehsay-yay*
tube	le tube	*luh tewb*
Tuesday	mardi	*mahrdee*
tumble drier	le sèche-linge	*luh sahsh lahnjh*
tuna	le thon	*luh tawn*
tunnel	le tunnel	*luh tewnehl*
TV	la télé	*lah taylay*
tweezers	la pince	*lah pahns*
tyre	le pneu	*luh pnuh*
tyre lever	le démonte-pneu	*luh daymawnt pnuh*
tyre pressure	la pression des pneus	*lah prehsyawn day pnuh*

U

ugly	laid	*leh*
umbrella	le parapluie	*luh pahrahplwee*
under	sous	*soo*
underground	le métro	*luh maytroa*
underground railway system	le réseau métropolitain	*luh rayzoa maytroapoleetahn*
underground station	la station de métro	*lah stahsyawn duh maytroa*
underpants	le slip	*luh sleep*
understand	comprendre	*kawnprohndr*
underwear	les sous-vêtements	*lay soovehtmohn*

undress	(se) déshabiller	suh dayzahbeeyay
unemployed	au chômage	oa shoamahjh
uneven	irrégulier	eeraygewlyay
university	l'université (f.)	lewneevehrseetay
unleaded	sans plomb	sohn plawn
up	en haut	ohn oa
urgent	urgent	ewrjhohn
urine	l'urine (f.)	lewreen
usually	généralement	jhaynayrahlmohn

V

vacate	évacuer	ayvahkeway
vaccinate	vacciner	vahkseenay
vagina	le vagin	luh vahjhahn
vaginal infection	l'infection vaginale	lahnfehksyawn vahjheenahl
valid	valable	vahlahbl
valley	la vallée	lah vahlay
van	la camionnette	lah kahmyoneht
vanilla	la vanille	lah vahneey
vase	le vase	luh vahz
vaseline	la vaseline	lah vahzleen
veal	la viande de veau	lah vyohnd duh voa
vegetable soup	la soupe de légumes	lah soop duh laygewm
vegetables	le légume	luh laygewm
vegetarian	le végétarien	luh vayjhaytahryahn
vein	la veine	lah vehn
vending machine	le distributeur	luh deestreebewtuhr
venereal disease	la maladie vénérienne	lah mahlahdee vaynayryehn
via	par	pahr
video recorder	le magnétoscope	luh manyehtoskop
video tape	la bande vidéo	lah bohnd veedayoa
view	la vue	lah vew
village	le village	luh veelahjh
visa	le visa	luh veezah
visit (verb)	rendre visite à	rohndr veezeet ah
visit	la visite	lah veezeet
vitamin tablet	le comprimé de vitamines	luh kawnpreemay duh veetahmeen
vitamin	la vitamine	lah veetahmeen
volcano	le volcan	luh volkohn
volleyball	jouer au volley	jhooay oa volay
vomit	vomir	vomeer

W

wait	attendre	ahtohndr
waiter	le serveur	luh sehrvuhr
waiting room	la salle d'attente	lah sahl dahtohnt
waitress	la serveuse	lah sehrvuhz
wake up	réveiller	rayvay-yay
walk	la promenade	lah promnahd
walk (verb)	se promener marcher	suh promnay mahrshay
wallet	le portefeuille	luh portuhfuhy
wardrobe	la garde-robe	lah gahrd rob
warm	chaud	shoa

warn	prévenir	prayvuhneer
warning	l'avertissement (m.)	lahvehrteesmohn
wash	laver	lahvay
washing-powder	le détergent	luh daytehrjohn
washing	le linge	luh lahnjh
washing line	la corde à linge	lah kord ah lahnjh
washing machine	la machine à laver	lah mahsheen ah lahvay
wasp	la guêpe	lah gehp
water	l'eau (f.)	loa
water ski	faire du ski nautique	fehr dew skee noateek
waterproof	imperméable	ahnpehrmayahbl
wave-pool	la piscine à vagues artificielles	lah peeseen ah vahg zahrteefeesyehl
way	le moyen	luh mwahyahn
way	la direction	lah deerehksyawn
we	nous	noo
weak	faible	fehbl
weather	le temps	luh tohn
weather forecast	le bulletin météorologique	luh bewltahn maytayoarolojheek
wedding	les noces	lay nos
wedding	le mariage	luh mahryajh
Wednesday	mercredi	mehrkruhdee
week	la semaine	lah suhmehn
weekend	le week-end	luh week-ehnd
weekend duty	le service de garde	luh sehrvees duh gahrd
weekly ticket	l'abonnement hebdomadaire (m.)	lahbonmohn ehbdomahdehr
welcome	bienvenu	byahnvuhnew
well	bien	byahn
west	l'ouest (m.)	lwehst
wet	humide	ewmeed
wetsuit	la combinaison de planche à voile	lah kawnbeenehzawn duh plohnsh ah vwahl
what?	quoi?	kwah?
wheel	la roue	lah roo
wheelchair	la chaise roulante	lah shehz roolohnt
when?	quand?	kohn?
where?	où?	oo?
which?	quel?	kehl?
whipped cream	la crème Chantilly	lah krehm shohnteeyee
white	blanc	blohn
who?	qui?	kee?
wholemeal bread	le pain complet	luh pahn kawnpleh
why?	pourquoi?	poorkwah?
wide-angle lens	le grand-angle	luh grohn tohngl
widow	la veuve	lah vuhv
widower	le veuf	luh vuhf
wife	l'épouse (f.)	laypooz
wind	le vent	luh vohn
windbreak	le pare-vent	luh pahrvohn
windmill	le moulin	luh moolahn
window (desk)	le guichet	luh gueesheh
window	la fenêtre	lah fuhnehtr
windscreen wiper	l'essuie-glace (m.)	lehswee glahs

windsurf	faire de la planche	*fehr duh lah*
	à voile	*plohnsh ah vwahl*
wine	le vin	*luh vahn*
wine list	la carte des vins	*lah kahrt day vahn*
winter	l'hiver (m.)	*leevehr*
witness	le témoin	*luh taymwahn*
woman	la femme	*lah fahm*
wood	le bois	*luh bwah*
wool	la laine	*lah lehn*
word	le mot	*luh moa*
work	le travail	*luh trahvahy*
working day	le jour ouvrable	*jhoor oovrahbl*
worn	usé	*ewzay*
worried	inquiet	*ahnkyeh*
wound	la blessure	*lah blehsewr*
wrap	emballer	*ohnbahlay*
wrist	le poignet	*luh pwahnnyeh*
write	écrire	*aykreer*
write down	noter	*notay*
writing pad	le bloc-notes	*luh blok not*
writing paper	le papier à lettres	*luh pahpyay ah lehtr*
written	écrit	*aykree*
wrong	mauvais	*moaveh*

Y

yacht	le yacht	*luh yot*
year	l'année (f.)	*lahnay*
yellow	jaune	*jhoan*
yes	oui	*wee*
yes, please	volontiers	*volawntyay*
yesterday	hier	*yehr*
yoghurt	le yaourt	*luh yahoort*
you	vous	*voo*
you too	de même	*duh mehm*
youth hostel	l'auberge de	*loabehrjh duh*
	jeunesse (f.)	*jhuhnehs*

Z

| zip | la fermeture éclair | *lah fehrmuhtewr ayklehr* |
| zoo | le parc zoologique | *luh pahrk zoaolojheek* |

Word list

15

Basic grammar

1 The article

French nouns are divided into 2 categories: masculine and feminine. The definite article (the) is **le,la** or **l'**:

le is used before masculine words starting with a consonant, **le magasin** (the shop)

la is used with feminine words starting with a consonant, **la plage** (the beach)

l' is used before masculine and feminine words starting with a vowel, **l'argent** (the money), **l'assiette** (the plate).

Other examples are:

le toit	the roof
la maison	the house
l'hôtel (m.)	the hotel
l'entrée (f.)	the entrance

in the case of the indefinite article (**a, an**):

un is used before masculine words, **un livre** (a book)

une is used before feminine words, **une pomme** (an apple)

des is used before plural words, both masculine and feminine, **des camions** (lorries), **des voitures** (cars).

Other examples are:

un père	a father	**une mère**	a mother
un homme	a man	**une femme**	a woman
des hommes	men	**des femmes**	women

2 The plural

The plural of **le**, **la** and **l'** is **les**.

The plural of most French nouns ends in **s**, but this **s** is not pronounced. However when the noun begins with a vowel or a silent **h**, then the **s** of **les** or **des** is pronounced z, **les affaires** (*layzahfehr*), **des enfants** (*dayzohngfohn*).

Other examples are:

le lit	*luh lee*	**les lits**	*lay lee*
la table	*lah tahbl*	**les tables**	*lay tahbl*
l'avion (m.)	*lahveeawn*	**les avions**	*layzahvyeeawn*
l'heure (f.)	*luhr*	**les heures**	*layzuhr*

Certain plurals end in **aux** (mainly words ending in '**al**')

le cheval	**les chevaux**
le canal	**les canaux**

3 Personal pronouns

I	**je**
You	**tu**
He/she/it	**il/elle**
We	**nous**
You	**vous**
They	**ils/elles**

In general '**tu**' is used to translate 'you' when speaking to close friends, relatives and children. **Vous** is used in all other cases. 'It' becomes **il** or **elle** according to whether the noun referred to is masculine or feminine.

4 Possessive pronouns

	masculine	feminine	plural
my	**mon**	**ma**	**mes**
your	**ton**	**ta**	**tes**
his/her/its	**son**	**sa**	**ses**
our	**notre**	**notre**	**nos**
your	**votre**	**votre**	**vos**
their	**leur**	**leur**	**leurs**

They agree with the object they refer to, e.g. her hat = **son chapeau**.

5 Verbs

parler		to speak
je parle	root + -e	I speak
tu parles	root + -es	you speak
il/elle parle	root + -e	he/she/it speaks
nous parlons	root + -ons	we speak
vous parlez	root + -ez	you speak
ils/elles parlent	root + -ent	they speak
parlé (past participle)		spoken

Here are some useful verbs.

être	to be
je suis	I am
tu es	you are
il/elle est	he/she/it is
nous sommes	we are
vous êtes	you are
ils/elles sont	they are
été (past participle)	been

avoir	to have
j'ai	I have
tu as	you have
il/elle a	he/she/it has
nous avons	we have
vous avez	you have
ils/elles ont	they have
eu (past participle)	had

faire	to do/make
je fais	I do
tu fais	you do
il/elle fait	he/she does
nous faisons	we do
vous faites	you do
ils/elles font	they do
fait (past participle)	done/made

6 Countries and prepositions

Names of countries take the article:

L'Angleterre	England
Le Canada	Canada
La France	France

in Paris	**à Paris**
in France	**en France**
in Canada	**au Canada**

7 Negatives

Negatives are formed by using:

ne (verb) **pas**	not
ne (verb) **jamais**	never

Je ne parle pas français.	I don't speak French.
Je ne fume jamais.	I never smoke.